DOWN
TO EARTH

OTHER NORTON BOOKS BY ERIK P. ECKHOLM

Losing Ground (1976)
The Picture of Health (1977)

DOWN
TO EARTH

ENVIRONMENT AND HUMAN NEEDS

Erik P. Eckholm

International Institute for Environment and Development

W · W · NORTON & COMPANY
New York · London

GF
41
.E24
1982

Published simultaneously in Canada by George J. McLeod Limited, Toronto.

Printed in the United States of America.

First Edition

W. W. Norton & Company, Inc. 500 Fifth Avenue, New York, N. Y. 10110
W. W. Norton & Company Ltd. 37 Great Russell Street, London WC1B 3NU
1 2 3 4 5 6 7 8 9 0

ISBN 0-393-01600-5

ISBN 0-393-30040-4 PBK.

Dedicated to Barbara Ward
(1914–1981)

CONTENTS

III. Conditions for Progress

PREFACE

IN 1980 Dr. Mostafa K. Tolba, executive director of the United Nations Environment Programme (UNEP), invited Barbara Ward to write a book for the tenth anniversary of the 1972 United Nations Conference on the Human Environment—the famous Stockholm Conference for which her book *Only One Earth* (co-authored with René Dubos) had been a highly acclaimed background resource. Because of her serious illness, she invited me to work with her on the project. Together we fashioned the general approach of *Down to Earth,* but declining health prevented her from working much on the manuscript. With Dr. Tolba's encouragement I proceeded on my own. Not long before her death on May 31, 1981, Barbara Ward dictated the foreword.

Research for this book was funded by UNEP, but it is not an official document; the views expressed are mine. Readers seeking more detailed technical information should refer to UNEP's new report on the state of the environment, *The World Environment 1972–1982* (edited by Martin W. Holdgate, Mohammed Kassas, and Gilbert F. White, and published by Tycooly International Publishing Limited, Dublin, Ireland).

My deep appreciation goes to Drs. Holdgate, Kassas, and White for their advice. Dr. Holdgate especially improved the manuscript with his meticulous critiques. I must also thank Dr. Tolba, Peter Thacher, and their colleagues at UNEP for their unofficial comments on the text. Nevertheless, responsibility for the contents is mine alone.

Portions of the manuscript were reviewed by Anil Agarwal, John Beddington, Justin Cooke, Cornelia Durrant, John Gulland, Carol

Karasik, Robert Luke, Michael M'Gonigle, Barbara Mitchell, Diana Page, David Runnalls, David Satterthwaite, and Anthony Seeger. To all, I am grateful.

I wrote *Down to Earth* while a Visiting Fellow of the International Institute for Environment and Development (IIED), the research and advocacy organization Barbara Ward had long directed. The IIED staffs in both London and Washington provided much good advice and a congenial, supportive environment.

Special thanks go to Jon Tinker, director of Earthscan, IIED's news and information service. He managed the project contract, and more important, was an invaluable interlocutor and editor. His intellectual imprint runs through every chapter.

I want to thank James and Kathleen Bishop, John Heermans, Frank Brechin, Robert Winterbottom, Chris Reij, Rob Bierregaard, Kent Redford, and others too numerous to list for their assistance during my visits to Niger, Upper Volta, and Brazil.

Andi Stein skillfully prepared most of the manuscript. Kathy Brown and Lynne Russell also chipped in at critical moments with much-appreciated secretarial assistance.

Valuable help with research and with the analysis of issues was provided by Robert Luke and Diana Page (Robert contributed significantly to Chapters 5, 6, and 7 in particular). Kathleen Courrier once again thought up a fitting book title. Thanks are due Worldwatch Institute for permission to draw on material from papers I wrote there in Chapters 2, 9, and 10.

Finally, I want to express my appreciation of Dr. Tolba's continuing willingness to sponsor unofficial analyses and public education efforts such as this book. The tradition began with the commissioning of *Only One Earth* by the secretariat preparing for the Stockholm Conference, and has been carried on by UNEP ever since.

In writing *Down to Earth* I have not presumed to try to match Barbara Ward's eloquence and erudition. But I have tried to be true to her vision of a more just and humane world. Her crystalline sense of morality never flagged, and will be missed.

Erik P. Eckholm
Washington, D.C.

FOREWORD
BY BARBARA WARD

IN JUNE 1972 the governments of the world met in Stockholm for the United Nations Conference on the Human Environment. During the decade since then we have gradually come to appreciate the extraordinary interdependence and fragility of that tiny part of our planet in which life is possible. A few thin meters of soil, a few miles up into the sky and a similar depth down into the oceans, encompasses virtually the whole of the biosphere in which we and other living things can survive.

Within this tiny realm the seaborne wastes of one continent become the marine pollution of distant beaches. Toxic fumes from an industrial complex fall as acid rain hundreds of miles away, poisoning lakes and streams. A few greedy nations can overfish the sea's wealth and deprive all mankind of valuable foodstocks. And the desperate search for farmland and fuelwood by poor families in many parts of the Third World leads to the destruction of forests, then soil erosion, floods, and drought.

In retrospect the 1972 Stockholm Conference should perhaps have been more of a turning point than it became. Those of us who were there experienced a quickening of excitement, a feeling that at last we were getting going. But this momentum quickly slackened.

The series of U.N. conferences that followed Stockholm in the 1970s had a common pattern—governments agreed on the nature of the problem and agreed on the solutions. But their actions rarely matched their promises.

For an increasing number of environmental issues the difficulty is not to identify the remedy, because the remedy is now well understood. The problems are rooted in the society and the economy—and in the end in the political structure. Foresters know how to plant trees, but not how to devise methods whereby villagers in India, the Andes, or the Sahel can manage a plantation for themselves. Biologists know where to draw boundaries for nature reserves, but cannot keep landless peasants from invading them to grow food or cut fuel. The solutions to such problems are increasingly seen to involve reforms in land tenure and economic strategy, and the involvement of communities in shaping their own lives.

One of the saddest of all metaphors is surely that of eating the seed corn. Yet the inexorable pressures of population on a limited environment and its resources are at the moment forcing hundreds of millions of people to do just this, to burn cow dung instead of using it to enrich the soil, to cultivate steep slopes until the precious earth is washed away down the rivers.

One phrase struck me most forcibly at the Stockholm Conference, a phrase the Chinese delegation first used, which was later incorporated in the official Stockholm Declaration: "Of all the things in the world, people are the most precious."

Before Stockholm, people usually saw the environment—many still do—as something totally divorced from humanity. To them the only *real* environment is a wilderness area, where all the people are excluded—except of course those who are rich enough to keep everyone else out. Stockholm recorded a fundamental shift in the emphasis of our environmental thinking. The meeting was rightly called the United Nations Conference on the *Human* Environment.

No matter how much we try to think of ourselves as separate sovereign entities, nature itself reminds us of humanity's basic unity. The vision of unity shared by so many of the great philosophers and so central to all the great religions is recognized now as an inescapable scientific fact. Could it be the vocation of this generation to give the planet the institutions of unity and cooperation that can express this insight? The need is all the greater since, during the same few decades that we have discovered the fragilities of our natural systems, so too have we invented, in nuclear weapons, a means of destroying ourselves and our environment together.

In the 1970s, after Stockholm, there was a growing realization of the basic and indestructible links between what humans do in one part of the world and what they do in another. This interconnectedness was one of the great insights of Stockholm, neatly summed up in the conference slogan "Only One Earth." There was a beginning of a sense of shared stewardship for our common planetary home.

Now, in the 1980s, some Western leaders are starting to abandon the concept of our joint voyage on Spaceship Earth, and to dismiss any concern for the environment or for the South as "do-goodism." They appear to regard the universe as expendable—as long as their tiny bit of it is not expended.

To call aid to the Third World a handout is primitive thinking. It conveys a petty vision, far from Stockholm's "Only One Earth"— a grudging, ungenerous view of a world filled with undeserving people clutching at our purses. This is coupled with a frightening tendency for some Western nations to turn their backs even on their own poor and underprivileged—who are almost always rich beyond belief compared to the relentless poverty of rural India or the slums and shantytowns of Jakarta, Mexico City, and Lagos.

In the immediate postwar years the American people through the Marshall Plan poured out their resources and their concern to help rebuild a shattered Europe. The gap between that sort of generosity and the North's collective meanness in the early 1980s leaves one wondering whether we are not now seeing the real consequences of Vietnam—a profound disillusionment with any kind of cooperative international action, and a falling back upon a crude, cynical nationalism.

For while the idea of a global interdependence was developing in the 1970s, so too was a reaction against this trend. The last few years have seen a rising resentment of the notion that we are all dependent on other people and other nations. This resentment is independent of ideology. It has been felt on the left and on the right, in the North and in the South.

We should not be surprised at this reversion toward a narrower nationalism. Big powers never want to be dictated to by little ones. And when it comes to governance of the global commons—the seas, the atmosphere, the forests, rivers, and rainfall that sustain human life —local pressures often tend to be stronger than any emerging international constituency. That, I fear, is the reality today.

Is this reaction against planetary awareness just a temporary setback? In my more pessimistic moments I fear that there may have been a genuine change in the tide in recent years. But we must remember that it took many centuries for nationalism itself to become the dominant world force. For a thousand years and more, until the Reformation, ideology and belief were the primary force.

Nationalism is a tough political power to replace. Throughout the twentieth century we have watched grudging efforts to modify the cruder forms of nationalism, and the continuing resistance to this process. This may explain the decade of U.N. conferences, where over a hundred governments have repeatedly voted in favor of resolutions on international action, but signally failed to do much to implement them. There is a curious tension between what governments subconsciously know to be the international realities and what they are prepared to accept in limitation of their own sovereign interests. Too often it is still only *my* earth, only *one hundred* earths.

We must be clear where the immediate responsibility for inaction lies. The peoples of North America, Japan, the United Kingdom, and the rest of Western Europe make up, together with a few oil states, the great majority of the world's rich citizens. Ours is the responsibility for the present appallingly skewed distribution of resources. The richest 20 percent, largely living in the West, have three-quarters of the wealth. The remaining three and a half billion of our fellow citizens must make do with the last quarter that remains.

And it is for the world's poor—the nations of the Third World, and the poor majority within those countries—that a decent environment is even more important than it is for the rich West. The poor are always nearer the margin, and the margins of our global environment are today smaller than they were ten years ago in Stockholm.

If the 1970s were for the United Nations the decade of conferences, it is perhaps encouraging that the 1980s have been declared the International Drinking Water Supply and Sanitation Decade. To move from the general understandings of Stockholm to the very specific problems of drinking water—with its close links to sanitation, waterborne disease, primary health care, infant mortality, and population growth—is a tremendous step forward.

In some Third World countries two of every five children die before they reach the end of childhood, and a prime factor in this mortality is polluted water. So long as parents experience the death of their first children, they will continue to bring more into the world —not out of folly or ignorance, but as an insurance for today's workload and tomorrow's old age.

From experience in Europe in the nineteenth century, and in parts of Asia today, we know that when basic health care, the beginnings of education, clean water, and hope and work are introduced, the birth rate begins to slow and then stabilize. And with this change the nightmare of a world that can no longer feed, clothe, shelter, or even supply a cup of clean water to its human population begins to fade.

Many cultures share a profound belief that water is the basic sustenance of humankind. That most fearsome image of pollution, the deliberate poisoning of the wells, has always haunted people. It is not chance that this was the first form of warfare to be outlawed.

To give the world clean drinking water and decent sanitation might cost us $80 million a day for the next ten years. This is trifling compared with the continuing hemorrhage of resources to the instruments of death—on which we spend a shameful $1400 million a day.

So far this insane scale of priorities remains acceptable to the rich —to the rich nations of the North, and to the rich minorities in the South. We must be thankful that the 1980s are opening with a practical focus on sanitation, and hope that in easing the daily grind of hauling and carrying water, in saving life, in giving a sense of being cared for, it will help to produce a more stable, a more peaceful, and ultimately a more human planet.

DOWN
TO EARTH

1 INTRODUCTION: GLOBAL ENVIRONMENT TEN YEARS AFTER STOCKHOLM

PLATO LAMENTED THE DESTRUCTION of soils and forests in ancient Greece. Dickens and Engels wrote eloquently of the wretched conditions spawned by the Industrial Revolution. But the surge in concern about environmental quality over the last two decades has been uniquely widespread and impassioned.

The United Nations Conference on the Human Environment, held in Stockholm in 1972, provided a focal point for the gathering environmental concerns of the 1960s. Inside the official conference hall representatives of the world's governments passed a lofty set of principles and voted for new forms of world cooperation.

Outside the official quarters thousands of groups and individuals displayed, through their enthusiastic lobbying and debates, the mounting strength of citizen action on environmental issues as well as the diversity of views propelling it. An inflatable whale, paraded through the streets, symbolized what many saw as the needless destruction of nature. Crippled victims of mercury poisoning from Minamata, Japan, embodied the dangers of unregulated industrial technology.

Particularly in richer countries, a combination of actual changes in the environment and changes in people's perceptions helped account for the new interest of the 1960s and 1970s. As news broke of one deadly incident after another, some feared that air and water pollution were getting out of control. The publication of Rachel Carson's *Silent Spring* in 1962 introduced many to the challenges posed by persistent toxic chemicals. Seagoing celebrities evoked the spectre of dying oceans; declining whale populations suggested human inability to control greed or to respect fellow creatures. Radioactive fallout from nuclear bomb tests brought home the message of a shared atmosphere. Projections of an exploding world population raised fears that the world would run short of food and resources, and that the last vestiges of wilderness would be overwhelmed.

People's ideas about what sort of environment was desirable and possible were also in flux. In the developed countries many began to feel that the unplanned growth of economies and populations would not necessarily improve the quality of life. The insights of ecology helped more people appreciate the interconnectedness of all life on earth.

Many in the Third World were initially skeptical if not hostile to the new devotion to the environment displayed by the affluent. Spokesmen for poor countries observed that their problem was too little rather than too much industry, and that some smoke in the air would be a small price to pay for lifting the multitudes from their gross deprivation. If we have environmental problems, such spokesmen said, they are a reflection of poverty: shantytowns where unsanitary conditions imperil health and degrade human dignity; forests razed and topsoil destroyed by the desperate, unskilled assaults of the needy.

Debating these issues during the preparations for the Stockholm Conference and after, Third World intellectuals broadened rather than repudiated the evolving environmental consciousness. For they too were often forced to look at their own circumstances in new ways —to examine the interrelationships between natural conditions and human conditions, and to focus on the quality of life rather than disembodied economic statistics.

The first in a series of major U.N. conferences held in the 1970s (later ones covered population, food, women's rights, desertification, human settlements, science and technology, and other topics), Stockholm was imbued with unique enthusiasm and hope. If environmental dangers seemed to loom large, so too did the promise of global cooperation to counter them. Representatives of the developed countries in particular worked to create new institutions for monitoring global environmental trends and for cooperation in protecting the oceans and other global commons. Those of the Third World hoped for significant new assistance to help wipe out sordid poverty without needless damage to ecosystems.

Events since 1972 have brought many people's ideas—both about the nature of the challenges and about the nature of required responses—down to earth. Progress toward global cooperation has been halting at best, many new environmental challenges have been identified, and international aid to the Third World has stagnated rather than multiplied.

Today, as the new U.N. report *The World Environment 1972–1982* makes clear, environmental trends per se do not appear to be quite as cataclysmic as they once did. Human civilization does not apparently face imminent doom because of pollution or the unraveling of natural systems. Yet many forms of degradation have been shown to have ominous long-term implications for society, and some are undermining human well-being right now. Damage to forests and soils is impairing the quality of life, especially among the poorest, and raising the costs of agricultural production. The pollution of air and water by both age-old and modern contaminants is taking a huge toll. The last decade's research has confirmed the possibilities of a large-scale reduction in genetic diversity and of human-caused disruptions of the climate. But most environmental problems defy simple explanations; they are rooted in a bewildering array of social forces and technological trends.

Outlining appropriate responses to environmental threats has also been difficult—and generating the political will to carry them out even more so. At the global level, a United Nations Environment Programme (UNEP) was established by the Stockholm Conference to prod the U.N. system and the world's governments into more sound environmental management. Although it has sponsored numerous successful activities, UNEP has not become the powerful global force some once dreamed of—nor, perhaps, could it have. For when their immediate economic and political interests are affected, national governments have proved unwilling to grant significant powers to an international authority. Even tasks that once seemed straightforward, such as global monitoring of trends in pollution and living resources, have turned out to be complex and expensive. Of countless possibilities, just what shall be monitored, for what purpose, and at what cost?

Needs for global cooperation aside, most environmental threats can be addressed effectively only at the national and local levels. But because of the links between resource trends and prevailing political, social, and economic structures, known solutions are often not applied. In both rich and poor countries, those working for improved environmental policies have often discovered the need to become involved in broader economic and political debates.

Without question, progress has been achieved on some environmental fronts over the last decade. Nearly all the developed countries began seriously to confront the threats of air and water pollution, with mixed results. But the registered improvements in environmental quality have generally been well worth the costs of their attainment. And, polls show, public support for spending resources to clean up the environment has remained strong even in the face of dismal economic conditions.

As we enter the 1980s the battles against most air and water pollutants have by no means been won; some recent gains could easily be undone if vigilance is relaxed, especially given the revived use of coal, a major source of pollution, as a fuel. Meanwhile, societies have hardly started the intimidating tasks of testing and regulating the tens of thousands of synthetic chemicals, some of them potentially dangerous, that permeate modern life. And the safe disposal of hazardous wastes remains more a goal than a common practice.

Still, the basic principle of public regulation of activities that threaten the environment has become firmly established in laws and institutions, even if special interests can sometimes subvert the decision-making process. Especially in the United States, but to an increasing degree elsewhere too, private citizens and nongovernmental organizations have played vital roles in promoting environmental policies that serve the public interest.

A decade back many Third World leaders were openly dubious about the relevance of environmental issues to their countries' development struggles. Today such doubts are rarely heard, though it would be an exaggeration to say that all such feelings have been dispelled. Brazil, for example, some of whose representatives at Stockholm characterized the hue and cry about pollution as a plot to hamper the industrialization of the South, founded a new national environmental agency shortly after the Stockholm Conference adjourned. Scores of other developing countries have over the past decade created environmental ministries or agencies and passed laws to regulate pollution. And some now require analysis of the expected environmental impacts of major investments. Many in the Third World have learned through unpleasant experience that unconstrained pollution can have savage effects without lifting the poor into affluence.

Third World governments have also been forced by events to notice a set of interrelated problems that in many ways present the world's premier environmental challenge. Famine amid the spread of desert-like conditions during a lengthy African drought in the early 1970s; disastrous increases in erosion, landslides, and flooding downstream of denuded hills in large areas of Africa, Asia, and Latin America; shortages and soaring prices for the firewood on which half of humankind depends for cooking and warmth—these were symptoms of the tragic cycle of degeneration undermining the livelihoods of hundreds of millions of the world's poor. Rapid population growth and lack of economic opportunities have pushed ever more people into "marginal" areas—desert fringes, mountain slopes, rain forest lands not suited to farming—where resource destruction may be the only feasible way of eking out a living. Some of the dispossessed migrate to urban slums and shantytowns, where they live amid environmental squalor of other sorts.

Many Third World leaders and international aid officials are paying significant new attention to the management of renewable natural resources, the often-forgotten underpinnings of much economic activity. In practice, solving problems of resource degradation often seems to hinge on providing a chance to participate more meaningfully in development to the marginal people who are now forced to damage their natural surroundings. Governments and aid agencies have found it harder to act on this aspect of the problem.

To be sure, neither the establishment of new government agencies nor renewed concern for natural resources is in itself proof of a turning tide. Unless governments have the political will to confront established interests and the political capacity to follow through with effective programs, the new rhetoric will remain hollow. Also, the poorest countries often lack the funds to address critical matters of resource degradation even when it may pay off handsomely over the long term. And despite dramatic declines in birth rates in some countries, continuing rapid population growth in others undercuts efforts to improve natural resource management.

Nevertheless the convergence of ideas about environment and Third World development over the last decade must be reckoned a historic advance for both fields. In the past those concerned about the preservation of nature and those concerned about economic progress have often been at loggerheads. Recently, many on both sides have begun to realize that they need the insights of each other if the goals of either are to be met.

The world conservation movement has for the most part focused on the need to protect endangered animals and to establish parks and preserves. But an animal cannot be saved apart from its habitat, and natural areas cannot last as fortress islands in seas of hungry people. Where large numbers lack a means to make a decent living, some are sure to invade national parks to grow food and cut wood. Desperately poor people cannot afford to worry much about what they see as useless tigers.

Instead of dwelling on the threat to the environment posed by development, many conservationists now recognize the need for development as a prerequisite of successful conservation. But not just any sort of pell-mell, lopsided development; the key is economic progress that is ecologically sustainable and satisfies the essential needs of the underclass. Analysis of Third World conservation problems leads inescapably to concern for social justice. Broader sharing of the fruits of development is important not only because it is morally right, but also because it is crucial to the protection of natural systems.

This newly sophisticated approach to environment and development was well reflected in the *World Conservation Strategy.* Released in 1980 by the major global conservation coalition, the International Union for Conservation of Nature and Natural Resources (IUCN), in cooperation with the World Wildlife Fund and UNEP, the *Strategy* attempts to provide guidelines for the management of the earth's living resources. In its statement of objectives it goes far beyond the usual conservation manifesto: its declared goals are to maintain essential ecological processes and life-support systems, to preserve genetic diversity, and "to ensure the sustainable utilization of species and ecosystems, which support millions of rural communities as well as major industries." As the *Strategy* declares: "The combined destructive impacts of a poor majority struggling to stay alive and an affluent minority consuming most of the world's resources are undermining the very means by which all people can survive and flourish."

Those involved with economic planning in the Third World have learned some lessons too. In general, modern air and water pollutants and toxic chemicals are less prevalent in developing countries. But most of these countries lack the technical personnel and institutional means for effective regulation of noxious effluents and dangerous products. Feeling the harsh pinch of economic backwardness, governments are often reluctant to apply strong antipollution standards to industries. Thus around the industrial centers that do exist pollution is often severe, harming nearby people and productive ecosystems alike. Workplace health hazards, scandalous enough in rich countries, are poorly regulated in most of the Third World.

The overuse and dangerous handling of pesticides are widespread. Moreover, chemicals are commonly marketed in developing countries that have been banned by developed countries or that have never been properly tested for safety or effectiveness. In addition to the direct health hazards for farmworkers and their families, pesticide misuse often leads to increased production costs via the classic treadmill of overspraying, evolution of pest resistance, and more spraying.

Awareness is spreading that large-scale development projects such as dams and irrigation developments can, when carelessly planned, cause severe ecological backlashes, damages that offset many of the benefits of the investments. As we enter the 1980s the major development lending agencies, with the encouragement of UNEP and nongovernmental organizations, have pledged to assess the environmental impacts of sensitive development projects before the bulldozers begin their work. But this promise has yet to be translated into widespread action—and few privately financed projects receive proper advance environmental analysis.

Finally, in much of the Third World the destruction of the natural resource base on which development depends has become obvious even to the ecologically illiterate. Expensive dams and canals fill with silt at twice the expected rate. Record floods wipe out crops and villages. Crop yields decline on overburdened soils. Climbing wood prices disrupt construction programs and put unbearable burdens on the poor.

Some planners have recently begun to incorporate an ecological perspective into rural development activities. But solving the interlocking crises of rural poverty and environmental degradation depends as much on politically contentious socioeconomic reforms as on improved planning. In the early 1980s ideas are in the air that could lead societies toward development that is more ecologically sustainable and more socially just. But established patterns are not easily shaken.

Ten years after Stockholm's celebration of global consciousness, to what extent have environmental problems proved really global? Conditions in the common areas—the oceans, the atmosphere, and Antarctica—are naturally of worldwide concern. The worst fears about the health of the oceans have not materialized; serious pollution effects seem limited to relatively few coastal regions. Given the extreme difficulty of safely disposing of toxic and radioactive wastes on land, pressures may well rise to increase ocean dumping. So far, though, the limited national and international efforts at regulation, combined with the size and resilience of the oceans, have prevented major international problems. Where serious pollution does exist it is most logically addressed at the national or regional levels, as is being attempted by UNEP's Regional Seas program.

The problem of overfishing now falls mainly under national control. Whales, a global resource whose plight has generated exceptional public interest, have apparently been saved from extermination, though how far depleted stocks will recover is uncertain. The clampdown in the 1970s on overharvesting of whales was one of the great successes of the nongovernmental environmental movement, which effectively pressured governments to act.

Our expanding knowledge of the upper atmosphere has only underlined the interdependence of nations. Two decades ago the notion that governments would regulate substances in household spray cans out of concern for the stratospheric ozone layer might have struck many as science fiction; now nations are developing a world treaty to prevent ozone depletion. The rising combustion of fossil fuels is contributing to a buildup of atmospheric carbon dioxide that, most scientists agree, will eventually disrupt the world climate. This will undoubtedly be one of the major environmental issues of the decades to come, and no nation acting alone can prevent the changes or easily cope with their possible consequences. Meanwhile the discovery that acids in rain are often formed from pollutants emitted hundreds of miles away in foreign countries has raised new legal and moral issues.

Some environmental challenges, then, are truly international. But the immediate causes and consequences of others, including those that take the greatest known toll—such as contamination of habitats by human body wastes, destruction of soils and forests, and even most contamination of air and water with hazardous substances—are essentially local. Only the design and enforcement of appropriate local development patterns and regulations can improve things. An international treaty can do little to stop a desperate farmer in Colombia from clearing a steep hillside, or to save a factory worker in India from cancer-causing asbestos fibers in his workplace.

Still, some forms of local resource degradation are today so widespread that they add up to matters of global concern. Cropland degradation, wherever it occurs, contributes to increases in the real cost of producing food and other agricultural goods; in an interdependent world food market, people everywhere can be affected. The denuding of forest lands causes the greatest harm where it occurs, but rising wood prices in the world marketplace appear certain to be a source of inflation in the decades ahead.

The most rampant forest clearing occurs in the humid tropics, which house untold numbers of scientifically unexamined plant and animal species. As forests are felled, thousands of species may be wiped out. The resulting losses of organisms or chemicals of potential value to medicine, industry, or agriculture cannot be known. But the potential mass extinction of irreplaceable species and unique ecosystems should concern people everywhere—for both economic and ethical reasons.

The deterioration of natural systems in poor and marginal areas is at once a symptom and a cause of the extreme misery in which hundreds of millions live. The natural resource problems cannot be isolated from questions of economic progress, political stability, population growth, migration, and international aid—matters that figure prominently in international relations.

Hence many types of localized environmental degradation have global implications. To some degree their causes are also international. Through their purchases and the behavior of their multinational corporations, citizens of the North can affect environmental conditions in the South. Once-rich African and Southeast Asian tropical forests have been grossly depleted to supply wood to Europe and Japan. Central American forests are being imprudently transformed into pastures to supply hamburger to North America.

More important, the extent of the extreme poverty that gives rise to so much ecological damage and human suffering is influenced by international monetary, trade, and aid policies. The struggle to preserve global environmental quality is unavoidably intertwined with the struggle to improve the lot of the global underclass.

I. Human Conditions

2 THE GLOBAL UNDERCLASS

ABOUT 800 MILLION PEOPLE, nearly one-fifth of humanity, are so completely deprived of income, goods, and even hope as to put them in a special class. These the World Bank has called the "absolute poor." Their conditions were well described by Robert McNamara, who as president of the bank did much to focus world attention on this global underclass: "Absolute poverty is a condition of life so degraded by disease, illiteracy, malnutrition, and squalor as to deny its victims basic human necessities; a condition of life so limited as to prevent realization of the potential of the genes with which one is born; a condition of life so degrading as to insult human dignity." Roughly half the absolute poor live in the three South Asian countries of India, Bangladesh, and Pakistan. Large numbers live elsewhere in Asia, especially Indonesia, and in Sub-Saharan Africa, with the remainder scattered among countries in the Middle East and Latin America and the Caribbean.[1]

Struggling week by week to survive, caught in endless cycles of hunger, illiteracy, exploitation, and disease, the absolute poor have no time to worry about global environmental trends. Yet in many ways they are more deeply affected by environmental quality than are the affluent. Most of the rural poor live directly off the soils, forests, waters, and wildlife whose deterioration has become the object of so much international concern. Many are forced by circumstances beyond their control to destroy the very resources from which they must scrape their living. In the cities the poor live amid squalor, and are often the prime victims of industry's pollution too.

The persistence of extreme poverty reflects both international and national economic inequalities. The poorest half of the world's people live in countries that account for less than 5 percent of the world's income, while the richest 13 percent live in countries enjoying nearly 60 percent of the income. More than a billion people live in countries where the average annual income in 1981 was $220 or less, and where trends make a mockery of the term "developing countries." Over the next five years real per capita income in these poorest countries is expected to grow by an average of no more than 1 percent annually —a derisive two or three dollars extra per person each year. And several African countries face *declines* in per capita income.[2]

So foreseeable economic growth will not do much to reduce the ranks of the extremely poor. Even robust growth has often bypassed the underclass. To quote a World Bank report: "Although there has been encouraging economic growth in most of the developing countries over the past three decades, a very large portion of their people have not shared in its benefits. On average, the poorest 40 percent of their societies is not much better off than it was."[3] Global and national policies to spur faster economic growth in the poorest countries remain sorely needed. But the problem of absolute poverty points inescapably to the needs for greater equity and power-sharing within countries.

Experience in several places, such as Sri Lanka, the state of Kerala in India, and China, has proven that internal reforms in the distribution of services, assets, and decision-making power can relieve the grip of extreme deprivation even where average incomes are quite low. Thus while growth-oriented measures are desirable, so too are equity-oriented reforms. Too many people, especially the rural landless and tribal peoples, have been casualties rather than beneficiaries of prevailing Third World development patterns.

The following pages include discussions of four overlapping but conceptually distinct elements of the global underclass: the hungry and undernourished, the rural landless, the urban squatters and slum dwellers, and tribal peoples. Why so much attention to the plight of these groups in a book about the environment? Some of the world's most severe environmental problems, those involving the degradation of natural resources in the tropics, cannot be solved in the absence of economic progress among the absolute poor. Economic development may carry its environmental risks, but as the discussions in this book on forests, soils, and biological diversity underscore, a lack of development for those on the bottom carries unavoidable environmental costs. Furthermore, achieving the international political consensus needed to confront shared environmental threats will be unlikely in a world of widening international disparities; the priorities of the developing countries will simply lie elsewhere. Thus inequality both within and among nations is a threat to the environment.

The most important reason for focusing on the plight of the absolute poor transcends ecological concerns. The struggle to preserve a decent environment is but one part of the struggle to create a decent world. Whose vision of a desirable future can countenance such utter degradation for so many? For reasons both practical and moral, those working to safeguard the environment must also work for a more just social order.

Pictures of the bleak faces and grotesque bodies of the starving usually impinge on the lives of the better-off during famines. But famines are temporary phenomena, usually brought on by drought or war in combination with governmental indifference or incompetence. In an era of lightning communications and worldwide transportation there is no technical reason why famines should exist at all—and in fact their toll has fallen over the last century. But the emergency aid measures that forestall famine do nothing to alleviate the fundamental food problem: the chronic undernutrition suffered by many of the world's destitute. (I use the term "undernutrition" in order to distinguish this state from "overnutrition"—the form of malnutrition that shortens lives among the rich.)

Describing the extent of undernutrition is a complex and necessarily imprecise business. The poorest of the poor, the undernourished are almost by definition beyond the grasp of government programs and statisticians. Even the clinical definition of undernutrition is sometimes revised and often disputed.

On average, the residents of the poorer countries consume much less food than do residents of richer countries. The average per capita consumption of calories in developing countries is only about two-thirds that in developed countries, of protein only one-half, and of high-quality animal protein just one-fifth. If all the grain fed to livestock and poultry and then consumed indirectly by people is added in, the citizens of developed countries can be said to consume three times the food of those in developing countries.[4]

However, the extent of undernutrition is more a function of income and consumption patterns within than among countries. A developing country like China can have low averages of income and calorie consumption, but because of relatively equal distribution, little undernutrition. In a country with great income disparities like Brazil, considerable undernutrition may coexist with comparatively high average income and food-consumption levels. In the rich countries undernutrition is sometimes found among unusually isolated and poor people—but obesity is more often the life-threatening nutritional affliction of poor people in rich societies.

The United Nations Food and Agriculture Organization (FAO), analyzing national food supply and distribution patterns, has roughly estimated the numbers of the undernourished. In the mid-1970s, according to their calculations, about 415 million people—one-tenth of humanity—consumed less than the "minimum critical diet" below which health may be endangered. Around two-thirds of these victims of the modern social order, 286 million of them, lived in Asia, with the bulk of these found in the populous and poor South Asian countries of India, Pakistan, and Bangladesh. Sixty-eight million Africans, forty-one million Latin Americans, and nineteen million residents of the Near East were believed to be undernourished.[5]

Using a somewhat different approach, World Bank analysts have measured the prevalence of "calorie-deficient diets" in forty developing countries. (While shortages of protein or of specific vitamins and minerals are common, outright shortages of calories account for most of the Third World's undernutrition.) They estimate that 500 million people, close to half the populace of the studied countries, consume less than 90 percent of the calories recommended by the U.N. expert committee that sets global standards on this matter.[6]

The ill effects of undernourishment are often nearly invisible. Outside of famine zones and refugee camps, overt starvation is uncommon. People, especially adults, often somehow adjust to levels of food consumption that scientists say are clearly inadequate. But this is no cause for complacency; the adjustment is usually a costly one. Chronic undernutrition can mean chronic health problems, a higher chance of death from disease at any age, heightened odds of mortality for mothers during childbirth and their babies, and a reduced capacity for work. Routine diseases such as diarrhea and measles are routine killers among the undernourished. And the issue is more than one of biological survival; because of undernutrition, hundreds of millions of people have little chance of achieving their full human potential.

Much hunger is seasonal, and occurs when outsiders are least likely to see it. About one-fifth of the world's people live in rural areas with pronounced dry and wet seasons. During the dry months the land looks most desolate and life looks most harsh. But, ironically, it is usually during the life-giving rains that people are worst off. In more isolated areas food stocks from the previous year's harvest become depleted just as the labor requirements for the future crop peak. The nutritional consequences can be severe. A study in rural Gambia, for instance, found pregnant women—who should have been putting on pounds—to be losing weight during the rains, imperiling their own health and that of their babies. Personal hygiene also tends to retrogress in muddy and flooded habitats.

In the rainy season the dirt roads that link villages with the outside world are often impassable and always unpleasant to traverse. The visits of government officials, foreign experts, even doctors become much less frequent than they are in drier periods, giving rise to what British social scientist Robert Chambers has called the "tarmac bias" in official perceptions of poverty.[7]

For at least ten million people, nearly all of them children, the situation is quite visibly grim for those who care to look. Needing twice as many nutrients per unit of body weight as their elders do, growing children are particularly vulnerable to severe undernourishment. Children among poorer groups in much of Asia and Africa and pockets of Latin America and the Caribbean display the bloated bellies, emaciated limbs, and hollow stares of extreme nutritional distress. Community surveys have revealed that from 1 to 7 percent of preschool children in various developing countries weigh less than 60 percent of their expected level. Those who survive this wretched state face life with stunted growth and, according to some evidence, with impaired mental capacities. Tens of millions more children suffer from less severe degrees of undernourishment that saps their resistance to disease.[8]

If the proportion of the world's population that is undernourished is well below the popular conception that "half the world is starving," it still remains unconscionable—unconscionable because so unnecessary. According to UNICEF, a transfer of just 2 percent of the world's grain output to the plates of the poor would largely eliminate undernutrition.[9] And one-third of the world's grain is fed to livestock and poultry each day. The numbers show beyond doubt that the root cause of today's hunger is not a global imbalance between the supply of food and the number of mouths to feed.

Redistribution of food supplies on the needed scale would not, however, be as simple as it may sound. Two percent of the approximately one and a half billion tons of grain produced each year is no small quantity. Getting it to the right people at the right time would be extraordinarily expensive and, more important, well beyond political and organizational capacities in much of the world. Moreover, the ultimate impact of such massive food handouts on needed agricultural progress within the regions of hunger could well be negative, as farm prices and pressures for agrarian reform were reduced. Properly designed food aid, especially that aimed at mothers and infants, used for relief in emergencies, and used as wages for construction of infrastructure, has its place. But a central lesson of the last few decades has been that the hunger problem cannot be fully isolated from the basic problems of poverty and underdevelopment that are its source. The persistence of undernutrition in a world that produces ample food for all is only one of the more heart-wrenching consequences of global development patterns that leave hundreds of millions of people with no opportunity to be productive.

People who consume too little food also tend to have too little clean water, too little decent housing, too little schooling, even too little entertainment. Economists have observed that many supposedly undernourished people spend any extra money on things other than food. Sometimes, in fact, people who receive food in aid programs sell it and use the money to buy other goods. However, this should not be taken as evidence that such people are well nourished. The costs of undernutrition can be subtle while other needs can be pressing— and in any case humans do not live by bread alone. No one should be forced to make the choices that those on the bottom must make daily.

One thing is sure: the blight of hunger will not be banished from the earth if business continues as usual. In their 1980 study of calorie deficiencies for the World Bank, Shlomo Reutlinger and Harold Alderman found that although a continuation of historic rates of economic growth and income-distribution patterns would result in a reduction of the proportion of developing-country residents who are undernourished in 1990, the absolute number would rise. Confirming what radical critics of the food economy have long been saying, they concluded: "The normal course of development, even with a vigorous expansion in food production, is not likely to solve the nutrition problem."[10] Nutritional data are merely confirming what earlier studies of general economic trends revealed: under the conditions prevailing in most developing countries the wait for the benefits of unregulated economic growth to trickle down to the poor is apt to be long if not altogether futile.

While agricultural progress in the developing countries is clearly not sufficient to eliminate hunger, it remains a necessary part of the solution. This is true for several reasons. First, if global food output lags behind the growth in demand, prices will rise, pulling the cost of adequate diets beyond the reach of ever more people. The developing countries constitute the world's greatest reservoir of unexploited food-producing potential; their success in boosting production is a matter of concern both to themselves and to the world at large, which will face the inflationary consequences of failure. Second, given the rather slim odds that global wealth will be spread more equally in the near future, each country has an obligation to pursue a food strategy that has a realistic chance of meeting basic internal needs—and in most cases this means growing much more food domestically. Many countries will lack the foreign exchange to import large amounts of food in the decades ahead even if ample surpluses should be available on the world market. Third, a broader development strategy that gives the poor the income to buy adequate diets will in almost every case be centered on agricultural development. Growing more food and giving more people the means to buy it should be part and parcel of the same process.

The food-production record of many developing countries over the last two decades has been fairly respectable. Since the early 1960s output in Latin America and Asia has climbed faster than the population, resulting in a net increase in average supplies per capita. The extent to which the economic benefits of these sizable production increases have been widely shared, reducing the numbers of the hungry, varies by country. But almost certainly a decline in per capita food output would have caused serious harm to the poor.

Unfortunately just such a decline has occurred in Africa, where dismal agricultural performance and extremely rapid population growth have combined to reduce per capita food output by more than 10 percent over the last twenty years. In several African countries even the absolute level of food production has fallen under the impacts of agricultural mismanagement and ecological degradation.[11]

Third World food demands rise relentlessly, not only because of population growth but also because of rising incomes and changing tastes, especially in the cities. The net effect is steeply rising food imports for the developing countries as a whole—imports that are already draining foreign-exchange coffers and thus reducing opportunities for productive capital investments. By 1981 the developing countries were importing 100 million tons of grain a year.[12]

Projections to 1990 and beyond, which show imports continuing to soar, paint a picture that is not likely to materialize.[13] Third World consumers will have to compete with affluent citizens of Western Europe, Japan, and the Soviet Union for food supplies that largely come from North America. While further increases in exports from the United States, Canada, and a few other countries are certainly feasible, production costs are rising in the wake of the oil-price jumps —and serious questions are being raised in the United States about the impact of all-out production efforts on long-term soil productivity. All in all, the financial capacity of many poorer countries fully to meet their projected food deficits with imports is questionable. Or if they do so, it will be at the expense of broader economic progress. Either way, the scope of undernutrition is not apt to be narrowed.

A preferable path—indeed, the only path that leads to a future one can view with anything other than foreboding—is for the developing countries to accelerate domestic food output (and at the same time to decelerate the growth in demand by slowing population growth). The technical potential exists for massive rises in food production, particularly where water resources have not yet been harnessed for irrigation. But the costs will be high. By one recent estimate investments in Third World agriculture must more than triple in the 1980s if the projected deficits are to be avoided—this at a time when massive new energy investments are also needed and foreign aid funds are less adequate than ever.[14] Beyond the traditional investments in infrastructure and services, greater attention must be paid to watershed management, forestry, and soil conservation in order to safeguard the agricultural resource base, and new farming systems must be developed that depend less on fossil fuels.

As important as the scale of agricultural investment is the way it is spent. If agrarian reforms, smallholder progress, employment creation, and the spread of opportunities are stressed, hunger can be wiped out. If matters of equity are ignored, undernutrition will surely persist despite rapid growth in food production.

Most of the world's absolute poor live in rural areas, and most of them are either landless laborers or people who lack secure access to enough farmland to support themselves at a decent level. Spreading landlessness is a root cause of many other ills, including runaway urbanization, uncontrolled international migration, mass underemployment, and the destruction of natural resources.

In the rural Third World today the control of farmland remains the principal key to wealth and power. In the absence of widespread industrial growth, most rural residents must make a living in agriculture if they are to make a living at all. Yet perhaps 600 million people live in rural households that are either completely landless or that lack secure rights to adequate farmland. They are struggling to improve their lives through farming without control of the basis of agricultural life. Many sell their labor to more fortunate farmers for a pittance; others rent land at exorbitant rates under sharecropping terms that smother incentives for investment and innovation; still others scratch what produce they can from inadequately sized family plots and seek employment elsewhere to make ends meet.[15]

Discussions of the rural poor too often lump them all together as "small farmers." This indiscriminate use of the term can be dangerous, because it conceals the major stratifications that pervade most rural societies. Many families with small landholdings can indeed benefit from technical assistance. However, in the words of Milton J. Esman of Cornell University, the stereotypical small farmers "are seldom the majority of rural households and they are certainly not the poorest."[16]

Landless laborers, sharecroppers, and marginal farmers together constitute the majority of rural residents in most countries of Asia and Latin America, and they are rising in number in Africa, where land inadequacy has only recently begun to emerge as a major problem. These people, the dispossessed of the earth, have generally been bypassed by economic development and in some cases have been harmed by it. While the picture is by no means simple or uniform, studies in a host of countries—including Bangladesh, Indonesia, Malaysia, Pakistan, the Philippines, Thailand, and India—indicate that the incomes of many rural groups have declined in absolute terms over the last two decades, often in the face of considerable national economic growth.[17]

In noncommunist Asia, reports the FAO, some 30 percent of the rural labor force is now completely landless. Perhaps as many more are farming marginal plots or renting under oppressive conditions. Through most of Asia the average farm is quite small by international standards, and among those fortunate enough to own farmland, ownership in Asia tends to be more broadly based than it is in Latin America. Inequality among landowners is nonetheless substantial, and the concentration of large holdings in a few hands joins population growth as an explanation for widespread landlessness. Some 11 percent of Bangladesh's families own more than half the country's land. In India in 1971, 70 percent of the farms were smaller than two hectares and included just 21 percent of the total farmland, while 4 percent of the farms were larger than ten hectares and occupied 31 percent of the farmland. In the Philippines in 1971, 5 percent of the farms were larger than ten hectares but they accounted for 34 percent of all cropland. By contrast, in South Korea, where significant land reforms have been carried out, 92 percent of the farms were three hectares or smaller in 1974, and they accounted for 93 percent of all farmland.[18]

In Latin America, according to the FAO, 7 percent of the landowners possessed a startling 93 percent of the arable land as of 1975. Throughout most of South and Central America, small numbers of giant estates occupy the better farmlands and coexist with large numbers of miniscule farms that are often unable to support a family.[19]

Landlessness and land concentration have long plagued portions of North Africa, and until recently Ethiopia was notorious for the near-feudal conditions under which many of its peasants labored. Throughout much of Sub-Saharan Africa, however, traditional tenure systems, in which land is owned by the tribe and allocated to individuals for use but not for sale, have predominated. The apparent availability of large "unused" areas has further fed the notion that landlessness is not a threat in Sub-Saharan Africa.

This relatively benign image of African tenure problems is increasingly misleading. The empty spaces create a mistaken impression. In vast areas of Africa the climate, soils, or other ecological factors make farming or even sustained grazing impossible. Elsewhere the soils and meager rainfall necessitate lengthy fallow periods if soil productivity is to be maintained.

The truth is that land scarcity is emerging as a problem in more and more parts of Africa. Where populations are pressing against the arable land base, a common result has been a transition from tribal to individual land rights—accompanied by the usual patterns of land accumulation by the wealthy, absentee landlordism, tenancy, and landlessness. These trends have progressed furthest in areas growing commercial export crops, such as West Africa's cocoa regions and East Africa's coffee lands. But they are fast appearing in peasant food-crop areas as well.

The problem of landlessness in Sub-Saharan Africa may be most advanced in Kenya. Farms bigger than 100 hectares occupy one-fifth of the country's cropland, and the large farms are getting larger. Yet more than half the country's farmers hold just two hectares or less, accounting for under 15 percent of the total cropland. By the early 1970s nearly one-fifth of rural households were landless. Notes John Cohen of Harvard University: "The Kenyan goal of small, relatively prosperous landowning farmers with a stake in a stable capitalistic system and an interest in progressive farming practices is increasingly threatened by the rise of land concentration, exploitive tenancy, landlessness, and other patterns which seem to go hand-in-hand with the tolerance of unregulated freehold tenure in the agrarian nations of the developing world."[20]

Kenya provides an ominous portent for the rest of black Africa. Doubling every twenty-four years, Africa's population is outpacing the expansion of cropped area, which increased by only 12 percent between the early 1960s and 1975. Increasing land scarcity and competition are inevitable throughout much of the continent, and in the absence of national policies to control private land accumulation and tenancy practices, as well as to slow population growth, Africa will develop the same land-based social conflicts and production inefficiencies that have long been apparent in Latin America and Asia.

Worldwide, the number of landless and near-landless people appears to be growing fast. Demographic pressures alone almost guarantee this: despite considerable migration to cities or foreign countries, rural populations are still growing at close to 2 percent a year in much of Africa and Asia. Even where they are feasible, land-settlement schemes cannot absorb more than a small fraction of the tide of potential farmers. The contribution of population growth to landlessness is often supplemented by other developments within the agricultural economy: land accumulation by better-off farmers; emergency sales of land by marginal owners; the spread of large commercial farms, sometimes foreign-owned; and the eviction of tenants by landowners fearful of tenancy reforms or seeing a chance to profit from the use of new technologies. While estimates of the magnitude of these trends toward inequality are not available, recent evidence from Asia in particular suggests that over the last decade and a half of rapid agricultural growth, land concentration has generally increased, boosting the proportion of insecure sharecroppers and landless laborers. At the same time economic policies in most developing countries have not promoted widespread nonfarm employment opportunities that could provide alternative livelihoods for agriculture's refugees. By the end of the century it seems probable that one billion or more residents of the rural Third World will lack secure access to farmland.

Spreading landlessness will manifest itself in many ugly ways. Obviously, it is a major link in the chain of circumstances that produces soaring rural-urban migration in many Third World countries (and illegal international migration as well). Those trying to cope with the afflictions of mushrooming shantytowns increasingly realize that the urban prospect may be hopeless if more is not done to spread opportunities in the countryside.

Ecological degradation is an even more alarming symptom of mounting landlessness. Lacking land or jobs in traditional farming areas, peasant farmers clear and plant lands that should never be farmed. They move into rain forests, destroying diverse ecosystems in what often turn out to be futile attempts at sustainable farming. Sometimes within sight of huge, underutilized agricultural estates in valley floors, desperate farmers in South and Central America plow up mountain slopes so steep that the topsoil washes away within a year or two.

In semiarid zones of Africa and Asia, land-hungry farmers plant in low-rainfall zones which, when the inevitable drought comes, turn into dust bowls. Meanwhile, they squeeze herders into ever more restricted areas and the problem of overgrazing is intensified. The emerging inadequacy of the land base in relation to population and technology is often partially concealed by a destructive form of involution: a steady decline in the soil-preserving fallow period.

The lopsided landholding patterns of much of the Third World are also inefficient economically. Other things being equal, large estates tend to produce less per unit of land than owner-operated small farms do. At the same time existing tenancy arrangements in some areas, such as Bangladesh and the state of Bihar in India, inhibit technical innovation. Where tenant farmers must buy all inputs and take all risks, must give over half their produce to the landowner, and are moved about from plot to plot each year, the adoption of new seeds and fertilizers—let alone the expenditure of time on soil-conservation measures—is unlikely.[21]

In addition, a skewed landholding pattern contributes to unemployment. Virtually everywhere, more labor is expended per unit of land on small farms than on large ones. In Kenya farms of under four hectares average nine times more labor input per hectare than do farms of forty hectares or more. Partly because of this they also produce six times more per hectare. In Colombia small farms use labor five times as intensively as large farms and thirteen times as intensively as cattle ranches.[22]

The economic significance of broadly shared agricultural progress —of which the fairer sharing of agricultural assets may be a prerequisite—goes beyond the direct benefits in terms of output and employment. With rising incomes and secure prospects, the rural poor demand simple consumer goods and farm implements, supporting the emergence of local industries and handicrafts. Productive, equitable agriculture and small-scale industries can reinforce each other, promoting a sustainable process of growth and a climate of progress in which people's receptivity to family planning may rise as well. Hence, because of the secondary and long-term benefits, agrarian reforms often make economic sense even where population pressures and land scarcity mean that land redistribution cannot provide plots to all who want them. Through their indirect effects on employment and industry, land reforms can ultimately help even those who do not receive land.

The effects of landlessness and grossly skewed landownership patterns on political stability must also be noted. Questions of land availability and distribution lie at the heart of recent political violence in Central America and portions of India; these examples provide a taste of things to come in many more places as well. Struggles for control over land and its fruits are certain to become more acute in country after country.

Reforms in land distribution, tenancy, and agrarian support-systems; economic development patterns that provide broad opportunities to earn a reasonable income; a slowing of rapid population growth —all three are elements of a strategy to forestall the spread of landlessness and its myriad ill effects. And progress in each of these areas is linked to progress in the other two.

The rural landless have their counterparts in the slums and shantytowns of Third World cities. Because the urban poor are so much more visible and politically threatening, they tend to receive disproportionate attention from the media and politicians in comparison with the more numerous, and usually worse off, rural poor. Nonetheless hundreds of millions of city dwellers live in physical environments that can only be described as abysmal. Daily life is for many a desperate and precarious affair; lacking economic security and political power, they are buffeted about by forces completely beyond their control.

That the urban areas of the Third World have been growing at a rapid clip is well known. Urbanization is one of the great social phenomena of the century, with the proportion of the world's people living in urban settlements rising from 14 percent in 1920 to 41 percent in 1980. In Latin America, as in the developed regions, the process is more advanced and over half the population already lives in cities. In Asia and Africa the proportion remains lower; about 30 percent of the population of the Third World as a whole now reside in cities. But about one-third of these live in the squalid slums and shantytowns that have optimistically been dubbed "transitional settlements" in U.N. documents.

Between 1970 and 1980 the urban population of developing countries grew by 4 percent a year, an increase of 320 million city dwellers over the decade. (By comparison, cities in the developed world grew at a rate of 1.2 percent annually.) This growth simply overwhelmed governmental capacities to provide basic services and to promote the construction of adequate housing. Slums and squatter settlements comprised the fastest growing sectors of Third World cities.

If urban growth of 320 million over the last decade could give rise to such widespread official despair about urban prospects, not to mention so much human degradation, then what will be the consequences of the growth expected over the next two decades? The United Nations projects the urban population of the Third World to increase by more than one billion between 1980 and 2000. By the end of the century sixty developing-country cities will count more than four million residents each, eighteen of them more than ten million.

Substandard housing is the most obvious consequence of runaway urbanization. While data are hard to come by, available information suggests that housing conditions deteriorated in most developing countries in the 1970s—contradicting the developed-country trend. Most cities face gross shortages of low-cost dwellings even as high-priced housing lies vacant and urban land lies idle. According to one survey, reported at the 1976 United Nations Conference on Human Settlements (Habitat), anywhere from 35 to 68 percent of the households in selected cities were unable to afford the cheapest available conventional housing. Even government-subsidized "low-income" dwellings are too expensive for large numbers of people.

In response, some crowd into inner-city slums. Housing occupancy in the West is measured in terms of rooms per person, that in the Third World in terms of persons per room. Forty percent of India's urban population lives in one-room houses containing an average of 4.6 people; more than half the families in many Nigerian cities occupy one room. Half the urban houses in Indonesia contain more than one family. Overall, it is not uncommon to find four or five people living in each room of old tenement buildings in Third World cities.[23]

With the old slums overflowing, huge numbers of people become squatters on vacant lands or buy illegally subdivided plots and build their own dwellings—anything from tarpaper shanties to sturdy and livable structures. The most disadvantaged people tend to wind up on dangerously steep hillsides or in flood zones, where natural hazards join overcrowding and the lack of sanitation to endanger health. Because they live in illegal areas, squatters are seldom served by convenient water connections, let alone sewage disposal facilities or garbage collection. In many cities they must pay exorbitant rates for water that is carted in by private vendors, and thus end up paying more per unit for this basic need than do the rich. They are often victimized by severe air pollution and waterborne toxic chemicals—the effluents of others' affluence.

In 1980 half of Mexico City's fourteen million residents lived in shantytowns with few basic services, and 10–15 percent lived in overcrowded central-city tenements. As of 1975 four-fifths of the 650,000 people in Guayaquil, Ecuador, lived either in substandard slums or in shacks built over swamps or land subject to frequent floods. In the Philippines in 1979, four million urban dwellers were crammed into slum buildings or lived in squatter settlements.[24]

Why people migrate to such conditions has been the subject of considerable research and debate. One major reason is the lack of economic opportunities in the countryside. At the same time the hope of landing a well-paying job and the attractions of the modern world in the city play some role too. The actual economic prospects migrants find in the cities are often dismal; in general, unemployment and underemployment are rampant. Few can afford to be truly unemployed, but those who spend long days collecting cigarette butts so they can extract and sell the tobacco in them, or who hawk chewing gum for sixteen hours daily, can hardly be said to have productive jobs. Even so, when the rural economy is as stagnant or rigidly stratified as it is in many countries, the move to urban slums is usually a rational economic choice. If just one family member eventually finds a modern-sector job, the group can be better off than before. Moreover, miserable as urban living conditions may appear, mortality rates in city slums are usually below those among the rural poor, and opportunities for education much higher.

Despite the high-blown speeches at the 1976 Habitat Conference, few governments have elaborated realistic strategies for confronting the urban settlements crisis. With rare exceptions, programs to build low-cost public housing have scarcely dented the problem; often even subsidized public housing can be afforded only by the middle and upper income groups. Experience shows that where people are provided some security of tenure and minimal assistance with other services, quite remarkable self-help efforts can materialize, making squatter areas "transitional" in a genuine and positive sense. As a recent study by the International Institute for Environment and Development concluded, public controls on urban land speculation, measures to provide cheap residential plots, programs to provide security of tenure on illegally occupied lands, loans for self-help activities, support for production of inexpensive building materials, and measures to provide basic water and power supplies to the urban poor will do far more good than housing programs per se.[25]

While major shifts in government programs and priorities within the cities are called for, many analysts doubt whether Third World cities can withstand the pressures projected for the coming decades. Realistic projections of industrial growth do not provide hope that modern jobs will open up on anywhere near the required scale. The combined cost of food, fuel, and water is becoming unbearable for many of the urban destitute, and the prices of such goods seem destined to keep rising. In many countries the effort to meet these minimal needs is inflicting broader social costs as well, as food and oil imports soar and precious forests are razed to supply fuelwood or charcoal to urban residents. A shift in development priorities to the countryside—combining faster economic growth with more equity— may be the only feasible way to slow the wave of migrants. Regeneration of rural areas is the key to a better life in the cities as well.[26]

Tribal peoples constitute a significant and often-ignored element of the global underclass. Although a precise definition of the term is elusive, tribal peoples are ethnically distinct populations that in many cases live in geographic and political isolation from the dominant society. Many still practice some form of sustained-yield, low-energy

agriculture such as shifting cultivation or nomadism, or they live by
hunting and gathering. They tend to have little political power and
little chance to participate meaningfully in the decisions that determine their fates.

They differ from the rural peasantry in their comparative lack of
integration into the national economy and their identification with a
separate, traditional religion and leadership. Their land needs for
subsistence and cultural survival are much larger than those of peasant farmers. As tribal peoples' contacts with the dominant society
increase, the conditions of those who survive tend more and more to
resemble those of the nontribal peasantry and the urban poor. However, because of their particular cultural and ecological vulnerabili-
ties, tribal peoples require special forms of assistance and protection
if interactions with outsiders are not to have catastrophic effects on
personal and group well-being.

According to a recent estimate by Survival International, nearly
200 million people, or 4 percent of the global population, can be said
to live in isolated or dominated tribal cultures.[27] This total includes
the better known groups such as the remaining few million Indians
of South America and the tens of millions of tribal people, mainly rain
forest dwellers, living in Southeast Asia. In black Africa, where most
people identify with a tribe, deciding who to include under the label
is difficult, but such groups as the nomads of the Saharan fringes, the
Pygmys of central Africa, and the Khoi-San peoples (Bushmen and
Hottentots) of southern Africa are included in the list.

Some of the more numerous tribal peoples are not well known
internationally. In India, for example, about forty million people are
ethnically and culturally distinct "tribals," and they generally share
the bottom rung of the socioeconomic ladder with the "untoucha-
bles," the lowest caste in the prevailing Hindu culture. Thirty-six
million in China, twenty-two million in the Soviet Union, and one and
a half million in North America live in tribal cultures.

New tribes are still being discovered in the Amazonian and Southeast Asian rain forests. One small group contacted in the Philippines
in the 1960s, the Tasaday, was so totally isolated that it used Stone
Age technology. Even today road-building crews in the Amazon basin
can come across a previously unknown tribe. And some tribal groups
are being physically decimated as a result of the intrusion of modern

civilization. Occasionally by the design of those who covet their lands, but usually because of the callousness of governments, corporations, colonists, and even missionaries, tribes fall prey in appalling numbers to simple infectious diseases to which they lack resistance. To give but one example: a Nambiquara village of 120 in Brazil's Western Amazon lost six members to hired gunmen in 1967, then suffered a measles epidemic in 1971 that wiped out every child under age fifteen. Overall, the Nambiquara tribe's numbers have been reduced from 10,000–15,000 at the turn of the century to just 530 today under the combined impacts of disease, violence, and the carving up of their lands by ranchers and colonists.[28] In the Amazon and elsewhere, "protected" tribal lands are often demarcated and redemarcated according to the convenience or greed of others rather than the needs of the natives.

Whether carried out by public or private entities, development projects that affect tribal lands—commonly hydroelectric dams, mining schemes, and large-scale agricultural enterprises—are often pursued in a manner insensitive of the basic rights and needs of the native inhabitants. Anthropologist Anthony Seeger, former head of a private Indian-support group in Brazil, has described the typical scenario:

The government defines economic priorities in conjunction with national and international business interests; social costs, especially with respect to native populations, are ignored; foreign money is obtained; projects are started; and only then is the presence of Indians acknowledged. Then it is a "problem" which needs quick resolution in the interests of development. . . . Contact with isolated tribes is over-hasty; transferral out of their homelands is the favored solution; large-scale population losses and cultural derangement are the common result.[29]

His description of events in Brazil could just as well be applied to experiences in many other countries of Latin America and Asia.

For native peoples, integration with the dominant culture generally means new forms of hardship and degradation. Peonage, debt bondage, and other forms of severe economic exploitation are not rare. Tribal peoples tend to become the lowliest of laborers, often in plantations or timber industries drawing on the very natural resources amid which they historically lived. Some wind up in city slums and work as servants or prostitutes. As their isolation is reduced, tribal people undergo what Latin American social scientists have called marginalization, a transition from a state of isolated independence to one of exploited dependence.

Culturally they fare little better. Where physical extinction no longer threatens, cultural extinction remains a constant possibility. Missionaries and insensitive educators, along with modern technologies and communications, can destroy the traditional culture without providing a workable new spiritual basis of existence. Tribal people are often pressured to adopt the traits of the dominant culture, but they remain despised by others and the objects of severe discrimination even when they do so. Alcoholism, mental disorders, and social disintegration are the common fates of "acculturated" native people. Many lead lives of dependency and despair on reservations; others disappear into the ranks of the rural and urban poor.

The destruction of indigenous cultures entails major costs for global society. The irretrievable loss of diverse traditions, philosophies, and languages certainly impoverishes human culture and our potential knowledge of ourselves. But the costs are in the material realm as well. Having mastered the art of survival in what are often harsh, marginal environments, tribal cultures constitute a priceless and unique repository of ecological knowledge. Modern scientists have hardly begun to learn about the qualities of the plants, animals, and soils of the rain forests and deserts where so many of the remaining tribal peoples live. Medical researchers have only recently appreciated the likelihood that numerous useful drugs will be discovered through the investigation of native medications. And undoubtedly many new sources of food and other economically useful products remain to be discovered in the rain forests. Untold thousands of tropical plant species are known to native peoples but not yet to modern scientists.

Even more valuable than their intricate knowledge of particular species may be the understanding of the dynamics of ecological systems that some tribal peoples have. Modern man has not had great success in finding sustainable ways to use the rain forests and the desert fringes. Many of the native dwellers of these zones have, by necessity, developed a sensitive understanding of the ecological interdependencies and seasonal variations, and know how to exploit the land without destroying it. The contrast is illustrated by events in Peru, described in a 1981 World Bank review of the problems of tribal peoples. Recent colonists in one rain forest area have been unable to feed themselves, even with outside assistance and inputs. In between outside food deliveries, they survive by bartering with or stealing from the nearby Indians, who produce a food surplus on similar lands without any outside inputs.[30]

In marginal environments, whose exploitation becomes more necessary each year, the desirable agricultural patterns of the future will almost surely combine modern technology with the insights of native cultures. The agroforestry systems now being touted as the key to rain forest agriculture, for example, are little more than intensified versions of traditional shifting cultivation. Those working to solve the desertification and overgrazing problems of the Saharan fringes in Africa now recognize the value of the knowledge of the nomads who have survived there so long through drought and breadbasket years alike.

The ecological knowledge of tribal cultures, most of which lack written languages, is seldom recorded on paper. It is passed by word of mouth. As the culture disintegrates, the accumulated knowledge of centuries is lost to humanity forever.

This is not an argument for working to preserve tribal societies as static artifacts for others' study and profit. The issue is not whether the dominant society should decide to preserve tribal cultures in a pristine and isolated state, although this option should be available to groups that choose it. Rather it is whether tribal peoples will be given more control over a process of evolution and integration that at best is bound to be extraordinarily painful and conflict-ridden. With basic protection against land-grabbing, violence, and economic exploitation, and institutions of government that allow self-determination, tribal peoples can work out their own paths of adaptation, and do so with a dignity that is too often denied them..

3 THE POPULATION FACTOR

IN HISTORICAL PERSPECTIVE, rapid population growth has been a brief and abrupt phenomenon. Two thousand years ago humans scarcely numbered 250 million; only in the early 1800s did the figure reach one billion. A second billion was added in one hundred years, a third in thirty years, and a fourth in just the fifteen years from 1960 to 1975. Today's world population of four and a half billion will rise to nearly six billion by century's end.

The era of the population explosion will necessarily be a short one. Exponential growth cannot long be sustained without producing stupendous and unsupportable numbers of people. The adjustment toward a new era of roughly stable population size has probably already begun. On some unknown day, most likely in the 1960s, the global growth rate peaked at somewhere near 2 percent and has declined somewhat since then. Still, the momentum of population growth remains awesome. The latest U.N. medium projections, which assume major continuing progress in fertility reduction over the decades ahead, show the world population stabilizing only after reaching 10.5 billion in the early twenty-second century.[1] (Like all such projections it is highly speculative, involving judgments about human behavior over the coming century.)

The world population is now growing by about 1.7 percent a year. But global averages do not convey the story. The developed countries are growing by just 0.6 percent annually. Several European countries have stable or even declining populations, and fertility in several other richer nations is below replacement level, the two-child average at which zero growth will eventually come about. The less-developed countries, containing three-fourths of the world's people, are growing at an average of more than 2 percent a year. Because of their faster pace of growth, the less-developed countries will account for close to four-fifths of the world's people by the year 2000.

Growth rates and trends vary considerably among the developing countries. China, the home of one billion, or two of every nine human beings, has acted aggressively to curb both birth rates and death rates, and now has growth of about 1.2 percent a year—down from more than 2 percent just one decade back. India, the other demographic colossus with nearly 700 million people, has much higher birth rates as well as higher death rates and is growing at about 2.2 percent a year. But Asia as a whole has an average rate of increase of under 2 percent, and the trend is downward.

Latin America's average growth rate, 2.3 percent, is also gradually falling. Africa, with the highest birth rate, a high but still falling death rate, and little family planning, is the fastest growing continent and will be for decades to come. Already expanding at what for demographers is a breathtaking 3 percent a year, Africa may well experience an even higher rate of increase in the near future.[2]

These differences in growth rates seem small until their implications over time are calculated. One of the real impediments to progress against the population explosion has been the lack of public appreciation of the simple arithmetic of exponential growth. A 3 percent growth rate means a doubling every twenty-four years; a 2 percent rate, a doubling every thirty-six years. And the built-in pressures for rapid growth will not end with the first doubling. One country, Kenya, is now growing at 4 percent a year, which will lead to a doubling in just eighteen years. If this rate were maintained for a century, which obviously it cannot be, Kenya's 1981 population of 16.5 million would multiply by fifty-one times to 840 million.

Also poorly understood is the inexorable growth momentum built into a youthful population. Some 45 percent of Africans, 40 percent of Latin Americans, and 37 percent of Asians are under fifteen years of age. (Only 24 percent of the developed world's people fall into this category.)[3] As these young people enter their childbearing years, the rapid spread of birth control has become essential just to keep from losing ground.

The recent U.N. medium projection of a world population stabilizing at 10.5 billion is lower than earlier estimates were, reflecting the recent fall-off in the global growth rate. Still, it hardly provides cause for complacency. Shifting from global generalities to the outlook for particular regions shows why. The U.N. projections show Africa's current population of 470 million rising to 2.2 billion—more than a quadrupling—before stabilizing in the twenty-second century. The population of Latin America multiplies more than three times, from 364 million to 1.2 billion. Asia rises from its present total of 2.5 billion to nearly six billion.

Examining where and when the next six billion people are supposed to appear, and comparing the results with what we know about the likely economic and ecological conditions that will greet them, raises unsettling questions. Will the projected numbers really materialize? If so, what will be the consequences for individual countries and for world order? The longer countries wait to confront the population factor, the more wrenching the process of demographic adjustment will be.

Population control burst forth in the late 1960s as a contentious international political issue. Emotional debates about whether rapid population growth is a problem at all, and if so, what to do about it, raged in development forums. These debates seemed to crescendo at the World Population Conference held by the United Nations in Bucharest in 1974.

Even at Bucharest, however, a political defusing of many key issues began to emerge. Amid the cacophony, the nations of the world collectively pronounced in Bucharest that "all couples and individuals have the basic right to decide freely and responsibly the number and spacing of their children and to have the information, education, and means to do so." Although too many governments have not yet acted to guarantee this basic right, its acceptance at the global political level was a historic event.

One factor broadening the support for birth control has been the mounting evidence of its health significance. Statistics now reveal the direct health costs of *not* promoting family planning and making it available to all regardless of ability to pay. Women who bear children too early or too late in life, women who bear too many children, and women who bear children too close together endanger themselves and their babies. The health consequences of unlimited fertility are particularly harsh for women and babies suffering the other environmental effects of poverty at the same time. Moreover, in the many countries where ready access to contraceptives and safe abortions does not exist, poorer women suffer extraordinary death rates at the hands of illegal abortionists. In short, like clean water and nutritious food, family planning is necessary to good health.[4]

For millions of the poorest women in Africa, Asia, and Latin America, teenage marriage is followed by two or more decades of nearly uninterrupted pregnancy and lactation. Often combined with hard labor and poor nutrition, continuous childbearing can produce women in their thirties with the enervated bodies of the aged, women who are especially susceptible to disease and early death themselves, and who give birth to weak babies.

Concern about the economic and ecological impacts of rapid population growth has led a rising number of governments to set goals for reducing the national population growth rate and to actively encourage couples to have smaller families. Many governments find that their efforts to increase savings for investment, to reduce unemployment, to provide universal education, to protect forests and croplands, and to reduce dependency on food imports are overwhelmed by surging human numbers. Rapid population growth per se is rarely the sole cause of failures to meet development goals. But it usually makes things worse.

Some have said that each baby is born not only with a mouth for consuming but also with two hands for producing. But the relevance of this statement to most developing countries is dubious. Too many of today's infants will never go to school, will have no land to farm and no access to a job productive enough to lift them from sheer poverty. As Vice-Premier Chen Muhua said in her 1979 explanation of China's aggressive birth-control policy, "When an infant grows up and reaches working age, he obviously cannot play the role of producer unless he possesses modern scientific, technological knowledge. . . . Without sufficient raw materials, without being equipped with sufficient advanced tools and machinery, he still can't fulfill his role as producer of material goods."[5]

The question is not whether population growth will slow, but how. And it is this matter of how—of strategy for cutting birth rates—that has engendered the greatest controversy: the so-called development versus contraception debate. Those of the first school, pointing to the "demographic transition" from high to low fertility of the West as it modernized, argue that the population problem will largely take care of itself when the world's poor enjoy the fruits of development. More refined versions of this approach stress the particular socioeconomic factors that lead parents to want large families—among them the needs for labor, for old-age security, and for certainty that some children will survive amid high mortality—and argue that targeted economic reforms and progress offer the only real answer.

Those of the second orientation, while not denying the critical need for development progress, stress the role of rapid population growth in hampering that progress. They argue that many couples in the developing world are already receptive to birth control when it is made freely available, and that propaganda to increase such receptiveness is in any case justified by overriding social needs, not to mention personal health and the human right to plan families.

Unfolding events have confirmed the obvious: both perspectives contain truth. Statistical surveys and observed trends show that both economic progress and family planning programs contribute to fertility declines. In a major review of the factors associated with recent fertility declines in developing countries, W. Parker Mauldin and Bernard Berelson found that social factors such as better health, higher adult literacy, more widespread education, and higher proportion of nonagricultural employment were significantly correlated with falls in fertility. But well-organized family planning programs had a significant impact too. The study's key finding was that broader social progress and family planning programs go best together, yielding more rapid declines in fertility than reliance on one or the other alone.[6]

As a rule, birth rates have fallen most rapidly in countries where the benefits of development have been most widely shared and have reached the poor majority on the bottom. However, generalizations about incomes and family size do not hold up well. Thus in Kenya rapid improvements in health and child survival have not yet led to the expected drop in fertility; Kenyan couples seem to want more babies than ever, and Kenya's population growth is higher than that in other much poorer African countries. In Indonesia demographic researchers have been surprised by the high receptivity to family planning among extremely poor people.[7]

Apparently the cultural, economic, and ecological forces at play in a given place are more relevant to today's population question than any sweeping historical theories. Moreover, the sad fact is that, for many countries, to wait for future affluence to solve the population problem would amount to committing social suicide. Their situation is without historical parallel; both the rates of population growth they face and the obstacles to development they face are higher than those ever confronted by the developed nations of the West.

People-oriented development and family planning provide mutually reinforcing benefits. Certain aspects of development—improved health, better education (especially of women), improved employment opportunities for women—are important in their own right, and can also establish a climate of progress in which desire for birth control rises. At the same time public education about the implications of high fertility for the family and society, and easy access to contraceptives for all people regardless of income, are crucial whatever a country's level of development.

Proposals to inundate the poor with contraceptives in the absence of strong development efforts have been called a form of oppression. But failure to guarantee access to modern birth-control methods too is oppression. The rich always find a safe way to limit births when they want to.

Theories aside, large numbers of women in developing countries today would like to limit their fertility but are not doing so—in many cases because they lack the knowledge and means. Evidence from the World Fertility Survey—the largest social science research project ever undertaken, involving surveys of women in sixty countries over the last decade—suggests the existence of a large unmet demand for family planning, especially in Asia and Latin America. The situation in many African countries, where traditional notions about the desirability of high fertility remain strong and organized family planning efforts are nonexistent, is less encouraging.

Analyzing interview results from fifteen Asian and Latin American countries, the United Nations Population Division observed that the proportion of married women wanting to cease childbearing "is surprisingly high, ranging from 30 percent in Nepal to 72 percent in Korea." As expected, the larger the existing family the more likely the desire to have no more children. Thus among women with five living children the proportion wanting to cease childbearing ranged from 66 percent in Nepal to more than 90 percent in Thailand and Sri Lanka. But the desire to limit births was surprisingly high among women with just two living children—at least 20 percent of such women in all the surveyed countries, and half or more in several (Bangladesh, Colombia, Korea, Sri Lanka) wanted no more children.[8] Moreover, figures like these greatly understate the demand for contraception because they do not account for women who want more children but wish to space the births.

Analysis of data from five Asian countries indicated that half or more of those saying they wanted to end childbearing were not using contraceptives. Clearly, not all this contradiction between desires and behavior can be explained by a lack of access to birth-control services. But in some cases this must be a dominant factor; in Nepal, more than three-fourths of women had never even heard of modern birth-control methods. In Pakistan years of public education had yielded a general awareness of the possibility of birth control, but only one-third of women knew where to go for assistance. Education has outpaced the spread of family planning services. However, even where they are widely available, cultural obstacles, including the attitudes of men, often inhibit the wider use of contraceptives.[9]

In many countries, attitudes about birth control seem to be going through a transition period in which several factors—among them knowledge about modern contraception, desires to limit births, improved child survival, and the convenient availability of family planning services—reinforce each other. In fact, as demographer Charles E. Westoff has argued, based on World Fertility Survey results, proximity to family planning services helps to create a demand for them; as people become more aware of the possibility of doing so, they become more interested in limiting family size.[10]

In the less-developed world, more than sixty countries, including nearly all the largest ones, have sanctioned family planning programs. However, the degree of political support given, and the effective reach of the programs, vary wildly. Governmental efforts are not the whole story. Private organizations, ranging from the International Planned

Parenthood Federation (IPPF) and its affiliates to countless local community groups, have played heroic roles in spreading the benefits of family planning, sometimes in the face of official indifference or hostility.

Today, 95 percent of the world's people live in countries with organized programs of some sort. But still, according to IPPF estimates, about 390 million women who were at risk of getting pregnant in 1980 were not using contraception. An undocumented but certainly large share of these women lacked knowledge of or ready access to effective means of preventing unwanted pregnancies. Furthermore, one-third of the world's women live in countries where abortion is still illegal—and hundreds of millions more lack access to safe abortions.[11]

Population programs are most common and advanced in Asia, where the pressures of people on limited resources have long been visible. In 1952 India became the first developing country to formulate an official population policy and establish a government-sponsored family planning program. If it has not brought dramatic results, the program has not been without impact. India's birth rate is considerably lower than that in the neighboring countries of Pakistan and Bangladesh, where policy statements have not been backed by anywhere near the organizational efforts seen in India. Widely reported incidents of forced sterilization helped stall the Indian program and bring down the Gandhi government in 1977. But now, shocked by census results that reveal only slight progress in reducing growth over the last twenty years, the Indian government is renewing the birth-control campaign. One notable point in South Asia: Where infant mortality has been sharply cut, as in Sri Lanka and the Indian state of Kerala, population growth has slowed most.

In terms of programs and results China's record of the last decade is unparalleled. Having made contraceptives and abortion universally available and backed this up with economic incentives and peer pressures for small families, China has pulled down its birth rate with incredible rapidity. Despite its comparatively youthful age structure and despite a per capita income of only $230, China may well be on the way to achieving its goal of zero population growth by the year 2000. It is doubtful, of course, that such dramatic progress would have been possible without the broader socioeconomic reforms that have occurred in China.

Elsewhere in Asia, Indonesia has become known for unusual success in introducing birth control to a largely rural, extremely poor populace, and motivating them to use it. Reliance on community-based organizations for education, social pressure, and delivery of services seems to be the key. Likewise, promotion of family planning by women's groups in much richer South Korea has been extremely successful.[12] Thailand and Taiwan have made impressive headway too, while the city-states of Singapore and Hong Kong have achieved birth and death statistics comparable to those of the West.

Among Latin American countries, Colombia has long stood out for its efforts to disseminate family planning services and the results are apparent: the birth rate is well below that in neighboring countries with comparable per capita incomes. Cuba has provided access to family planning as it improved the lives of the poor, and has the lowest birth rate in the Caribbean.

Mexico, abruptly reversing its earlier pronatal policy in 1972, is now working to bring contraceptives within reach of its entire population and is actively promoting smaller families; the birth rate has begun to dip. Brazil, South America's giant, has lacked a nationwide family planning program, although some people have had access to contraception through commercial channels and the efforts of private groups. Recently the government indicated a desire to move ahead in this area despite the continuing opposition of the Catholic church. Still, among the larger nations of the world Brazil is second only to Nigeria as a laggard in the development of modern population policies and programs.

Governments of the Arab world, save for Egypt, Tunisia, and Morocco, have done little to support birth control. But the greatest paucity of organized programs is in Sub-Saharan Africa. Most governments have shown little interest in the subject, and the rest have not put their ideas into practice. Kenya led the way in 1967, when it launched Sub-Saharan Africa's first official family planning program. However, the availability and quality of services have been grossly inadequate; fewer than half the respondents in a recent survey even knew where they could go for advice and supplies. More important, there seems as yet to be little real public demand for contraception in Kenya, though attitudes may be changing among younger people. In the early 1970s the government had hoped to push the national growth rate down from 3.5 percent to 3.0 percent by 1980. Instead the figure has risen to 4.0 percent, probably the world's highest rate of natural increase and a statistic that raises serious doubts about Kenya's development prospects.

The limited programs of a few other Sub-Saharan countries only underscore the central message: Africa is essentially a void when it comes to organized family planning efforts. If further progress in pulling down the continent's death rates is not accompanied by the spreading availability and use of contraception, extraordinary population pressures may push many countries ever deeper into economic and ecological mires. If experience elsewhere in the world is any guide, desired family size, which is uniquely high in Africa, will soon begin to fall. The provision of a family planning infrastructure along with the other elements of primary health care would ensure that contraception is available as the demand is created. Many African leaders do not seem to realize that by the time physical pressures and social dislocations force them to turn their attention to the demographic factor, it will be too late to forestall huge increases in human numbers.

Although nothing can substitute for a national commitment to family planning, international support is also vital to progress in the poorer countries. In 1980 international population grants of some $450 million were provided to developing countries, of which $150 million was channeled through the United Nations Fund for Population Activities. More than one-third of the total was provided by the United States, which has been the undisputed leader in population aid. The World Bank provided another $111 million in loans in the population field.[13]

These sums, which accounted for about 2 percent of all international development aid, are not commensurate with the existing demand from developing-country governments, let alone the global social need. Contrary to the belief widespread in the early 1970s that population assistance is being forced on the Third World, "international support for population policies is flagging at precisely the time when the commitment to, and political acceptance of, family-planning policies is spreading," in the words of the Brandt Commission. For example, the United Nations Fund for Population Activities, which has been quite successful in introducing demographic concerns and programs to politically wary countries, has recently been able to meet only two-thirds of the requests for assistance it receives from governments.[14]

Research on more convenient and safer methods of contraception merits higher global support as well. Though all the modern methods in wide use are much safer than the alternative of unrestricted childbearing, each has drawbacks. A study sponsored by the Ford Foundation in the mid-1970s found the global research expenditure on fertility control and contraceptive safety to comprise less than 2 percent of governmental medical research funding. It concluded that "to exploit adequately existing knowledge and opportunities," research expenditures in this field should be at least tripled. Unfortunately, contraceptive research funding since then has fallen in real terms.[15] Because of the uncertain profit-making potential of the kinds of contraceptives most needed in developing countries, private firms are not filling the gap. Governments are shirking their responsibility, thereby perhaps missing opportunities for progress that would be of immense global benefit.

As population-related pressures build and public attitudes about birth control change, the issue that will increasingly confront governments is not whether to provide family planning, but how hard to promote its use. In this respect China serves, depending on one's point of view, as either a shining example or an ominous portent. In an effort to safeguard the country's socioeconomic gains, the Chinese leadership has set once-unthinkable population goals and is taking stringent measures to achieve them.

Childbearing decisions that were once the province of the couple are now the subject of detailed social planning, backed up by the power of the state. Foreign demographers were skeptical when China began working to establish a two-child family norm in the early 1970s. But since 1979 the Chinese leadership has moved well beyond that ambitious goal, intensively promoting the *one-child* family. Economic rewards are provided to those who pledge to have one child, while stiff economic penalties are assessed those who bear more than two. Party workers and neighbors apply social pressures on recalcitrant couples, visiting them in their homes and trying to elicit pledges to have only one child. Local groups are allotted stringent "birth quotas" by central planners, with the group then deciding who should have children in a given year. Some production teams have an officer who keeps track of the menstrual periods of the team's women, reporting missed periods to the brigade. Extreme pressures to undergo sterilization after the second child and to abort unplanned pregnancies have been reported from some areas.[16]

Public acquiescence in measures like these would be inconceivable had not China achieved good public health and provided old-age security through communal organizations. Still, the new birth-control campaign is culturally jarring even for this relatively homogeneous, community-oriented society. The government's perception of social imperatives has led it to make unprecedented intrusions into private life. If few outsiders relish the thought of such measures, few can wish to confront the population-resource challenge faced by the Chinese. With a billion people, only half as much arable land as the United States, and extraordinary poverty to overcome, the Chinese leadership has recognized the lateness of the hour and acted to salvage the country's prospects for future prosperity.

How many other countries will, by ignoring the dimensions and implications of today's demographic trends, one day find themselves similarly boxed in, forced to take radical and unpalatable counter-measures? How many countries might unknowingly be near that day already? The costs of procrastination in confronting the population factor will extend well beyond the realms of environment and economics.

4 HEALTH AND THE HUMAN ENVIRONMENT

"HEALTH," according to the constitution of the World Health Organization, "is a state of complete physical, mental and social well-being and not merely the absence of disease or infirmity." Sadly, the person who can measure this priceless good has not yet put pen to paper. Our picture of health in societies must largely be extrapolated from our knowledge of diseases and deaths. Luckily, data on life expectancy and major causes of death reveal a lot about prevailing social and environmental conditions; a society's ways of death reflect its ways of life.

Nearly all disease is linked to the environment in the broadest sense of the term. The noted geneticist Theodosius Dobzhansky has observed that "genes determine not 'characters' or 'traits' but reactions or responses." Heredity determines susceptibility to afflictions, but the individual's interactions with his social and physical milieus influence whether or not that potential is realized. Thus while most people are susceptible to lung cancer, few who do not smoke are likely to develop it. Even bacterial and viral infections affect individuals differently according to their physical and perhaps mental conditions.[1]

To say that most illness is environmentally triggered is not to say that most illness can be wiped out. Old disease agents are evolving and new ones appearing as time passes and technologies change. Infectious disease is a fact of life, and some afflictions are genetically programmed. The probability of some diseases rises with age no matter how prudent and pollution free a person's life.

Focusing on the underlying sources of disease and death patterns does, however, point the way toward healthier societies. Much of the suffering and early death occurring in the world today results from circumstances over which humans have influence. This is true in rich as well as in poor countries, although the social and physical conditions of the latter exact an infinitely higher human price.

A comparison of life-expectancy figures from around the world provides some indication of the different environmental impacts of poverty and wealth. The global average life expectancy at birth is around sixty-two years. In all the developed countries and a handful of more advanced developing countries in Asia and Latin America, life expectancy exceeds seventy. In nearly every country of Sub-Saharan Africa, as well as some of the most wretchedly poor countries of Asia (Afghanistan, Bangladesh, Kampuchea, Laos, and Nepal among them), life expectancy is in the forties. In India, Pakistan, and Indonesia, the figure is near fifty—comparable to life spans in Great Britain and the United States at the turn of the century. Elsewhere in Asia, figures in the fifties and sixties are recorded. Latin America's average life expectancy is in the low sixties, but two of the region's poorest countries, Bolivia and Haiti, rank nearer the world's worst-off places, with average life spans of close to fifty.[2]

Apparently as a result of both genetic and lifestyle differences, women in developed countries tend to outlive men by some six years. Women seem less disposed to the heart attacks that kill so many middle-aged men, but also are less apt to smoke, to die in car crashes, to be murdered, or to be exposed to deadly poisons on the job. In most of the Third World, too, women outlive men. But in some parts of Asia and possibly North Africa, the reverse is true. Reliable studies in India, Iraq, Pakistan, and Sabah (East Malaysia) have found females to have shorter average lives than males. The apparent reasons include discrimination against young girls within families in the allocation of food and care, and the high hazards of repeated childbirth.[3]

Deaths among infants in their first year of life, more than anything else, account for international variations in life expectancy. In some countries of Northern and Western Europe and in Japan, fewer than one in a hundred babies dies in its first year; for the developed world as a whole, the loss is one in fifty. In the poorest African and Asian countries, one in five infants dies—and the rate is even higher in the poorest areas within these nations. Among less-developed countries as a group about one in every nine newborns fails to reach age one.

The survival prospects of rich and poor also differ strikingly among the one through four age group. Deaths among small children are extremely rare in developed countries—under one per thousand per year, and accidents rather than disease are the leading threat. But in the Third World, surviving infancy is no guarantee of a long life. Because of the interacting impacts of undernutrition, poor sanitation, and parasites, one in forty small children in the poorest developing countries dies each year—and again the loss rate in poorer regions and among the lowest income groups can be far higher. In parts of Latin America, nutritionist Alan Berg has noted, "the making and selling of minicaskets are common sights." Half of all Third World deaths are among infants and children under five, compared to only 2–4 percent of deaths in Western countries.[4]

Altogether, according to the World Health Organization, about seventeen million infants and children under age five died each year in the late 1970s. If the excellent health conditions of Northern Europe had prevailed throughout the world, only two million such deaths would have occurred.[5] Hence fifteen million deaths of babies and small children—more than forty thousand a day—can be regarded as preventable. All other global health problems pale before this one. Yet because they are so commonplace these forty thousand daily scandals do not provoke the global outrage they should.

In general, incomes correlate with health status. Residents of richer countries enjoy higher life expectancies, and within countries income levels usually affect health. In Brazil, for instance, life expectancy among the lowest income group in the northeast is a shameful forty-three years, compared to sixty-seven years among the highest income group in the south.[6] Thus looking at the gloomy economic prospects for the least-developed countries and the global underclass wherever they are, it would be easy to give up all hope of significantly improving the dismal health of the destitute quarter of humanity.

But such despair would be ill-founded. Many examples prove that great improvements in quality of life—indeed in the chance for life itself—are possible at relatively low income levels. In Sri Lanka, adequate diets, rudimentary medical care, and education have been spread quite widely. Despite a low average income of $230, life expectancy is sixty-four and the infant mortality rate is forty-two per thou-

sand. In Pakistan, in contrast, where per capita income is higher at
$270, life expectancy is only fifty-two, and 142 of every thousand
infants dies before age one. In China, where the per capita GNP is
a mere $230, the life expectancy is a high sixty-eight. These and other
examples show that if social organization is directed toward the right
ends, respectable health standards can be achieved despite poverty
and under differing political systems. The wise society can be healthy
without necessarily being wealthy.

The inferior health of some poorer people in rich countries reveals
still other dimensions of the health-income relationship. In the United
States, for instance, blacks and some other minority groups suffer
higher infant mortality and lower life expectancy than average. By
absolute global standards their basic needs for food, clean water, and
medical care are usually met. But second-class citizenship takes its toll
by other means. Economic frustration, the effects of racial discrimination, and other pressures of the grinding poverty faced by a disproportionate share of blacks contribute to what might be termed social
demoralization. Health-impairing behavior patterns—high rates of
alcoholism, of teenage childbearing, and of interpersonal violence, for
example—are a common result. Also, the poor in rich countries, like
the poor everywhere, are apt to live in the most polluted zones and
to have the most dangerous jobs. Clearly, the health costs of poverty
derive from more than the absence of basic physical goods.

The combined impacts of undernutrition, infections spread by
human excrement, airborne infections, and parasites account for
nearly all the childhood deaths in developing countries. Rooted in the
social ecology of poverty, these threats can seldom be countered with
medical weapons alone.

Undernutrition's drain on health is subtle. Starvation is rare, even
among children. But a lack of adequate amounts and quality of food
increases both the frequency and severity of diseases. For the child of
poverty, what should be a simple bout with measles, the flu, or diarrhea can become a life-and-death struggle.

The pervasive effects of undernutrition were revealed in the Pan
American Health Organization's investigation of childhood mortality
in fifteen countries of the Americas, published in 1973. The study, still
the most thorough of its kind, found that undernutrition or immature

births (including premature and underweight births, both often linked to nutrition) were the *primary* cause of 6 percent of the deaths among infants and small children. However, nutritional deficiencies or immature births were *associated* with 57 percent of those deaths.[7] Hence undernutrition probably contributed to more than half of all child deaths in Latin America, where diets are generally better than in Africa and much of Asia.

The pernicious effects of undernutrition precede a baby's birth. Much evidence suggests that women who themselves were undernourished and unhealthy during childhood are more apt to give birth to underweight babies—which in turn are more apt to die in infancy than more robust infants. More obviously, an inadequate diet during pregnancy increases the chances that a woman will give birth to an underweight baby.

Once born, infants everywhere are exposed to a wide array of infectious agents. The less sanitary the habitat, the more numerous and varied the exposures; the less well-nourished the baby, the greater the likelihood of serious illness.

For the first four months or so mother's milk is usually quite sufficient for healthy growth. But for millions of low-income women, "modernization" has meant a shift to bottle feeding despite their inability to afford enough packaged formula, their lack of facilities for sterilizing bottles, and their lack of access to pure water. Unnecessary undernutrition and accelerated exposure to life-threatening germs are the common results. Aggressive commercial promotion of infant formula seems to have encouraged this disastrous social trend—and because of this has become the subject of an international code of conduct on the marketing of baby foods, which was adopted by the World Health Organization in 1981. Many Third World countries are belatedly working to regulate the promotion of infant formula and to educate people about the benefits of breastfeeding. Since most of the rural poor in particular have not yet switched from breast to bottle, preventive actions now can forestall future tragedies.

Even where infants are breastfed, other foods must eventually supplement and then replace mother's milk. Most of the infant deaths linked to undernutrition occur during or soon after weaning. The new foods are often inadequate, and exposures to infectious agents multiply at this time.

The resulting threats take many forms, but none is more wide-spread and deadly than diarrhea. Known to the well-off as an occasional nuisance, diarrhea is in fact one of the world's major killers, taking at least five million children's lives a year.[8]

When unsanitary bottle feeding has not wreaked havoc in early infancy, diarrhea strikes most frequently during weaning, as contact with unsterile foods and contaminated containers begins. The bacteria and viruses that cause "weanling diarrhea," as it is known, are usually spread via human excrement. Where toilet facilities are filthy or nonexistent, ample water for cleaning utensils and hands is unavailable, and sanitary habits are not the norm, repeated episodes of diarrhea are inevitable among the young, who lack the partial resistance that develops with age. Poor nutrition increases the dangers of the disease, which in turn can exacerbate undernutrition by reducing food consumption and impairing intestinal absorption of nutrients. In an environment of poverty, acute, potentially fatal attacks of diarrhea recure often, and a low-grade indisposition can last for months at a time.[9]

A simple, low-cost treatment that cuts diarrhea's death toll has recently been developed. A simple sugar-and-salt drink, made from water that can even be polluted provided it is first boiled, rehydrates the body in the same way as intravenous feeding. The availability of such practical, life-saving medical measures lends urgency to the U.N.'s goal of providing "primary health care"—relying mainly on community health workers and simple technologies rather than scarce doctors and elaborate hospitals—to people everywhere by the year 2000. Still, treatment is not prevention. Only improvements in the environment and in nutrition can slash the devastating frequency of illnesses in the Third World. That modern medicine can work wonders was underscored by the global eradication of smallpox in 1977. Immunization against measles, polio, and other specific diseases are saving lives and should be saving more. But many of the afflictions killing Third World children cannot be prevented or cured with medical technologies alone.

Infectious agents of all sorts thrive in dirty habitats. One study of forty-five Guatemalan babies recorded a total of 2500 episodes of infectious disease in the first three years of their lives—an average of one illness every three weeks per infant. Throughout the Third World, debilitating parasites such as guinea worms or the nematode worms (roundworm, hookworm, and whipworm) are picked up from the soil and around wells; nematode worms now infect close to one-third of the entire world population.[10]

Reasonably clean and plentiful water, clean excreta-disposal facilities, and the practice of sanitary principles are together essential to better health. These three needs are to some degree indivisible; providing clean water or latrines or health education without the other two often proves ineffective in cutting disease rates. The failure of societies to devote greater resources to meeting these fundamental health needs ranks alongside the persistence of undernutrition as a measure of inhuman priorities.

More than half the people in the Third World (excluding China) do not have reasonable access to safe water supplies. Three out of four have no adequate waste-disposal facilities—not even a bucket latrine. The situation is generally much worse in rural than in urban areas—although city slums in the Third World are almost universally sordid and, because of the close human concentrations, are especially vulnerable to epidemics. Also, aging and leaking city water systems in many cases provide only intermittent service and contaminated water to people who are listed as well served in the statistics.[11]

According to government-supplied (and in some cases suspect) U.N. data, as of 1980, 25 percent of the Third World's urban population (again excluding China) lacked reasonable access to water, while 71 percent of the rural population was so deprived. Tens of millions of rural women and children spend long hours each day carrying heavy loads of water on their heads or backs. In cities, members of poor families walk to distant standpipes, or where none are accessible, pay dearly for water from mobile vendors. Whether the price is exacted in hours of backbreaking women's labor or in scarce family funds, the consequences for sanitation are the same: clean water is too precious to be used routinely for washing as well as for cooking and drinking. Family health suffers as a result. Studies indicate that beyond a minimal level of purity, the quantity of water available to families (for hygienic uses) may be more important to good health than its quality.

Convenient access to abundant water does not guarantee good health where excrement disposal is unsanitary. According to government-supplied and undoubtedly overoptimistic U.N. figures, 47 percent of urban and 87 percent of rural Third World residents lacked decent waste-disposal facilities in 1980. People defecate in farm fields, canals, streams, vacant lots—everywhere depositing the germs and parasites that make untreated human waste the world's deadliest environmental pollutant. As the main conveyor of the diarrheal and other intestinal disorders that kill tens of millions each year, human excrement takes a toll that dwarfs any known impacts of industrial pollutants.

During the decades of the 1960s and 1970s the percentage of Third World residents with ready access to clean water and sanitary facilities rose significantly. But as populations soared, the absolute numbers lacking these necessities still climbed. Against this backdrop, the United Nations declared the 1980s the International Drinking Water Supply and Sanitation Decade. The hope—known to be hollow even as it was announced—was that Third World governments and international aid donors would drastically step up their investments in water and sanitation, providing these goods to all by 1990. Achieving this goal would require a threefold to fivefold increase in expenditures over the 1979 investment level of $6–$7 billion, one-third of which was provided as international aid. It would also require ending the urban bias in water and sanitation spending, wider use of simple technologies, and pursuit of new forms of community involvement and education to ensure that new wells and latrines are better maintained than they have often been.

The needed funds sound large until they are compared to other global expenditures. Meeting the financial needs of the Decade would require global spending of some $80 million a day—this in a world that lays out more than $250 million a day on cigarettes and $1.4 billion a day on arms.

No genuine political commitment to providing universal access to water and sanitation has emerged among aid givers or most Third World governments. Still, many of the latter have been provoked for the first time into drawing up national strategies, and many donors are reexamining water and sanitation policies. It appears possible that a new spurt of activity will at least prevent the absolute number of people deprived of safe water and sanitation from rising further during the 1980s.

On top of the omnipresent threats of infection and undernutrition, residents of developing countries must contend with a number of parasitic and other types of diseases whose scope is largely limited to the tropics—and which, as a result, have not received the degree of scientific study accorded the main killers of the temperate-zone rich. Inaugurating a new program of accelerated tropical disease research in 1975, WHO noted that the global research budget for six major tropical diseases was then only $30 million, compared to nearly $1 billion spent in one country, the United States, on cancer research alone. Research on the prevention and cure of these six diseases— malaria, schistosomiasis, filariasis, trypanosomiasis, leprosy, leishmaniasis—and others is now intensifying.

The new research emphasis comes at a time when, partly because of inept human ecological interventions, several tropical diseases are spreading. Schistosomiasis (also known as bilharzia, a debilitating and sometimes fatal parasitic disease spread via human wastes and aquatic snails) and filariasis (one type of which is spread by mosquitoes that breed in polluted puddles in cities) now afflict at least 200 million people each. And malaria, whose toll was cut by massive antimosquito campaigns in the two decades following World War II, staged a deadly resurgence in the 1970s.[12]

Malaria's comeback has been especially marked in South and Southeast Asia and in Central America. In India alone the number of reported cases rose from 40,000 in 1966 to 6.5 million in 1976. In Africa little progress was ever made against malaria, and that is where it causes most harm: according to WHO, malaria kills at least one million Africans under age fourteen each year.

The spread of malaria has several causes. Following initial control successes, many governments became complacent and reduced support for mosquito-spraying programs. But a number of recent campaigns have been stymied by frightening new impediments: resistance to pesticides among the target mosquitoes, and to antimalarial drugs among the malaria parasites. By the mid-1970s, reports WHO, one-fifth of the world's malarious areas faced resistance either to pesticides or drugs. A decade earlier such resistance problems affected only 1.5 percent of the infested zones. Luckily no large area has yet faced both types of resistance at once—though present trends suggest the probability that this will happen sooner or later.[13] Massive, often careless spraying of DDT and other pesticides in agriculture seems often to have been the major factor triggering resistance in mosquitoes—a costly side-effect never added into the balance sheets of the commercial plantations that apply pesticides to crops so haphazardly throughout the tropics.

In addition, tropical forest colonization and other land-clearing activities sometimes create new habitats for malaria-carrying mosquitoes. In some new settlements in Brazil's western Amazon Basin, half the people catch malaria. The disease has also ravaged colonists in Indonesia's outer islands.

Unlike malaria, which threatens all social classes, schistosomiasis is essentially a poor person's disease. It can only persist where sanitary facilities are bad, since the parasite's eggs must be deposited directly into waterways by human wastes. Also, only people who themselves spend time walking or bathing in the canals, slow-moving rivers, and lakes that harbor the alternate hosts (certain types of snails) can pick up the disease. These preconditions are easily met among most of the global underclass.[14]

Where the parasite is prevalent—throughout Africa, and in parts of Latin America and West and Southeast Asia—newly built reservoirs, ponds, and irrigation canals often provide new avenues for disease transmission. Every major impoundment in Africa over the last few decades has been blighted by the disease. In some areas, such as around Sudan's giant Gezira irrigation scheme and on the borders of Ghana's Lake Volta, virtually all children are infected. In some African villages, blood in a young boy's urine is regarded as normal —and in a tragic sense, it is.

Stung by past health disasters, international aid agencies have become more wary of tropical water projects and are apt to work to prevent the introduction of schistosomiasis into new reservoirs and irrigation systems they help build. However, no available preventive measures are foolproof or cheap. And thousands of small-scale waterworks are constructed in the Third World with little or no attention paid to the health implications. All over West Africa's Sahelian region, for example, small dams are being built for agricultural purposes —but no meaningful programs to prevent or treat schistosomiasis exist. Small water bodies in the region are widely infested with the disease. Its spread is simply accepted as part of the background noise of development, a sad commentary on some people's notion of development.

The upper classes in the poorest countries, and a rising share of the populace in newly industrializing "middle income" countries, display health patterns more and more like those of affluent Westerners. Heart disease and cancer are often the main causes of their premature death. Third World elites often aspire to the same high-fat, high-calorie diets and sedentary lifestyles that undercut well-being in the developed world. The smoking habit is especially well entrenched among the Third World's upper classes and is spreading in many regions. The international cigarette companies, sometimes in partnership with local government-owned firms, are doing their best to ensure this; with the cigarette market stagnant or declining in the West, developing countries present the sales frontier. Cigarette commercials in the Third World strive to associate smoking with modernity and urbanity just as the more highly educated and affluent groups in the West are kicking the habit.

With modernization have also come the assorted health hazards of industrial pollution and toxic chemicals. Although these threats are not yet so ubiquitous in poor as in rich countries, where factories exist and dangerous technologies are used in the Third World they are far less likely to be properly regulated.

Another of the modern world's most deadly technologies, the automobile, likewise inflicts great damage in developing countries. Compared to the situation in rich countries, Third World cars and trucks must dodge more pedestrians, bicyclists, and animals on the road. Fewer public resources are devoted to traffic signals and road design, and traffic safety laws are less often enforced. Thus in Brazil the number of traffic deaths per automobile is ten times that in the United States.[15]

For an unknown but certainly growing number of the world's poor, modern insult is being added to traditional injury. They not only lack access to pure water; what they drink may be laced with heavy metals. Plantation workers and their families often live and work amid overly applied, overly dangerous pesticides. Those lucky enough to land a factory job can face exposures to chemicals or deadly fibers at levels long since banned in the West. City dwellers breathe foul air created by cars in which they will never ride and by factories whose products and profits will never touch their lives. These luckless people must struggle simultaneously against ancient wants and the hazards of a space age that has passed them by.

In developed countries today, just two disease categories—cardiovascular afflictions and cancer—account for more than two-thirds of all deaths. Cardiovascular diseases alone take half of all lives in North America, Europe, and Japan. Coronary heart disease (which leads to heart attacks) is the number one problem in most countries, but is overshadowed by strokes in some.

A high incidence of heart disease per se would not necessarily be a sign of social dysfunction; failure of the heart is often the immediate cause when a person "dies of old age" after a long and healthy life. Moreover, some people are genetically destined to suffer arterial problems. But hundreds of thousands of cardiovascular deaths can rightly be called premature. In typical developed countries, half or more of the deaths from coronary heart disease involve people under age seventy-five, and at least 15 percent occur among people under fifty-five. Because of a combination of genetic and lifestyle factors, heart attacks especially threaten middle-aged men.

The timing and overall incidence of cardiovascular diseases are unquestionably influenced by personal lifestyles. Usually resulting from a lifelong accumulation of arterial damage, heart attacks and strokes can seldom be blamed on any one cause. However, a variety of traits have been associated statistically with risk of cardiovascular disorders: obesity, high blood cholesterol, high blood pressure, diabetes, alcoholism, sedentary living, a stress-ridden personality, and cigarette smoking. These various "risk factors" combine with a vengeance. A forty-five-year-old American man who smokes doubles his risk of a heart attack. If he also has high blood pressure and high blood cholesterol, his increase in risk is fourfold.[16]

In the mid-twentieth century death rates for cardiovascular diseases, even taking account of the decline in other health threats, rose relentlessly in the developed world. Then in the 1960s the rates peaked in many countries. In the United States and Japan cardiovascular death rates have fallen by close to 20 percent since the mid-1960s.[17]

Improved medical measures explain only a small fraction of the prevented deaths. Something in the social environment has clearly changed. The key factors cannot easily be identified. But the correspondence between the decline in premature deaths and changes in behavior patterns known to be linked to arterial conditions is too great to ignore.

In the United States the sudden and steep drop in heart attacks occurred along with several relevant social trends—dietary shifts that reduced average cholesterol levels; a decline in the proportion of the population that smokes; a cultural turn toward more exercise; and mass treatment of high blood pressure. Remarkably enough, the turning point in heart attack deaths coincided almost exactly with the 1964 issuance of the famous surgeon-general's report on the hazards of smoking, and of the American Heart Association's recommendations for reduced consumption of saturated fats and cholesterol. The appearance of benefits so quickly may not be as far-fetched as it seems. In Scandinavia during World War II, a war-induced cut in the richness of diets was associated with an almost immediate drop in the incidence of heart disease.[18]

Cancer accounts for about one-fifth of the deaths in developed countries. Its toll in poor countries is significant too, and about one-tenth of the world's fifty million annual deaths are attributable to cancer.

Probably more than any other disease, cancer is associated in the public mind with environmental causes—and with good reason. The prevalence of different types of cancer varies widely among societies; and when people migrate to new places, their patterns of cancer incidence change along with their cultural practices and physical surroundings. Studying differences in cancer patterns around the world—for example, stomach cancer rates are high in Japan, lung cancer rates high in the United Kingdom, and liver cancer rates high in Mozambique—researchers infer that 60–90 percent of all cancer must have environmental origins. The environment of concern here is of course an all-embracing concept, including all the natural and the man-made materials that people eat, breathe, or touch; sunlight (whose radiation causes skin cancer); even childbearing patterns (which affect women's hormonal balances and in turn the odds of certain types of cancer).[19]

The major proven cause of cancer is cigarette smoke, which alone may cause about 20 percent of the cancers in many developed countries. Eight or nine out of ten lung cancers are attributable to smoking, which also promotes cancers of the mouth, throat, esophagus, bladder, kidney, and pancreas. Tobacco smoke acts synergistically with such other environmental insults as alcohol, radiation, and asbestos, posing extraordinary dangers among some unfortunate groups.

Diets influence cancer rates in many mysterious ways, and may well become the primary focus of future cancer-prevention programs. The high fat content of typical Western fare is suspected of promoting a number of common cancers—of the breast, ovary, and uterus in women, and of the prostate gland and testis in men—by altering hormonal balances. Various theorists link the high fat content or the low fiber content of the Western diet to cancer of the colon, one of the most frequent killers. Whether either or both factors are the true culprits has not yet been proven.

Chemical food additives warrant close scrutiny and regulation, but have not yet been associated with any observed human cancer trends. A natural food contaminant, aflatoxin, which is produced by a mold growing on damp peanuts and grains, has been linked to high liver cancer rates in Africa and Southeast Asia. Marked variations in the incidence of stomach and esophageal cancer around the world are almost certainly related to eating practices. Among the factors under scrutiny are local beers in southern Africa, pickled fish in Southeast Asia, and certain herbal teas in several places.

In the West at least, dietary factors appear to contribute to as many as half of all cancers in women and one-third in men. But there is no dietary equivalent of the cigarette. A multitude of dietary components and eating practices will have to be uncovered through patient medical detective work—and their elimination will depend on changes in entrenched cultural practices.

Pollution of the air and water seems to contribute to a small fraction of cancers. But cause and effect is hard to prove, especially given the long lag times that can separate exposure to carcinogens and the onset of disease, and the presence of so many possible cancer causes in the modern environment. The major proven impacts of modern chemicals and industrial substances have been among workers exposed to high concentrations for extended periods. Occupational exposures to asbestos alone, which peaked in developed countries in the 1950s but continue at dangerous levels in some Third

World factories, may account for anywhere from 3 to 18 percent of U.S. cancer deaths today, thirty years after the main exposures. Those working in a variety of other industrial processes too have belatedly discovered the invisible dangers of their jobs.

So far the U.N.'s International Agency for Research on Cancer (IARC) has listed about 160 substances as presumed carcinogenic threats to humans. But only about one-eighth of the 55,000 chemicals in commercial use have ever been tested for cancer in animals. And hundreds not yet on the IARC danger list have shown troublesome signs in animal tests. The impact of prolonged low-level exposures to mildly carcinogenic substances is not well understood, nor is the possibility of hazards when otherwise benign substances interact. Fears that more cancer "time bombs" like asbestos are now in public circulation cannot be dismissed out of hand.

More than 65 percent of the cancer deaths in many developed countries involve victims under age seventy-five. Cancer is also the leading disease cause of death among children in affluent societies, although it falls well behind accidents as a threat to this age group. In theory a majority of premature cancer deaths can be prevented. An end to smoking, dietary changes in line with emerging research results, a political willingness to spend more on chemical testing and to act on the results, the cleanup of workplaces—these are among the measures that must be taken now if cancer's toll in the decades ahead is to fall.

Environmental pollutants have caused afflictions other than cancer. That air pollution helps cause and intensify chronic respiratory ailments—emphysema, chronic bronchitis, asthma—is well established. Lead from car exhausts and old paint is suspected of subtly disturbing the nervous systems of some inner-city children. Japan's dramatic outbreaks of heavy-metal pollution—the destruction of the nervous systems of hundreds who ate mercury-laden fish from Minamata Bay, and the epidemic of itai-itai (literally "ouch-ouch") disease among hundreds whose bones agonizingly disintegrated because of cadmium in their food and water—became worldwide symbols of industrially induced disease. And localized tragedies because of contamination by one chemical or another, usually because of inevitable "accidents," frequent the pages of present-day newspapers.

What is not known is the health impact, singly and in combination, of long-term low-level exposure to the many synthetic chemicals, metals, and other pollutants that permeate modern life. Certainly few serious, widespread health damages have been proven. But eternal vigilance, and the uncompromising application of pollution controls where human damage is threatened, are in order if we are to breathe easy.

In many countries, populations are gradually aging as birth rates and the toll of infectious disease decline. Viewing the demographic trends and the soaring costs of medical care, some have begun to worry about the mounting health-care burden posed by the aged. The spectre is evoked of societies staggering under the weight of huge numbers of chronically ill people racking up stupendous medical bills.

Fortunately, the medical evidence permits us to imagine a more appealing future. Reducing deaths among the young and the middle-aged need not mean a jump in the proportion of the debilitated and the senile. Research over recent decades indicates that the same social, environmental, and personal measures that reduce premature disease and death also lead to better health among the aged. Heart failures, cancer, and other so-called degenerative diseases will not disappear, but the period of incapacity at the end of healthy lives can be shortened or eliminated.

The quest for immortality remains as futile as ever; no evidence suggests that the last century of sensational medical progress has allowed a higher proportion of people to live beyond a hundred. Only one in ten thousand residents of the developed countries passes that threshold. Rather, the notable rise in average longevity reflects the reduction in mortality among infants, small children, and the middle-aged. Dr. James F. Fries of Stanford University has calculated that under medically ideal social conditions, the average life span might be around eighty-five.[20] Whether or not he is right about the number, his broader point holds up: what appears feasible is not a great extension of each person's time on earth, but rather a great improvement in quality of health during that time. We can build societies in which most people die, as his biographer said of Wordsworth, "of nothing serious"—after long lives, vigorous to the end.

Meeting this goal requires meeting many conditions first. All children would be born into families with enough income to afford good nutrition, sanitary housing, and elementary medical care. Their parents would practice family planning, avoiding births too early or late in the mother's life. During pregnancy their mothers would eschew tobacco, alcohol, and unnecessary drugs, and avoid exposure to toxic chemicals on the job or in the environment.

During childhood all people would acquire habits that prevent or delay the onset of chronic afflictions later. Regular exercise, a wholesome diet that is low in fats, and nonsmoking would be family norms. A sense of personal responsibility for maintaining health would carry over into adult life.

At the same time governments would recognize the impact of public policies on individual lifestyles. Nutrition education and crop subsidies would reflect medical findings rather than the pressures of food growers and packagers. Strong antismoking campaigns would be maintained and high taxes would force smokers to pay the full smoking-related costs that society is now forced to bear. Safety features in automobiles would be mandatory.

Governments would also confront head-on the environmental health threats that individuals can do little or nothing about. Workplace hazards, risks associated with manufactured products, air and water pollution, and toxic-waste disposal would be tightly controlled.

As people aged, continuing the healthy personal habits they established in childhood would be crucial. The maintenance of physical activity may be especially important. As Dr. Fries writes: "Premature organ dysfunction, whether of muscle, heart, lung, or joint, is beginning to be conceived as stemming from disuse of the faculty, not overuse. . . . The body, to an increasing degree, is now felt to rust out rather than to wear out."

As the links between mental and physical well-being become more apparent, the importance to lasting health of social contacts and stimulating mental activity is growing plainer. With the aged proportion of populations rising, extended family relationships withering, and retirement from work taking place with decades left to live, the search for good health must carry us far afield from customary medical and environmental issues. A new view of the physical, intellectual, sexual, and occupational potentials of the aged is emerging. Social institutions must be either created or revitalized to help old people maintain their physical and intellectual vigor and the social interactions that sustain the human animal.

Even as most of humanity begins to grapple with the health challenges of the twenty-first century, those in the underclass remain victims of timeless hazards. The unnecessary daily deaths of 40,000 infants and small children must rank as the world's number one health concern. Resulting from unnecessary hunger and filth, these deaths—and the indifference with which they are accepted—call into question the humanity of the living. Or they tell us something dark about the meaning of humanity.

II. Natural and Unnatural Conditions

5 OCEANIC AFFAIRS

THAT THE SEAS were endlessly bountiful was long an article of faith. This assumption even underlay the early development of the international law of the sea. In his 1608 treatise *Mare Liberum,* the foundation of oceanic custom and law for the next three and a half centuries, Hugo Grotius cited the unlimited abundance of fish as one reason for unregulated fishing. The freedom of all to fish outside narrow coastal waters—the three-mile reach of a cannon—became established practice.

Not long after Grotius wrote, his initial assumptions were being proven faulty. Seeing catches off Newfoundland decline, seventeenth-century European fishermen began trailing southward to the banks off New England. A pattern was set that has persisted up to the present: overfish one stock, then move on to other species or regions.[1]

The oceans are large, their productivity is enormous, and this pattern did permit enormous growth in the world fish catch until quite recently. But at last the burgeoning world demand, served by ever-improving fish-catching techniques, has begun to press against the expansive limits of the seas. In the 1970s, as the global catch leveled off, new attention was focused on the legacy of depletion and on the need to put fisheries exploitation on a sustainable footing. A new legal regime, under which states regulate fishing for 200 miles off their coasts, has replaced the traditional free-for-all. This historic shift has set the legal stage for more rational management of fisheries.

A new order in the seas has come none too soon; the list of depleted fish stocks is long. In the Atlantic the catches of traditionally popular food fish such as cod, halibut, herring, and haddock have all declined. By the 1970s in fact, nearly every major species traditionally sought in the northern Atlantic waters was overfished, and some stocks had collapsed. Nor has overfishing been limited to prime food fish or to the waters adjacent to Europe and North America. The long-distance fleets of developed countries, and in some cases local fishermen using traditional methods, have helped impoverish fish stocks in the far corners of the earth. Hake, sardinella, and pilchard have been devastated off African coasts. The catch of Thai fishermen in the Gulf of Thailand dropped in 1979 after years of reckless growth; with mature fish of the valuable types dwindling, trash fish, sold for fertilizer or animal feed, now fill 60–70 percent of the fishermen's nets. Ominously, half of this low-value portion of the catch is immature individuals of the desired species. Prime fish have become rare around the larger settlements on the Amazon River.[2]

Perhaps the signal event in world fisheries in the 1970s was the collapse of the anchovy catch off the coast of Peru. There a rich upwelling of nutrients had sustained one of the earth's great concentrations of exploitable biomass. Taking advantage of the rising demand for fishmeal in Europe, Japan, and North America, where it was fed to poultry and pigs, Peru in the 1960s developed the world's largest fishery. In some years these anchovies accounted for one-fifth of the entire global fish catch, and in value they surpassed copper as an export for Peru.

Biologists warned of the dangers of overfishing, but the press of an industry trying to recoup large capital investments and the lure of extra foreign exchange led the Peruvian government to take undue risks. The catches of 1967, 1968, 1970, and 1971 all exceeded the estimated maximum sustainable yield of 9.5 million tons. Then in 1972 came nature's backlash. A shift in the ocean currents that periodically reduces marine productivity in the area occurred—but this time the anchovies did not later spring back as they always had before. Apparently the population of mature anchovies had been so badly diminished that, under the extra pressure of the current shift, it could not produce a large new brood.[3] On land, fortunes were lost, hundreds of fishermen lost their jobs, and the world protein feed market received a nasty jolt. To the dismay of the Peruvians the anchovies have not recovered despite years of close protection. The catches in 1978 and 1979 were just 1.4 million tons. (A recent surge in the catch of sardines, which are apparently filling the ecological gap left by the anchovy decline, is softening the economic blow.)

In the two decades leading up to 1968 the world fish catch climbed steadily at a rate of 6–7 percent a year. Then fluctuations and unprecedented declines began to occur. The catch temporarily peaked at seventy million tons in 1970; this total was not again achieved until 1978, as slow growth in other fisheries gradually made up for the loss of the once-gigantic anchovy catch. The global catch in 1979 reached seventy-one million tons. Analysts of the United Nations Food and Agriculture Organization (FAO) believe a new growth trend of only 1–2 percent a year has emerged. Thus over the last decade the per capita supply of fish on a worldwide basis has been falling, in sharp contrast with the previous experience.

The outlook is for slow growth at best. In many areas, newly responsible and effective regulation of fishing will hold down catches; elsewhere, fully exploited or overexploited stocks will not support higher catches anyway. The FAO calculates that the catch of conventionally fished species could in theory be increased by twenty to thirty million tons over its current level. Perhaps half this increase would result from restored productivity of stocks now depleted by overfishing, the rest from harvesting the few remaining underexploited stocks.[4] Even if it materializes, this will not be much of an increase considering historic growth rates and the rising world demand for fish. For all practical purposes the growth era is over.

Technological optimists have pointed to krill as the answer to the fish problem. Tiny shrimp-like creatures of the Southern Ocean around Antarctica, krill are incredibly numerous. One recently sighted swarm covered several square miles at depths of 60–600 feet —ten million tons of biomass in a single school. Early in the 1970s some said that catches of 50 million or even 100 million tons a year might be sustainable, to be processed into high-protein foods and animal feeds. Some dreamed of a cheap new source of protein for the world's poor.

One no longer hears such claims about krill. For one thing it has become apparent that a huge krill harvest could jeopardize the recovery of the whale populations of the Southern Ocean, many of which feed on krill. (In recognition of this link, the convention to regulate exploitation of living resources recently signed by the Antarctic Treaty powers stipulates that catch quotas for one species must not jeopardize the productivity of other species in the Antarctic ecosystem.) For another thing the economics of krill harvesting, processing, and marketing have proved less favorable than some envisaged. Rising fuel costs have undercut the viability of such long-distance fishing, and no large market for krill-based products has yet materialized. Krill harvests, while increasing, have so far reached only a few hundred thousand tons, taken mainly by the Soviet Union and to a lesser degree by Japan. If a significant fishery does develop, it will be a high-cost one of little direct relevance to the world's hungry.[5]

Aquaculture—raising fish or shellfish rather than hunting them in the wild—has more promise as an instrument of Third World development. Annual production through aquaculture may now exceed five million tons and is especially significant in China and Southeast Asia. The potential exists for major increases throughout the Third World, and aquaculture has received serious attention from international aid agencies in recent years.

Not surprisingly, one consequence of the stagnation in world fisheries is rising real prices. In Japan, where fish consumption is high, average fish prices rose between 1961 and 1978 at a rate 6.5 percent higher than the overall inflation rate. Statistics are not available on price trends in the Third World, but the general trend is certainly upward.[6]

Low-income consumers everywhere are of course the major victims of rising fish prices. And fish tend to play a more important nutritional role in the diets of the poor than the rich. Fish provide 55 percent of the animal protein in Southeast Asia, 35 percent in Asia as a whole, and 19 percent of the animal protein in Africa. In Europe the corresponding figure is 12 percent; in South America, 7 percent; and in North America, just 5 percent. Even regional figures can mislead; in many poorer communities fish are virtually the only source of animal protein.[7]

While pollution and habitat interference have wiped out fish in many areas, overfishing has been by far the major threat to global fisheries up to now. With the declaration of 200-mile fishery zones by coastal states over the last decade, an institutional setting finally exists that could lead to control of this ancient malfeasance. Earlier efforts at international cooperation in limiting catches usually failed because of competition and mistrust. Under the new system a single government bears responsibility for a given area and has a direct interest in enlightened management—although short-term politics and greed can always supersede common sense.

If they are to take full advantage of the new regime many developing countries must improve their marine research, regulation, and enforcement capacities, and also improve domestic fleets. Too often foreign fleets, operating under license or in joint-venture arrangements with local partners, make serious inroads into local stocks while the main profits flow abroad. In many areas the livelihoods of small-scale traditional fishermen have been wiped out by the incursions of modern boats owned by foreigners or local elites. Fisheries "development" often destroys the welfare rather than enhances the techniques of low-income traditional fishermen.

The problems of migratory species such as tuna remain unresolved and will continue to cause international disputes. The whales too have a story of their own, which is recounted below. But nearly 99 percent of the current oceanic catch comes from within the 200-mile coastal zone. If countries take advantage of the new opportunity for sound management, the global fish catch, now worth more than $50 billion a year, can be sustained and possibly increased.

Among global environmental issues the plight of the whales has stirred unrivaled public passion. To many people the depletion of whale species after whale species over the last five centuries epitomizes the inability of humans to control their greed and to live in harmony with nature. The political struggle to save the whales has been the stuff of high diplomacy and has spawned one of the world's most potent networks of nongovernmental pressure groups. It has also given rise to international eco-sabotage, the blowing-up of the notorious pirate whaler *Sierra* in 1980.

Although the history of whaling is a sad one, recent developments point toward a happy ending. Controls are now being applied that should prevent extinctions and permit the eventual restoration of many whale stocks. If the past destruction of whales is a symbol of humanity's failures in relations with nature, the current progress in salvaging these mammals should inspire hope for the future. Because of public concern and organization an ecological perspective seems likely to prevail over myopic commercialism.

Until quite recently such an optimistic forecast would have seemed ludicrous. Providing meat, fats, and valuable oils in large quantities with each kill, whales have long held special commercial appeal. For centuries the established pattern was for whalers to destroy one stock and then move on to another. European whale hunters began operating from coastal bases as early as the fourteenth century, and as early as the sixteenth century the North Atlantic populations of some species were impoverished. In the 1700s high-seas fleets roamed the North Atlantic and then the seas of the world; by 1900 some whale stocks in the Northern Hemisphere had been gravely reduced. Early in this century technological improvements permitted larger scale long-distance operations that by necessity began to concentrate their efforts in the Southern Hemisphere.

Apart from some futile measures in the 1930s, efforts to bring whaling under control did not begin until 1946, with the signing of the convention that established the International Whaling Commission (IWC).[8] This commission has since included most but not all whaling nations, as well as many countries with an interest in whales but no commercial hunting.

The record of the IWC in the next two and a half decades was, to say the least, sorry. Although a few stocks received protection, one result of the commission's catch quotas and seasonal limits was to spur competition among national fleets to develop more efficient ships and capture a larger share of the collective quota for themselves. Limits were sometimes violated, and in any case the application of catch quotas tended to follow rather than to prevent the depletion of stocks. Scientific knowledge of stocks was inadequate; political bargains and conflicts prevailed and in some years no limits were set at all for whaling in Antarctic waters—the principal remaining whaling zone. Whaling by nonmember countries increased, sometimes with the covert support of IWC member states. Right through the initial quarter-century of so-called regulation, the catches of several whales —among them the blue, fin, sei, and humpback—followed the classic pattern of overshoot and collapse.

By the late 1960s outrage about the sham controls was rising among scientists and a world public increasingly concerned about the environment. In 1970 the United States banned domestic whaling and the importation of whale products. The main whaling countries,

Japan and the Soviet Union, faced mounting international criticism. A major turning point in the politics of whaling came in 1972, when the United Nations Conference on the Human Environment in Stockholm called for a ten-year moratorium on commercial whaling. The resolution had no legal force but a powerful political impact.

Although the whaling countries have staved off a total moratorium in close votes of the IWC, over the last decade a new pro-conservation climate has emerged and the regulation of whaling has been greatly tightened. The annual meetings of the IWC have been opened to outside observers and its decisions have received wide public scrutiny. A growing number of nonwhaling nations have joined the IWC, adding weight to the conservation perspective.

A "new management procedure," under which quotas are supposed to be set according to scientific advice, has improved the protection effort, though political bargaining over quotas and gaping holes in scientific knowledge continue to mar the process. As whaling has declined so has the supply of data on whale stocks; in the absence of solid information, quotas are usually set at prevailing catch levels. But new scientific data generally lead to downward revisions of quotas. The policing of regulations is also a problem.

The overall permitted catch of whales has been pushed down from 46,000 in 1973 to 14,000 in 1982. Improved measures to discourage member-country collusion with whaling operations outside IWC control have been adopted. In 1979 the IWC prohibited long-distance factory-ship whaling in all waters save the Southern Ocean off Antarctica, and created a whale sanctuary in the Indian Ocean. The screws on whaling have been tightened from other quarters as well: several countries have banned whaling within their 200-mile offshore zones, and trade in products from most whales has been prohibited under the provisions of the international endangered species convention (CITES).

As one outgrowth of the Stockholm Conference, UNEP and the FAO are jointly developing a global plan of action for the conservation, management, and utilization of marine mammals. One of their primary goals is to improve the scientific knowledge of whale population trends and dynamics. Woeful inadequacies in knowledge persist, permitting what many regard as dangerous loopholes in the protection system. Over time these U.N. agencies hope to create a global framework for considering appropriate management procedures and goals for whales and other marine mammals such as dolphins and seals.[9]

For some whale populations the extra protection of the last decade has come just in time. The populations of most of the larger whale species are at a low fraction of their original levels. Many are presumed to be gradually expanding as a result of recent protection measures, but given the slowness of their reproduction and the difficulties of data collection, solid proof of stock recovery has generally been lacking.

The blue, humpback, fin, and sei whales remain seriously depleted. Hundreds of thousands of sperm whales are known to exist in some regions, but the impact of continued hunting is disputed. Male sperm whales of the necessary social and sexual maturity are relatively scarce because of past overfishing. Hence, according to ecologist John Beddington, the population will probably decline for years even in the absence of hunting. In 1981 the IWC took the more prudent course, reducing sperm whale quotas in all but one region to zero.

One species, the bowhead whale, is believed to be in danger of total extinction, having been reduced by nineteenth-century whaling to as little as 2–3 percent of its original numbers. Unfortunately the catching and consuming of bowheads plays a central role in the culture of certain Alaskan Eskimos, who demand the right to continue with limited kills. This clash of human and ecological interests has produced major splits within the environmental movement and one of the more anomalous sights of modern diplomacy: Eskimos flying halfway around the world to argue in IWC meetings for preservation of a traditional cultural practice. Under recent compromises, which have satisfied neither the Eskimos nor the scientists working to save the bowhead, the Eskimos have been permitted the landing of up to seventeen bowheads a year. But the whale stock, believed to number only about 2000 in the North Pacific, remains in precarious shape and the controversy is bound to persist, a tragic legacy of past misdeeds.

On the other side of North America, the taking of humpback whales by native Greenlanders has also stirred controversy. But the biggest threat to the humpbacks of the Northwest Atlantic (where their largest remaining stock resides) results from direct competition with modern fishermen. Capelin, the main food source of the humpback whales, have been overfished and now hungry whales are often caught in nets, to the detriment of both whales and fishermen. Destructive competition between various marine mammals and humans for dwindling fish supplies has erupted in other places, including Scotland and Japan, and looms on the horizon elsewhere.[10]

A smaller whale, the minke, is now more plentiful than ever in the Southern Ocean, and accounts for most of the world's annual permitted whale kill. When larger whales were numerous the minkes did not present attractive targets. Also, they have benefited from the ecological gap created by the near extermination of blue whales, with which they compete for food. Thus a harvest of minke whales is not only sustainable, but also, some argue, possibly desirable in order to facilitate the recovery of the magnificent blue whales, the largest creatures ever to have lived on earth. The populations of both species cannot be maximized, and leaving the system alone will probably not bring back the original equilibrium.[11]

Thus, having played god with the whales for so long and so badly, we may not be able to escape this role. The prospect of a rising human catch of krill, the main food for Antarctic whales, further complicates the matter; close monitoring of the Antarctic ecosystem and conscious decisions about the desirable mix of species will be necessary.

While the minke whales present a unique dilemma, the debate over their harvest is provoking the opening salvos in what is certain to become a bitter debate over fundamental values. With the whales facing annihilation, wide agreement on the need to curb whaling was easy to obtain. But over time, as stocks gradually recover, the case for a complete whaling ban on ecological grounds weakens. Questions far more contentious than species preservation must be confronted, questions that require political rather than scientific resolution.

To many in the antiwhaling movement the killing of whales is simply objectionable. Many put whales in a special category apart from other exploited animals because of their intelligence, gentleness, and other appealing qualities; some go beyond this to see whale protection as part of a more basic philosophical challenge to the dominant economic worldview. No compelling reason exists to continue commercial whaling, it is argued. The economic benefits are slight, substitutes exist for all whale products, and the profits from whaling go to richer countries that can easily do without them. Many strong humanitarian, ethical, and esthetic arguments can be marshalled against whale killing. So why continue the practice?

Opposition to whaling on ethical grounds cannot, in the final analysis, be reconciled with the approach being proposed even by conservation-oriented resource managers. The U.N.'s draft global plan of action on marine mammals cites with approval the definition of conservation in the *World Conservation Strategy,* a document prepared by the major world conservation organization, the International Union for Conservation of Nature and Natural Resources (IUCN):

Management of human use of the biosphere so that it may yield the greatest sustainable benefit to present generations, while maintaining its potential to meet the needs and aspirations of future generations. Thus conservation is positive, embracing preservation, maintenance, sustainable utilization, restoration and enhancement of the natural environment.

The concept of sustainable utilization clearly implies the possibility of harvesting for economic benefit. Sensitive planners do recognize that the uses and benefits of a resource include much more than its value as a dead product; as the draft U.N. plan points out, nonconsumptive uses of whales, such as organized whale watching, the filming of natural populations, and the capture of live specimens for aquariums may now rival in economic value the $200–$300 million taken in by commercial whalers each year. For many people just the knowledge that creatures as fascinating as the whales roam the seas has great value; intangibles like this too should play a role in resource-management decisions. But the draft U.N. plan also points out that controlled commercial whaling is compatible with most of the nonconsumptive uses of whales—and that if whale stocks were to be fully restored, the value of sustainable catches would probably multiply at least tenfold.

Current political winds suggest that a temporary moratorium on commercial whaling could well be imposed in the early 1980s. Apart from the minke whales, a special case, something quite close to a whaling ban had already been put in place by 1981. The unifying rationale behind these restrictions has been the need to let depleted stocks recover. Resolution of the more fundamental arguments over values has been postponed.

An approach to managing whales that treats them like other

exploited resources need not ignore esthetic and ecological concerns. But to those who oppose whaling on ethical grounds, the effort to balance such concerns with economic goals is inherently objectionable. Given the contradictions among public interests in whales, defining widely agreed goals and strategies will be some challenge. The U.N. draft plan asks: What is "the significance for management of the discovery of the whale song"? Who is going to answer that question?

Haunting indeed is the image of great oceans turned into dead seas. So too the fear that toxic chemicals and spreading oil slicks might upset the web of life in the oceans—or even cut humankind's supply of oxygen as phytoplankton smother.

But reports of death at sea are greatly exaggerated. Marine life has proved more resilient than some scientists expected. True, aquatic ecosystems have been severely damaged near some industrialized areas, and their produce near some coastlines has become unfit for human consumption. Pollution from oil production, transportation, and accidents has killed birds and shellfish and reduced tourism along some shores. But oil pollution has probably not yet had lasting impacts on a significant scale.

Traces of DDT have been found in remote corners of Antarctica, illustrating the global nature of oceanic pollution. Yet in the waters off North America and Europe, DDT concentrations declined in the 1970s. Less encouraging, DDT levels may well be rising off Third World coasts, and concentrations of PCBs (polychlorinated biphenyls, a class of highly toxic and long-lived industrial chemicals) seem to be holding constant in Northern Hemisphere waters and are damaging some fish and marine mammals. Still, no evidence shows that the open-ocean concentrations of metals, save lead, have risen significantly above the natural levels. Overall, available data suggest that most ocean life has scarcely been affected by pollution up to now.

This conclusion gives grounds for relief but not for complacency. Our knowledge of trends in the levels of various pollutants, and of changes pollutants cause in marine ecosystems, remains disgracefully inadequate. Our picture of oceanic health is far too spotty to justify any relaxation of efforts to cut the flow of persistent toxic substances into the waters that cover 70 percent of the globe. As the experts compiling UNEP's 1982 review of the state of the environment observed, many scientists feel uneasy taking at face value the lack of evidence of pollution damage. Even if measured concentrations are low, chronic effects could appear slowly and then be virtually irreversible. The most stringent precautions are therefore essential, particularly in view of the enormous deficiencies in our knowledge. Moreover, without our knowledge pollutants may subtly hamper the recovery of overexploited fish stocks, or render fish populations more vulnerable to climatic extremes.

Even the more land-locked, severely polluted seas such as the Mediterranean and the Baltic have as yet shown no sign of an overall decrease in fish productivity because of pollution. However, the massive flow of industrial wastes and human sewage into these and other smaller seas has adversely affected sea life and threatened the health of swimmers.

Mainly because of the inflow of untreated sewage, for example, the waters off Poland's Baltic coast are seriously degraded. In the summer of 1981 the Polish government was forced to close numerous beaches because of high coliform bacteria counts in the water. Dangerous bacteria and viruses were found in the dead fish that turned up in rising numbers in fishermen's nets. Eels nearly died out, and the government offered fishermen a bounty to bring in remaining eels for burning since they were suspected of spreading human disease.[12]

Throughout the Baltic contamination has impaired the reproduction of aquatic mammals, probably contributing to the drastic declines recorded in the populations of harbor seals, ringed seals, and gray seals. About 40 percent of the female seals in some portions of the Baltic Sea exhibit pathological changes in the uterus, believed to be caused by PCBs.[13]

Worldwide, pollution has often caused harm in coastal areas near large cities, industrial centers, and the mouths of polluted rivers. Smelly, nearly lifeless waters fill many bays and harbors, and some sea life is so contaminated with chemicals, metals, or bacteria that its consumption by humans is (or should be) prohibited. At the same time the physical alteration of rivers, wetlands, and shorelines often destroys habitats or breeding grounds of valuable fish.

Shellfish are especially prone to accumulating heavy metals and other long-lived pollutants. In fact since 1976 the United States has maintained a "mussel watch" as a means of documenting pollution trends. The concentrations of several metals, radioactive materials, halogenated hydrocarbons (such as PCBs and many pesticides), and petroleum elements in the tissues of mussels and oysters are being monitored.

In the late 1970s, 26 percent of the shellfish grounds off thirteen U.S. states were closed to commercial harvesting because of unsafe contamination. Pollutants have virtually wiped out clams, oysters, and prawns in Japan's Tokyo Bay, and shellfish contamination exceeds permitted levels in several other of the country's coastal areas. The Japanese government has resorted to dredging Tokyo Bay and the Seto Inland Sea in order to reduce the levels of PCBs and heavy metals on the bottom. Nor is such damage limited to developed countries. Shellfish production along Mexico's eastern coast, for example, has been undermined by pollutants from sugar and pulp and paper factories.[14]

Three brief articles about the oysters of Hong Kong's Deep Bay, appearing in successive 1979 issues of the *Marine Pollution Bulletin,* illustrate not only the hazards that uncontrolled industrial pollution can pose but also the political pressures that can hamper protection of public health in any society.[15] The March issue of the journal reported the finding that oysters from Deep Bay contained cadmium levels of 1.0–1.38 parts per million (ppm). Some oysters sampled in the local market had cadmium levels as high as 5.4 ppm. The safe upper limit for food recommended by the World Health Organization is 0.5 ppm. The government's immediate responses were to announce that a person would have to eat six oysters a day for twenty years to be endangered—and to ask doctors to be on the alert for cases of suspected cadmium poisoning.

Two months later the *Bulletin* noted the Hong Kong government's discovery that sediments entering the Deep Bay oyster-farming area contained 520 ppm of chromium, the result of discharges from tanneries upriver. The WHO safety limit for chromium in drinking water is 0.05 ppm. At the time of the journal report, levels in the oysters had not yet been established, no restrictions had been placed on oyster sales, and great quantities were being exported in dried form or as oyster sauce. The government had just announced plans to test for other toxic substances in local seafood.

Worries about the safety of eating Deep Bay oysters soon became irrelevant. The August issue of the *Bulletin* reported that "an as yet unidentified source of marine pollution has destroyed 90 percent of the oyster farm crop in Deep Bay."

All this occurred in 1979, decades after Japan's well-publicized heavy-metal tragedies, in one of the world's more technologically and economically advanced places where governmental regulation is unusually efficient. In how many lakes, rivers, and bays of the Third World have seafood contaminants never been measured? How many governments are willing and able to act strongly to protect human health at the short-run expense of fishing industries or polluting factories even if dangers are discovered?

Economic pressures often lead governments to wish away pollution problems. The U.S. government reopened the multi-million-dollar commercial fishery in Virginia's James River in 1981 even though fish there still carried more of the nerve-destroying and carcinogenic pesticide Kepone than is supposedly allowed; the unsafe residues persisted five years after careless pollution from a small factory had been halted.[16]

Mindful of the human agony and the sordid international image engendered by the mercury poisoning of those who ate fish from Minamata Bay in the 1940s and 1950s, the Japanese government has monitored fish contamination and banned sales more conscientiously than most over the last decade. And there has been plenty of banning to do. In the 1970s fish in numerous rivers still contained impermissible levels of mercury despite the introduction of pollution controls.[17]

Severe mercury contamination of foods was recently discovered in the harbor and rivers around Bombay, India, a heavily industrialized area. Cluster bean pods, popular vegetables that are grown in nearby rivers, were found in 1979 to be dangerously high in mercury as well as cadmium, lead, and copper. Local fish are often mercury-contaminated, and along stretches of the River Kalu they no longer survive at all. Metals dumped in the rivers also find their way back onto land: milk from cattle that graze along riverbanks is laced with mercury, and crops in nearby irrigated fields are absorbing dangerous concentrations of heavy metals.[18] Outbreaks of Minamata disease in Bombay's teeming slums could easily go undetected.

Largely because of a succession of dramatic blowouts and spills, oil pollution has generated special worldwide alarm. And in fact the oil released into the oceans through accidents tended to rise over the course of the last decade. The 1969 blowout off Santa Barbara, California, which generated such enormous public concern at the time, involved the release of only about 77,000 barrels of oil. But a 1979 tanker collision in the Caribbean resulted in the discharge of more than two million barrels, and the 1979–1980 blowout of Mexico's Ixtoc 1 well dumped a record 3.1 million barrels of oil into the Gulf of Mexico.

Birds are usually the most visible immediate victims of oil spills. Tens of thousands, their feathers clogged with oil, have died after each of the larger accidents. Less obvious damage generally befalls underwater life too. Studies carried out six months after the 1978 grounding of the tanker *Amoco Cadiz* off the coast of France revealed that 30 percent of the local fauna and 5 percent of the flora had been destroyed—although the only commercial fishery to be harmed was the oyster business. Reproduction and growth of several fish species was impaired that year. All in all, though, the encouraging news from studies after oil spills has been the impermanence of the impacts. Near-total recovery seems usually to have occurred.

Still, spills can have serious human consequences, especially off Third World coasts where economically marginal people live directly off marine resources. For example, thousands of low-income Nigerian fishermen lost their livelihoods for months in 1980 following an explosion at a Texaco rig, which spread oil slicks over sixty miles of shoreline and up into the Niger River delta for twenty miles.[19]

Chronic low-level oil pollution, which occurs where tankers commonly wash their ballast tanks and around terminals, refineries, or other industrial sources, has some scientists more worried than accidental spills do. Hydrocarbon pollution over long periods may well cause the slow degradation of ecosystems. Soviet scientists have argued that prolonged oil contamination causes a decline in primary productivity, a shift in the composition of the phytoplankton, and ultimately reductions in fishery potential. Data in support of this thesis have been collected in the Black Sea, the Sea of Azov, and off the Atlantic coast of the United States. Other experimental evidence indicates that petroleum elements can disrupt the early life-stages of fish.

Worldwide, oil production in offshore wells is rising fast, raising the odds of blowouts. Furthermore, drilling is on the increase in frigid northern regions where the natural decomposition of spilled oil, so essential to holding down its damage to living things, proceeds far slower than in warmer zones. Some governments and oil companies have their eyes on Antarctica too, where increased risks and magnified impacts of spills can be expected. (Rules to govern Antarctic oil exploitation have not yet been agreed upon by the Antarctic Treaty powers.)

Thus the ecological hazards associated with oil production and transportation may well increase over the next two decades. Still, at present more than half the oil-derived pollutants entering the seas come from sources on land. The control of petroleum discharges along coasts and into rivers, as well as of hydrocarbon emissions from cars and factories that reach the seas by air, remain vital along with the safe regulation of tanker traffic and offshore drilling.

Engineering works often undermine fisheries, sometimes in ways that economic planners fail to foresee as they calculate the costs of new construction. All over the world huge areas of tidal wetlands, the fertile transition zones between land and sea, have been ditched or filled in to support settlements or farmlands, or simply as a convenient way to dispose of solid wastes. The spawning, nursing, or feeding grounds of numerous marine species are thus lost, as are critical flows of nutrients into coastal waters. Upstream diversion of river waters can cause harmful rises in the salinity of estuaries; construction, deforestation, and farming can cause increases in sediment deposits that bring extra nutrients into estuaries but extinguish sea life. The biological impacts of wetlands degradation are usually irreversible.

By 1950, 90 percent of the tidal marshlands in the northeastern United States had been ditched, altering ecosystems and especially harming clam fisheries. Construction upstream of Magorda Bay, Texas, caused sedimentation that buried more than 6000 acres of productive oyster reefs over a thirty-six-year period. Land reclamation in Tokyo Bay has eliminated many once-rich fishing grounds. Around Manila, Philippines, land reclamation to support commercial buildings is destroying the livelihoods of traditional fishermen from nearby villages.[20]

The mangrove forests that cover many shoreline areas of the tropics and subtropics, through nutrients in falling detritus, provide the basis of the food chains that support a majority of nearby marine species. Yet according to a recent global survey, "vast areas [of mangrove] are being destroyed either intentionally or as a secondary result of other activities." Cutting for timber, upstream diversions of fresh waters essential to the needed coastal salinity balance, and land reclamation are among the major causes of mangrove and related fisheries losses. Often those who damage mangrove forests seem unaware of the economic and natural costs they are inflicting.[21]

Recent research on the diets of Amazonian fish, a critical protein source for communities along the river, has revealed the dangers of meddling in ecosystems we do not understand. Biologist Michael Goulding has documented what local tribal groups have long known —that many key fish species feed on fruits dropping from trees in the Amazon's extensive floodplains.[22] These same floodplains are often touted as the frontier of agricultural development, the one large area in the Amazon Basin where soils are fertile enough to sustain grain cultivation and grazing. But because of the detrimental impact on fisheries, extensive clearing of the floodplain forests would exact previously unimagined biological and economic costs.

Throughout the world the production of fish from inland lakes and rivers is barely holding ground against the negative impacts of dams, channels, and other physical alterations as well as pollution. Statistics on inland fisheries are notoriously incomplete, but at least seven million tons of fish, one-tenth of the global catch, comes from inland waters. These fisheries are especially crucial to the nutritional and economic status of millions in the Third World. Yet, as a recent FAO report observed, the "catch from river systems is declining so fast in many areas of the world that even the realization of potential increases in catch will not counter-balance the loss."[23]

The most productive rivers are those with marked cycles of seasonal flooding—precisely the rivers that put a gleam in the eyes of engineers. New fisheries created in man-made lakes seldom offset the multitude of biological products lost because of altered river flows. In China, fish production from lakes and rivers (not counting aquaculture) fell from 600,000 tons in the 1950s to 300,000 tons in the 1970s. Wetland reclamation, flood-control works, chemical pollution, and the overharvesting of wild fish eggs for use in aquaculture all contributed to the decline.[24]

Few systematic efforts have been made to add up the economic costs of pollution and other human activities that destroy fisheries. According to one study, about 8 percent of the total annual value of the finfish and shellfish catch along the Atlantic and Gulf Coasts of the United States—$41 million out of $561 million—was being lost in the mid-1970s as a result of pollution and physical modifications of coastlines. In the same period the U.S. West Coast fishery was reduced in value by 18 percent, $45 million a year. The contamination of San Francisco Bay oysters and the decline in salmon catches because of river damming and landfills between them accounted for the bulk of that total. Another study of shellfish losses in the United States as a whole concluded that the potential production of oysters, clams, and mussels from grounds placed off-limits was $29 million in 1975.[25]

In Japan and elsewhere, pollution is suspected of helping cause red tides, sudden blooms of red plankton that poison many fish. In 1972 when they reached a peak, thirty-three red tides reduced fish catches by $25 million. Near-shore oil pollution in Japan in 1973 caused an estimated $6 million in direct damage to fisheries.[26]

In many regions detailed analyses of the costs of pollution would undoubtedly provide economic justification for more aggressive controls. Some of the costs cannot be fully quantified. The social loss when beautiful beaches and rivers are fouled involves much more than the value of dead fish and missed tourism. And in some cases runaway pollution has destroyed the stability and livelihoods of communities, exacting a human price that fisheries data cannot capture.

Thanks to the Consumers' Association of Penang, rare documentation is available from Malaysia of the kind of tragedy that has undoubtedly stricken numerous other unsung groups around the world. The village of Kuala Juru, at the mouth of the river Sungei Juru, had for generations been known for its expert fishermen and plentiful catches. But mindless "development" nearby has undercut the economic and social stability of the village's 300 residents. In 1968 an ill-designed bridge disrupted river flows and caused a suffocating buildup of silt in prime fishing zones. Then in the early 1970s factories in a new industrial park upstream began dumping oil, heavy metals, and assorted other toxic wastes into the river—often in violation of the laxly enforced pollution laws. Within a few years villagers found that thirty species of fish, including the more desirable ones, had disappeared from accessible waters. The few surviving species were of low value and smelled repulsive when cooked. Incomes in the village fell by more than four-fifths, and a traditional way of life was destroyed. As the villagers' desperation became nationally known in 1976, some governmental assistance was finally received—to initiate cultivation of the pollution-resistant sea cockle for sale in nearby markets. Meanwhile the flow of poisons into the river continued. According to a 1976 Malaysian government study, "at least eleven Malaysian river basins are at present facing water pollution problems of a serious magnitude."[27]

Although ocean pollution has its global aspects, the main problems are local and regional, and the main sources of contamination are on land. Thus global approaches to the control of ocean pollution face inherent political and practical limitations.

A treaty limiting the dumping of certain toxic materials and highly radioactive wastes into the oceans was developed during the preparations for the Stockholm Conference, endorsed by the world gathering, then opened for signature in London in late 1972. This London dumping convention constituted historic recognition of countries' common interests in preventing contamination of the seas, and has been ratified by close to four dozen countries including all the key industrial states. Like other subsequent treaties it created a "black list" of substances whose disposal at sea is prohibited, and a "gray list" of materials requiring permits and special care.

The treaty has its weaknesses. Enforcement is up to individual governments whose technical capacities and political commitments vary widely. No list of specific proscribed materials can adequately cover the myriad chemical brews spewing out of modern industries, and dangerous compounds can slip through the regulatory cracks. The considerable pollutants pouring into the oceans from outfalls—drainpipes extending anywhere from hundreds of yards to several miles at sea—are not covered by the treaty even though the dumping of the same materials in the same place from a ship is. And many observers feel that the European countries which have been dumping low-level radioactive wastes in the Northeast Atlantic under the aegis of the London convention are not living up to their obligation to monitor the ecological impacts. Still, overall the London convention was an important milestone in the protection of oceanic life.

The draft U.N. treaty on the Law of the Sea, negotiations on which may be completed in 1982, encourages the further evolution of international controls on marine pollution. Its widespread ratification would effectively broaden the reach of the London dumping convention, strengthen the ability of coastal states to combat pollution from passing ships, and generally promote further discussion of actions needed to protect the marine environment. Under the draft treaty the rules that will be devised to govern deep seabed mining must include environmental safeguards.

The events along coastlines and within national borders that mean most to the health of the oceans have generally been beyond the reach of international negotiations. Some regional efforts to combat land-based pollution have been made. The states around the Baltic have a treaty aimed at limiting the inflow of pollutants. Many European countries have ratified the 1974 Paris convention on land-based sources, which obligates them to control the flow of specified toxins into adjacent Northeast Atlantic and Arctic waters.

Following what has proven to be a shrewd political strategy, Maurice Strong, UNEP's first executive director, initiated a systematic regional approach to ocean protection under U.N. auspices. The Regional Seas Program, certainly UNEP's major success, is bringing together states bordering ten different shared seas or coastlines, states that have an interest in cooperating for their own good. The Mediterranean Action Plan is the most fully developed to date. Plans have also been adopted for the Red Sea, the Persian/Arab Gulf, the Caribbean, the West and Central African coastline, and the East Asian Seas, and are under development in several other regions.[28]

While the specific elements of each plan differ, a common general approach has been followed. UNEP provides the initial spark, bringing governments together and providing seed money for program development. But the governments of the region themselves take over funding and management, and they draw on the technical advice of a host of U.N. agencies. In each case UNEP has encouraged a gradual but broad-ranging attack on the threats to the shared sea. Cooperative monitoring and research, relying on the coordinated work of national institutions in the region, often represents a breakthrough in itself, and more important, will provide an agreed scientific basis for necessary pollution-control actions in the future. First a general convention, full of good intentions but with little bite, is drawn up. Then subtreaties called protocols are developed spelling out legal obligations in such specific areas as the dumping of toxic substances or joint responses to oil spills. The result is a flexible legal framework within which new legal agreements can be negotiated as needs demand and politics permit. Action plans also include cooperative research projects on the environmentally sound development of coastal zones.

Taking a regional rather than a global approach "allows us to focus on specific problems of high priority to the states," observes Stjepan Keckes, the head of UNEP's Regional Seas Program. The resulting political appeal has been amply illustrated at the meetings of the Mediterranean Action Plan, where representatives of hostile states—Israel and Syria, Egypt and Libya, Greece and Turkey, Morocco and Algeria—have all sat together. "Pollution is the unifying concept," says Keckes.[29]

And polluted the Mediterranean is. By 1976 when the initial convention was signed in Barcelona, offshore degradation was beginning to call into question the Mediterranean's role as the world's premier tourist region. Each year more than 100 million tourists visit the coast, joining the 44 million who live there. Untreated sewage from these legions pours into the sea, joining the detergents, pesticides, heavy metals, industrial chemicals, and oil that it receives annually. Particularly because of the lack of proper sewage treatment, human health has been endangered; outbreaks of hepatitis, dysentery, meningitis, cholera, and a host of other diseases have been linked to the dirty water. Dozens of beaches in Italy and Israel have had to be closed for health reasons.

The less degradable pollutants swirl about the Mediterranean, making the problems inescapably international. Since the sea's waters are only regenerated every eighty to one hundred years, it can scarcely cleanse itself.

In the Barcelona convention, sixteen countries ringing the Mediterranean accepted a general obligation "to take all appropriate measures . . . to prevent, abate, and combat pollution of the Mediterranean Sea area and to protect and enhance the marine environment in that area." Two protocols, one controlling dumping by ships and aircraft, the other concerning oil spills and other emergencies, were also signed. While useful first steps, they did not strike at the roots of the Mediterranean's ills, which are on the land whence flows at least four-fifths of the sea's pollution. In 1980 another protocol committing nations to the control of land-based pollutants was signed. The earnestness with which it is implemented—the total cost of cleaning up existing pollution sources will be well over $10 billion, and no timetable is specified in the treaty—will determine the ultimate success of the Mediterranean Action Plan. The plan is backed up by the research and monitoring activities of eighty-three institutions in the sixteen countries, as well as by other cooperative planning exercises.

Progress with the Kuwait Action Plan, established by a 1978 convention to protect the Persian/Arab Gulf, has been delayed but not halted by open war between two signatories, Iraq and Iran. The governments surrounding the gulf, alarmed by the ominous findings of recent ecological studies, have agreed to proceed. Shallow and nearly land-locked, the gulf has an unusually limited capacity to absorb pollution. It faces extraordinary pressures: massive oil-tanker traffic, meaning ballast-cleansing and accidental spills; and rapid coastal population growth and industrialization as the region's soaring oil revenues are invested. A protocol has already been signed in defense against oil spills. But the most significant commitment over the long term, if it is taken seriously, could be the article in the 1978 treaty saying that each nation "shall endeavor to include an assessment of the potential environmental effects in any planning activity entailing projects within its territory, particularly in the coast area, which may cause significant risk of pollution in the Sea area." Here, as in the Mediterranean, concern for a common body of water has led to concern about the ecological soundness of developments on land.

In the Caribbean Action Plan, which was initiated in 1981, the promotion of sound development has from the beginning been the primary focus of the involved governments, in part because no major sea-wide pollution problems are apparent. Treaties on combatting oil spills and pollution may eventually be forthcoming, but the main emphasis will be on coastal-zone management and development planning in the Caribbean islands. One particularly critical topic is the planning of tourism, a major industry, which needs to expand in a manner less destructive than it has been of the natural resources that attract vacationers. Questions of human settlements planning, watershed management and forest protection, and environmental health will also be investigated.

All the regional seas programs face a common challenge: how to move beyond platitudes to commitments of resources on a scale that will make a difference. It is one thing to put up a few million dollars for research, quite another to incorporate the findings into development planning and to enforce strong pollution-control programs. Still, cooperative research programs and consultative processes have been set in motion, and any results will be better than what has gone before. The greatest benefits may result from future damages avoided as a result of newly improved planning procedures. Ecologically sound planning of coastal development, and adoption of less polluting technologies up along the rivers that feed the endangered seas, are bound to benefit societies in many ways. As Peter Thacher, UNEP's deputy head and a main architect of the Mediterranean Action Plan, has said, "Ironically, the effort to protect the oceans may provide its greatest benefits on land."[30]

6 POLLUTION: OLD AND NEW DIMENSIONS

AIR POLLUTION in one form or another has accompanied human society from the beginning. Cooking over a wood fire often creates a smoky, unhealthy living environment. Still today smoke from burning wood or cow dung irritates the eyes and impairs the lungs of hundreds of millions of the poor. Many Third World cities and even entire rural valleys are blanketed by smoky haze, the poor man's smog.

At the same time, fire and smoke have usually been associated with food, warmth, and kinship. The idea that air pollution is a problem worth combatting arose with the spreading use of coal in the Middle Ages. As early as 1306 a proclamation by Edward I of England banned the burning of "sea-coales" by London craftsmen. But the forces of urbanization and industrialization were to prove more powerful than love of pure air.

The Industrial Revolution and related urbanization led to a drastic escalation in air pollution. Coal warmed homes, drove factories, and later generated electricity for industrial and residential use. In the nineteenth and early twentieth centuries many cities of Europe and the United States were covered with black shrouds of smoke. As leader of the Industrial Revolution, Great Britain also became the foremost air polluter. London became known for its "pea soup" fog, an unnatural phenomenon that added flavor to Sherlock Holmes mysteries but shortened the lives of Londoners. Someone coined the term "smog" to describe the combination of smoke and fog that frequently enveloped British cities. Industrial centers like Pittsburgh, Pennsylvania, developed an atmosphere so inky that automobile drivers were sometimes forced to use their headlights at midday.

Laden with compounds that, we now know, cause cancer and respiratory ailments, smoky air must have caused much disease and death. Yet the health costs of air pollution in the early industrial era were never measured. The dramatic fall in mortality from infectious diseases during this period, a consequence of improved sanitation and diets, concealed whatever negative impact dirtier air had on health.

Many cities such as St. Louis and Pittsburgh embarked on highly successful smoke-control programs in the 1930s and 1940s. London followed suit after a particularly deadly pollution episode in 1952. But in these cities and elsewhere, smoke and soot proved rather easy to control in comparison with other products of coal combustion.

Up to the mid-twentieth century smoke and sulfurous compounds were synonymous with air pollution. Thus in 1943 when residents of Los Angeles began complaining about a recurrent, irritating haze, pollution experts visiting from eastern cities blamed the new problem on sulfur dioxide. But even after industrial emissions of sulfur dioxide were slashed, the haze appeared with growing frequency. Finally the residents of Los Angeles, and ultimately people everywhere, had to face the fact that humans had developed a massive new means of polluting the air—the automobile.

Los Angeles introduced the world to photochemical oxidants— ozone and other compounds that form when hydrocarbons (mostly the product of imperfect combustion in vehicle engines) and nitrogen oxides (produced both by vehicles and electric power plants) react in the presence of sunlight. The term "smog" was soon applied to the yellow-brown cloud that hung over Los Angeles, and this new use of the word spread quickly, pushing its original sense into linguistic history. With the example of Los Angeles before them, pollution researchers elsewhere began to reassess local problems and often to identify photochemical smog in the air. As automobile use soared, the familiar haze appeared in city after city—Tokyo, Ankara, Mexico City, Melbourne.

Despite the successes registered against smoke, the pollution of city air by other products of coal combustion (above all, sulfur dioxide) and by nitrous oxides, hydrocarbons, and carbon monoxide continued to worsen in most countries in the 1950s and 1960s. At the same time public concern about environmental quality began to escalate, driven in part by the accumulating evidence of the health hazards and other damages caused by dirty air.

That periods of extreme pollution by sulfur oxides and particulate matter take lives, especially among those with heart or respiratory problems, had become apparent in well-publicized pollution episodes such as in the Meuse Valley, Belgium, in 1930 (6000 ill, 60 dead); Donora, Pennsylvania, in 1948 (6000 ill, 20 dead); London in 1952 (tens of thousands ill, 4000 dead); and in New York City in 1953, 1963, and 1966 (hundreds of extra deaths).

Recent emission reductions have cut the likelihood of such overtly deadly incidents. But strong evidence indicates that prevailing levels of air pollution contribute to the development of chronic respiratory diseases (emphysema, asthma, and chronic bronchitis) and of short-term respiratory afflictions as well. And in rural areas, those living near smelters and refineries often face increased cancer risks because of the toxic substances spewing from smokestacks.[1]

Rising concern about the physical discomfort and reduced visibility caused by pollution, and rising evidence of the damages being wreaked on crops and materials, joined health considerations to spur enactment of new antipollution laws. Over the last twenty-five years virtually all the more developed countries and many less-developed ones too have begun trying to regulate the flow of pollutants in the air.

Some successes have been registered. The Organization for Economic Cooperation and Development (OECD), comprising twenty-four countries in North America and Western Europe as well as Japan, has summarized the progress of air pollution controls in many developed countries.[2] In most cases pollution by sulfur dioxide and particulate matter (soot, dust, and other particles), the main original targets of clean-air laws, has been cut.

Sulfur dioxide emissions had been rising through the 1960s, but the trend was reversed in many countries in the 1970s. In Japan sulfur dioxide emissions fell by more than half between 1970 and 1975. Slowed growth in energy consumption, switches from coal to natural gas and oil, and switches from high-sulfur to low-sulfur coal and oil account for a greater share of the declines in sulfur dioxide emissions than does the adoption of sulfur-removing devices in smokestacks.

Thus if world energy developments lead to surges in the use of dirtier fuels, as appears likely, recent gains against air pollution could easily be wiped out.[3]

More significant than the decline in absolute emissions of sulfur dioxide have been the reductions in the average and peak levels of sulfur dioxide in city air. In large urban areas of the United States, measured levels of sulfur dioxide decreased by 67 percent from 1964 to 1979.[4] In addition to the benefits of installed emission-control equipment, construction of taller smokestacks and location of industry away from urban areas have dispersed the pollutants more widely. City health has undoubtedly gained as a result of dispersal tactics, but other problems, including acid rain and the spread of haze over large areas, have been aggravated.

Progress against smoke and large particulates has, in the industrial countries, been most marked of all. Emissions of particulate matter were cut in half in Germany and France between 1965 and 1975, and by 30 percent in the United States. Londoners now enjoy 70 percent more sunshine in December than they did in 1958. There and elsewhere the elimination of coal burning in urban homes accounts for much of the gain against smoke. The widely mandated adoption of emission controls by industries has also been vital.

With particulates as with sulfur dioxide, some of the solutions have carried their own hazards. Industrial control equipment effectively collects the coarser particles that impair visibility, but does not eliminate the finer particulates, emissions of which have generally risen. And fine particulates, which can penetrate deeply into human lungs, pose serious health threats.

Because of outdated factories, inadequate environmental regulations, the use of wood as a domestic fuel, and widespread burning of refuse in open incinerators, some Third World cities are blighted by dangerous levels of particulate matter and sulfur dioxide. A report from the U.N.'s global air-pollution monitoring project found particulate concentrations in Calcutta to be much the highest among the eleven cities covered.[5] Inefficient burning of coal and lignite gives Ankara some of the world's worst air.

The city of Cubatão, Brazil, which hosts twenty-four petrochemical and other industrial plants, has been dubbed the "valley of death" by environmental groups. Barraged with extraordinary levels of particulates and other pollutants, the city's residents suffer high rates of respiratory disease, and a rising incidence of miscarriages, stillbirths, and birth defects was noted in 1980. Lacking the power to force the companies (many Brazilian owned, some multinational) to clean up their operations, the national environmental agency has proposed physically relocating the 15,000 unfortunate inhabitants of an especially polluted slum.[6]

Success in the control of photochemical smog has been limited at best. Between 1970 and 1975 emissions of nitrogen oxides increased in Japan, Canada, the United States, Finland, France, Germany, the Netherlands, and Sweden, and held steady in the United Kingdom. Since then they seem to have leveled off in Japan and the United States, two of the countries with the worst smog problems.

The lack of progress stems from several factors. First and foremost is the rise in the automobile population, which offsets the limited installation of emission controls on new cars. The number of stationary sources generating nitrogen oxides, mainly power plants, also rose during the 1970s.

Satisfactory technological answers to the smog problem do not exist. In motor vehicles, measures that could cut nitrogen oxide pollution sharply would simultaneously boost carbon dioxide and hydrocarbon emissions. The devices applied to cars up to now have brought only limited benefits and deteriorate quickly. The large-scale removal of nitrogen oxide from utility smokestacks has not proven feasible either.

Tokyo has managed to cut the frequency of extreme smog emergencies. But by and large smog levels in climatically susceptible cities are holding constant or rising. In the absence of curtailments in driving and further conservation of energy, there is little reason to hope for any improvement in the years ahead.

Furthermore, field studies in North America and Europe have established that oxidants and their precursor gases can travel far. Thus residents of Massachusetts breathe smog formed from pollutants emitted 300 kilometers away in New York City. Airborne nitrates join sulfates to create the hazes that sometimes cover areas as large as Western Europe or eastern North America. The appearance of haze in Arctic regions has scientists worried too.

Nitrogen oxides, like sulfur dioxide, can be transformed into acids that fall with the rain far from their place of origin. And long-distance travel by heavy metals and other toxic substances flying out of industrial smokestacks has also been observed. Air pollution can no longer be addressed as simply a local urban problem.

The story of efforts to clean up rivers, streams, and lakes is less encouraging than that of air-pollution control. As developed countries have begun to confront water degradation over the last two decades, a few notable successes have been achieved. Fish have returned to London's River Thames, and contamination of water and wildlife by such notorious poisons as mercury and DDT has generally been reduced. But to the extent generalization is possible, the quality of inland waters in the developed world has at best held steady, with declines in some forms of pollution offset by increases in others. Also, many new waterborne hazards have been identified. The characterization of trends in U.S. waterways in the 1970s in UNEP's report on *The World Environment 1972–1982* would apply to many other developed countries too: "More rivers were moderately polluted in this decade than in the last decade, but fewer rivers were highly polluted."

Controlling water pollution has turned out to be more complex and expensive than many envisaged a decade ago. This does not mean that the scores of billions of dollars spent for this purpose have been wasted; to the contrary, significant further deterioration of water quality would have occurred in their absence. In the years ahead, however, the scope of the antipollution struggle must be broadened.

A 1979 report on water quality in the member countries of the OECD summarized the contradictory trends.[7] On the positive side, levels of the traditionally fought pollutants—suspended solids and oxygen-consuming organic materials, which come mainly from untreated urban sewage and industrial effluents—"have stabilized or fallen in several member countries." At the same time the widespread presence in waters of "micro-pollutants"—toxic chemicals and metals —and of disease-causing microorganisms has been discovered. Thermal pollution of waterways is also causing increased concern.

In general, pollution from so-called point sources like sewage pipes and factories "is under progressively better control." But the contamination of waterways from nonpoint, diffuse sources—runoff from farmlands, which tends to carry fertilizers, pesticides, and organic matter; and from urban areas, which often carries oil, metals, and other pollutants—"remains largely uncontrolled and is on the increase in most countries." And acids and heavy metals falling with the rain constitute additional nonpoint sources of water degradation.

The huge investments made in urban sewage-treatment systems, together with the regulation of more flagrant industrial effluents, explain the limited progress achieved against suspended solids and oxygen-demanding materials. The proportion of developed-country populations whose sewage received some treatment rose markedly between 1965 and 1975, though it still varied widely among countries. As of 1975, 80 percent of United Kingdom residents were served by treatment plants but only 10 percent of Belgians were. In most cases sewage facilities have received the bulk of the public investments aimed at environmental improvement over the last decade. The U.S. government, for example, made grants to local communities totaling $31 billion between 1972 and 1981 for the construction of waste-treatment facilities.

No acceptable alternative exists to pressing ahead with the costly extension and improvement of urban sewage treatment. But the recent realization that many waterways are polluted by hundreds of toxic substances including organochloride compounds, heavy metals, and organometalic compounds forces the opening of a new front in the battle against water pollution. Levels of toxic substances in rivers and lakes have in the past been little monitored, and the implications for human or environmental health of the traces of countless chemicals appearing in rivers are poorly understood. In 1981 the U.S. Environmental Protection Agency produced a preliminary list of thirty-four urban streams that are seriously contaminated with toxic chemicals but will enjoy little improvement under planned regulations.

The control of diffuse pollution sources also poses a great and so far unmet challenge. During storms, vast quantities of chemical fertilizers and pesticides flow into streams, particularly where the erosion of farm soils is rampant. Water rushing off cattle feedlots too carries nutrients and organic matter into waterways. Improvements in farm practices to reduce soil erosion and overuse of chemicals must be part of the answer. Achieving them on a wide enough scale is more difficult than requiring installation of a control device on a single factory drainpipe. Likewise, poisonous runoff from city streets and garbage dumps is hard to confront.

Phosphates and nitrates are prevalent in farmland runoff and also usually emerge even with treated urban wastewater. These two nutrients contribute particularly to the problem of eutrophication, in which algae proliferate and then decay in a water body, using up its oxygen and rendering it progressively less fit for fish life, recreation, or drinking.

While "biological oxygen demand" concentrations in the freshwater bodies of the developed world have been declining, pollution by nitrates is on the rise nearly everywhere. Outside of Sweden and Finland, which have engaged in large-scale efforts to reduce the flow of nutrients into streams and lakes, countermeasures have generally been too weak to halt the process of eutrophication. In the OECD countries, "almost all important freshwater bodies deteriorated during the 1965–1975 period."

Few Third World countries have compiled data on trends in the quality of inland waters. What information can be pieced together is not encouraging. Around industrial centers of the so-called middle-income countries, contamination of rivers with toxic chemicals, metals, and organic pollutants has frequently been documented. Thus a recent study of fifteen major Mexican rivers found them unfit for most uses; municipal wastes, the effluents of petroleum refineries and sugarcane processing plants, and farmland runoff all contribute to severe degradation. Colombia's Bogotá River has been called one of the world's most polluted rivers; sewage and industrial effluents turn its waters—waters that residents of downstream villages still drink—dark, smelly, and foamy. Heightened levels of mercury, copper, and arsenic as well as organic pollutants are found in the river.[8]

In many different countries industrial or agricultural pollution of lakes and streams has contributed to declines in inland fisheries. The effects of water pollution on human health generally have not been investigated.

Even in the poorer, less industrialized countries, waters around population centers are sometimes dangerously contaminated by human and animal wastes, pollution from small traditional industries, and unregulated pollution from those large-scale factories that do exist. Most Third World cities do not have sewage systems, let alone treatment plants, and many have not devised safe alternative methods of urban sanitation either. Hazardous conditions in surrounding canals and rivers are the result. Waters near agricultural plantations frequently receive high doses of deadly pesticides but nevertheless are used for bathing or sometimes even drinking by nearby peasants. Both the traditional and the modern sources of water pollution must be confronted more forcefully if development is to mean improvement in the quality of human life.

Developed countries' programs to curb air and water pollution have brought some gains but no dramatic breakthroughs. Recently, as the global economic malaise has drawn new attention to influences on economic health, antipollution laws have come under attack. Required investments in pollution control, some argue, have drained scarce capital from productive investment without providing comparable benefits in return.

While some particular regulations have undoubtedly had uneconomic impacts, sweeping condemnations of the pollution-control programs of the 1970s are simply incorrect. A reasonable assessment of the net benefits of recent environmental laws is provided by the OECD. The main economic association of the noncommunist developed countries, the OECD has never been accused of starry-eyed environmentalism. In a 1980 report, *Environment Policies for the 1980s,* the OECD secretariat characterized the impact of recent antipollution requirements:

Environment policies are increasingly perceived to be justified on economic, as well as social and ecological grounds. National studies, based now on several years of experience, suggest that total benefits are well in excess of the total costs of measures to abate pollution. Indeed, the present situation, wherein expenditures on pollution amount to 1–2 per cent of GNP and damage from pollution ranges between 3–5 per cent of GNP, entails a welfare loss and justifies an increase in expenditures on environment. Recent polls in some countries indicate that increases for this purpose would command broad public support.[9]

To be sure, even the limited environmental progress of the last decade has not come cheaply. But a failure to control pollution carries an enormous price in such forms as bad health and premature deaths, damages to materials and crops, losses of productive ecosystems such as fisheries, losses of recreational opportunities, and degradation of the esthetic quality of life.

Applying sensible pollution controls faces inherent political and analytical difficulties. The direct expenses of cleanup measures fall upon particular industries or groups, while the resulting benefits, even if much larger, are less visible and are spread widely in society. The affected industries have a strong political interest in opposing costly required investments, while no single group has an immediate material interest of comparable magnitude in imposing controls. Thus can the political process be distorted, resulting in weaker antipollution policies than are in the social interest.

Sound economic analysis of pollution regulations faces parallel problems. The costs of required controls are tangible and easily figured, but no ready means exist for totaling the benefits of pollution reductions. The temptation is to engage in overly narrow accounting, ignoring the unmeasurable, subtle benefits of a cleaner environment.

No objective means exist for ascribing value to all the costs of uncontrolled pollution, or to the benefits of reducing it. What is the price of a shortened human life? How does one evaluate the spiritual loss to residents of Tokyo whose sight of beloved Mount Fuji is obscured by smog? How can we measure the value of a restored and productive ecosystem? The final judgment about the desirability of antipollution measures, then, is inescapably a political one reflecting value choices. No economist alone can supply answers to the great environmental policy issues of the day.

Some analysts have tried to compare the costs and benefits of pollution controls. In 1978, according to the U.S. Council on Environmental Quality (CEQ), $21.4 billion in damages were avoided in the United States as a result of mandated reductions in air pollution. The bulk of these benefits took the form of improved health—fewer pollution-linked diseases and deaths—as well as avoided damages to materials, buildings, and crops, and increases in property values from cleaner air. Additional but unmeasured benefits resulting from improvements in visibility and reductions in acid rain and transboundary pollution flowing to Canada and Mexico were not included. These calculated benefits may be compared with the estimated costs of compliance with air-pollution laws in 1978 of about $17 billion.[10]

Such comparisons highlight the crucial role of public policy in promoting measures that serve the overall public interest despite the often raucous opposition of hard-hit industries. The workings of an unregulated private market simply cannot take account of the diffuse and intangible social interests affected by pollution. This does not mean that public regulators cannot take advantage of financial incentives and market-oriented controls. The "polluter pays" principle, which tries to build the costs of pollution into the prices of the goods whose production causes it, is being promoted by the OECD. Flexible economic incentives, which have been tried more widely in Europe than in the United States up to now, can sometimes provide a useful supplement to or substitute for the more common setting of rigid pollution-level standards.

Public policy can also be used to equalize the burdens imposed by antipollution laws, and to make those who profit from pollution activities compensate those who suffer the ill consequences. If the costs were distributed fairly through society, the antipollution struggle would place no serious burden on anyone. The $27 billion spent on pollution control in the United States in 1978 sounds large until seen in per capita terms. It amounted to just $120 per American—compared to a per capita income level of $10,000 that year.[11]

The government of Japan has made a pioneering effort to force those who pollute to share in the costs imposed on at least some of the victims. Under a 1973 law, individuals with certain pollution-related diseases are compensated for medical expenses and lost wages, and upon death their funeral costs are covered and their survivors receive special benefits. Eighty percent of the compensation funds are paid by polluting industries, with the rest coming from a tax on motor vehicles. Victims of pollution-related respiratory diseases as well as of specific poisons like mercury and cadmium have received aid. Obviously no such law can be applied flawlessly; the specific causes of too many diseases cannot be proven, and cancer has been exempted altogether from coverage. And compensation is no substitute for prevention. Still, this approach has the dual merit of encouraging industries to cut back their pollution and of lightening at least some of the financial pain pollution causes.

The costs and benefits of specific control measures aside, some have expressed concern about the broader economic impacts of recent pollution-control programs. Costly, "nonproductive" antipollution investments have been blamed for pushing up inflation and unemployment, reducing productivity, and generally hampering economic growth. Such arguments ignore the real if unmeasured "products" provided by a cleaner environment. Conventional economic accounting methods tend both to exaggerate the pluses of damage-causing activities and to undercount the minuses of a damaged environment.

Even in conventional economic terms, antipollution measures have not generally been burdensome. The environment ministers of the OECD countries, meeting in 1979, jointly stated that the previous decade's environmental measures "had generated significant benefits, without in most cases negative effects on the economy," adding that "the short-term net employment effects have been positive." They noted that "the impact on inflation has been on the whole moderate, averaging 0.1–0.3 per cent per annum; the impact of environmental policies on the rate of economic growth has been neutral, perhaps even slightly positive."[12]

The early 1980s are an appropriate time for reassessing environmental goals and the effectiveness of measures tried over the previous decades. But all too often pollution-control laws are used as scapegoats by special interests that seek relief from environmental requirements by blaming them for economic problems rooted elsewhere.

Strong national environmental policies have often prompted innovations in industrial technologies, resulting simultaneously in more efficient production and a cleaner environment. Stringent pollution standards force firms to reexamine the possibilities for waste recycling, materials recovery, and energy conservation. Michael G. Royston's book *Pollution Prevention Pays* documents numerous examples. The U.S.-based 3M company, which manufactures a variety of products in fifteen countries, saved over $20 million between 1976 and 1979 as a result of new recycling and other measures that significantly cut pollution. Ciba-Geigy, the Swiss chemical firm, has reduced emissions by up to 50 percent while saving about $400,000 a year and reducing energy consumption.[13]

When it comes to environmental contamination, an ounce of prevention is usually worth tons of cure. Douglas Costle, former administrator of the U.S. Environmental Protection Agency, has noted the high costs of negligence in three recent cases:

- The chemical wastes dumped carelessly in New York's Love Canal could have been disposed of in a secure landfill for $4 million. Instead, government agencies have had to spend more than $50 million to cope with the consequences of contamination; the offending company faces lawsuits running into the billions; and a thousand families have been physically uprooted, emotionally scarred, and in some cases had their health impaired.

- The PCBs illegally sprayed along North Carolina roads by a "midnight dumper" could have been disposed of safely for $100,000. Now the state must spend $2–$12 million for cleanup.

- Pollution of Virginia's James River and of the factory's working environment by the makers of the pesticide Kepone could have been prevented for $200,000. Instead the company has paid out $13 million in damages plus large undisclosed payments to nerve-damaged workers. Fisheries losses have totaled many millions of dollars; thorough cleanup of the river is unfeasible.[14]

Though extreme, examples like these illustrate a valid general point: preventing pollution in the first place usually makes economic as well as ecological sense. Over the last decade many new factories have incorporated antipollution technologies without great hardship. Usually, the factories causing the worst pollution, and those for which the economics of newly imposed standards are least favorable, are the older, outmoded ones. Retrofitting a plant to cut emissions tends to be more expensive and less effective than building cleaner processes into new plants. Third World countries that are only now industrializing thus have a chance to avoid some of the developed countries' expensive efforts to make up for past errors.

The long-standing debate about whether developing countries should use lax environmental regulations as a means of attracting sorely needed industrial investment continues to simmer. On the whole it appears that differing environmental standards are usually too minor an element in a multinational investment decision to be a significant determining factor. The once-feared flight of heavy industry to "pollution havens" in the Third World has not widely materialized.

Still, numerous examples have been documented of firms in poor countries cutting costs at the expense of worker health and the environment. One 1975 study of U.S.-based multinational firms revealed capital outlays for pollution control to be roughly double at home what they were abroad.[15] Environmental groups in Southeast Asia charge that polluting Japanese-owned industries relocating in poorer countries of the region often lack adequate emissions controls.

Variations in pollution standards according to local conditions do make sense. But the notion that poor countries should necessarily adopt lax pollution standards ought to be viewed with caution. Already the more industrialized developing countries are learning the sorry consequences of unregulated industrial buildups. Savage pollution in areas of Brazil, Mexico, India, and elsewhere has given rise to belated regulatory efforts, but often little can be done to offset the massive environmental and human damages being generated by existing plants. Third World countries that fail to impose reasonable pollution standards on companies investing today may well find themselves trapped in unpleasant and costly dilemmas a few years from now.

The true costs and benefits brought by polluting industries to the Third World deserve careful scrutiny. Where large numbers of people are poorly nourished and unhealthy to begin with, and where many depend directly on land and water resources for bare survival, the damages inflicted by air and water pollution can be high. The negative human impacts can be greater than in rich countries even if our present rudimentary accounting techniques imply the reverse.

The officials in capital cities who talk of the need to pay an environmental price for economic progress are seldom the ones who pay that price. More likely they are part of the group reaping the fruits of progress. The interests of village fishermen who will lose their livelihoods because of uncontrolled river dumping of industrial effluents can easily be overlooked as national planners strike their agreements with new industries. (Residents of one such threatened village in Indonesia recently took matters into their own hands, burning down the offending factory.)

Inevitably, industrial development in the Third World is going to have adverse effects on air and water resources. Ideally, it would come as part of a broader development process that cleans up the traditional environmental threats to health such as sewage-clogged gutters and smoky households. But in the late twentieth century it makes no sense to trade one set of outdated hazards for another. The developed world has learned of the genuine costs of ignoring the subtle and long-term effects of environmental contamination. For the Third World to try to cut corners in development by wishing away the pollution challenge would be bad economics as well as bad ecology.

Synthetic chemicals permeate modern life. At least 55,000 are produced commercially, and a thousand new ones are manufactured each year. In developed countries people are exposed to chemicals in the air they breathe, the water they drink, the food they eat, the drugs they take, and the products they handle each day at home and at work. In poorer countries fewer synthetic chemicals are in the environment, but the exposure of some workers and consumers to particular substances can be quite high.

Modern chemicals have undoubtedly brought major benefits. But an unknown proportion cause cancer, birth defects, or other human ills, or damage plants and animals. Having accepted the proliferation of chemicals without much control in the past, societies now face the expensive and complex tasks of identifying those that are dangerous and then deciding what to do about them.

The search for those that cause cancer, for instance, is still at an early stage. Often cancer appears years or decades after exposure to the causative agent. Where identifiable groups—usually workers in a particular industry—experience an unusual incidence of cancer, medical detectives can sometimes work backward to identify the offending substance. A handful of carcinogens have been fingered in this way, after they have already worked significant harm. But even this unsatisfying means of identification is ineffective for substances to which the general population is exposed over time; tracing cause and effect is impossible.

The best available method for determining whether a substance is carcinogenic is feeding it to animals in a controlled study. Any substance that causes cancer in animals is presumed by scientists to have the potential to do so in humans. The problem is that toxicity tests cost between $400,000 and $1 million each, and take up to five years to complete. For practical reasons most chemicals will never be so scrutinized. By comparing chemical structures, scientists try to identify the more suspicious substances that should receive priority for testing. Short-term, inexpensive tests using microbes and cultured cells also aid in the selection of suspicious chemicals.

The U.N.'s International Agency for Research on Cancer (IARC) keeps track of worldwide test results. The IARC has listed about 160 substances as posing probable carcinogenic hazards to humans. But fewer than one-eighth of the chemicals in commercial use have been subjected to animal tests, and many of these were not tested according to the latest standards. Hundreds of the tested chemicals have shown suspicious signs and need follow-up studies. Says the U.S. Office of Technology Assessment: "How many more carcinogens will be identified is uncertain, and what is known about the tested chemicals may be overshadowed by what is unknown both about untested chemicals and about complex human exposures and behaviors not amenable to laboratory testing."[16]

Cancer is not the only hazard to be watched for. In 1980 a special U.S. government committee on toxic substances characterized the broad challenge:

The magnitude of the toxic substances control problem, although not quantifiable with precision, is staggering in view of the number of substances whose risk should be evaluated, the rate of growth in both number and volume of chemicals, the various routes by which humans and the environment are exposed, possible synergistic or combined effects of the substances, and the effects that they cause—acute and chronic, immediate and delayed.[17]

Highly publicized chemical disasters—such as the showering of poisonous dioxin over portions of Seveso, Italy, forcing their abandonment; the evacuation of families from New York's Love Canal area because of the toxic wastes oozing around homes; and the many reported outbreaks of cancer, sterility, or nervous disorders among factory workers—represent only the visible part of the problem. The health effects of chronic, low-level exposures to numerous potentially dangerous substances, singly and in combination, are unknown. Fortunately, no major health impact among the public at large from ordinary exposures has yet become apparent.

Deadly incidents arising from careless regulation and use of toxic substances are common enough in Europe, Japan, and North America, where large numbers of scientists and public officials are working to prevent them. In the Third World, where the rush for economic growth has not usually been accompanied by development of technical skills and institutions for regulating modern technologies, toxic chemicals pose an increasing challenge. "The abuse of toxic substances in developing countries is certain to be a major environmental issue in the decade ahead," observes S. Jacob Scherr of the Natural Resources Defense Council.[18]

Although it received little worldwide attention, perhaps the worst toxic-substance tragedy to date occurred in Iraq in 1971 and 1972. Large quantities of wheat seeds were treated with antifungus compounds containing mercury. (Use of such fungicides had been prohibited in many countries.) Some of these seeds were mistakenly baked into bread. Over a three-month period more than 6000 neurologically damaged patients were admitted to hospitals. Many more stricken people could not get into hospitals because of overcrowding; in any case no effective antidote was available. Some 452 people died inside hospitals, and many others left them to die at home. This single incident took more lives than the world-famous cases of mercury poisoning in Japan.[19]

Anecdotal evidence suggests that in much of the Third World, careless or callous practices often characterize the handling of dangerous materials inside factories, the sale of dangerous drugs, and the sale of potentially hazardous consumer products. The problems, and their international connections, are perhaps best exemplified by pesticide practices.

Two decades after the publication of Rachel Carson's *Silent Spring,* more than half the world's countries do not have effective legislation to govern the use of pesticides. Many governments have little idea even of the kinds of agricultural chemicals being imported and sprayed in their countries. When the United Nations Food and Agriculture Organization polled member countries in the mid-1970s on the amounts and types of pesticides being applied, more than forty were unable to provide any of the information sought.[20]

Unfortunately, reliable worldwide statistics on trends in the application of different types of pesticides cannot be compiled. In the absence of stronger government disclosure requirements, the major pesticide manufacturers, who will enjoy world sales of nearly $13 billion in 1982, refuse to make public any breakdown of their production and sales. Reports from many Third World countries indicate the continuing use of persistent pesticides that have been severely restricted in developed nations out of concern for ecosystems, wildlife, and health. For example, DDT is still sprayed profusely in many places, especially on cotton and other plantations.

Environmental and consumer groups in Africa, Asia, and Latin America have also documented the widespread sale of even more dangerous compounds that have been banned in developed countries because they severely threaten human health, and of pesticides that have not been properly tested. True, the calculation of risks and benefits from using a particular pesticide may differ from country to country. But in many cases neither the government officials who approve the use of banned or untested pesticides, nor the farmworkers who apply them, know about the special dangers.

Even widely approved pesticides can be deadly when handled without proper care. Some of the less persistent chemicals now used instead of long-lived substances like DDT are, unfortunately, far more toxic for humans. The mixing, repackaging, and distribution of pesticides constitute major danger points in developing countries. Workers handling potent powders or liquids without even elementary protective gear are a common sight. Even when the proper uses and safety precautions are clearly stated on the containers in which materials have been shipped, distributors commonly put pesticides into small, often unlabeled containers for final sale. A University of California team visiting Pakistan in 1974 reported that "one customer, lacking a suitable container, unwrapped his turban, poured a granular pesticide therein, and replaced it on his head for transport." Instructions about safety and proper uses are passed haphazardly from dealers to farmers by word of mouth.[21]

Public concerns about wildlife and the health effects of pesticide residues in food provided the main initial impetus for closer regulation of pesticides in developed countries. But it is farmworkers who pay the major price for careless pesticide practices.

Conditions for farmworkers are bad enough in the United States, where scores of thousands are poisoned annually. But a 1976 WHO report on occupational health said that in some developing countries field surveys revealed "up to 40 percent of workers with symptoms of poisoning during the spraying period."[22]

Events in and around Central American cotton plantations over the last decade illustrate the multiple hazards of poorly controlled pesticide use. Faced with mounting pest resistance, growers in parts of El Salvador, Guatemala, and Nicaragua had to raise the number of sprayings per growing season from eight in the 1940s to more than fifty. Pesticide poisonings account for hundreds of deaths and thousands of illnesses annually among fieldworkers, many of them illiterate Indians working the fields barefoot. High concentrations of DDT in mother's milk have been recorded among farmworker families.

As pesticides sprayed on cotton fields wafted across the Central American countryside, mosquitoes became resistant, undercutting the malaria-control program. Cases of malaria multiplied. Meanwhile, milk, meat, and vegetables grown near the cotton fields were severely contaminated. Many shipments of beef bound for the United States were rejected because U.S. safety limits for residues were exceeded. The rejected meat reportedly found its way into local markets, where the control of pesticide residues in food is virtually nonexistent.[23]

Throughout the Third World the passage and enforcement of appropriate laws, the improved training of farm managers and workers, and above all the wider use of integrated pest management can cut the damages. But the inevitable hazards are intensified by the willingness of companies to take advantage of regulatory vacuums, and the double standard maintained by exporting countries in their regulations. Many examples exist of companies' failing to inform importers about the known hazards of their products and about the restrictions that have been placed on their use in technically advanced nations. The governments of exporting countries have generally refused to accept responsibility for the proper sharing of information about hazardous exports. The United States at least requires that foreign buyers of pesticides be informed if they are purchasing a banned product. The governments of Europe and Japan have not gone even that far. The possible damage to their own citizens from consumption of residues of banned pesticides in imported foods—a common phenomenon—has apparently made little more impact than the moral issues at stake.

The hazardous trade problem involves much more than pesticides. In most countries exported consumer products, foods, drugs, and industrial chemicals are largely exempted from the safety and environmental regulations imposed on products for the home market.

Recent strong regulations in developed countries governing the safe disposal of hazardous wastes likewise permit unrestricted exports. Some firms are known to be exploring the possibility of paying Third World countries to become chemical dumping grounds. When it comes to human safety and environmental protection, the morality prevailing in international trade is *caveat emptor.*

The rationale given for laissez-faire in trade is that each sovereign state is free to make its own judgments about risks and benefits and to regulate imported goods accordingly. In practice, considering the technical and regulatory weaknesses of Third World governments, the situation is primed for abuse.

Recognizing the dangers, both the United Nations Environment Programme and the United Nations General Assembly have called for the full notification of importing governments about the hazards of traded products. The Scientific Advisory Committee of UNEP's International Register of Potentially Toxic Chemicals (IRPTC) has gone further, calling for development of an international code of ethics on trade in hazardous chemicals, including adoption of a standardized international certificate containing toxicological information. But developed-country governments have so far failed to bring the scandalous trade in hazardous products under control themselves, and have shown no interest in meaningful international measures.

The long-term solution of course is for each country to develop the capacity to make and enforce appropriate domestic regulations governing the use of dangerous substances. Third World countries may be greatly assisted in this task by the IRPTC, which is just now getting off the ground. Its registry of toxicological information on more than 40,000 chemicals can be useful to all countries, helping them learn the results of studies elsewhere and avoid costly duplications of tests. But it can be especially useful to regulators in developing countries who have no large scientific establishment to back them up.

The IRPTC also publishes a periodic bulletin in several languages that reports on new scientific findings, poisoning incidents, and regulatory decisions in one country or another involving toxic chemicals. This can be invaluable for the isolated Third World official who otherwise could not keep abreast of the rapid developments in this field.

With hazardous chemicals as with more traditional pollutants, sound information about risks and benefits is necessary but not sufficient for effective control. Armed with the best available knowledge, governments must be willing and able to enforce measures that serve the long-term public interest even when the immediate costs seem high. The challenge of toxic chemicals is as much political as it is technical.

7 GLOBAL ATMOSPHERICS

ACID RAIN. In any era but our own these words would have sounded preposterous together. Rain gives life; rain cleanses and rejuvenates. Now some rain kills and corrodes.

Common air pollutants—sulfur dioxide and nitrogen oxides—can react with water in the atmosphere to form droplets of dilute acid. The pollutants or acids sometimes travel hundreds of miles before raining down; hence acid rain posses crucial issues of international law, responsibility, and equity. Who benefits from the activities that cause acid rain? Who suffers the ecological consequences? What recourse do the victims have when the foul rain results from activities in a foreign country?

Acid rain raises another issue common to many environmental threats. How much information is necessary to justify expensive countermeasures? As is usually the case with complex ecological matters, we neither know all the facts about acid rain nor understand all the implications of the data we have. And as is usually the case, the industries involved point to the uncertainties as reason for delaying antipollution measures.

But there is no disputing a central point: a major, destructive change has occurred in the rainfall over large areas of Europe and North America. Substantial biological and economic damages are already apparent. And although a link between pollutants from a particular factory and damage in a particular downwind area cannot be proven, we nevertheless know what the main sources of acid rain are.

As stated by a 1981 report of the U.S. National Academy of Sciences, existing knowledge of acid rain "is disturbing enough to merit prompt tightening of restrictions on atmospheric emissions of fossil fuels and other large sources." The same report also notes that because of the combined effects of traditional air pollution and acid rain, continued emissions of sulfur and nitrogen oxides "at current or accelerated rates . . . will be extremely risky from a long-term economic standpoint as well as from the standpoint of biosphere protection." A Canadian official has put it more forcefully: "We cannot wait for a perfect understanding of the acid rain phenomenon before moving to control it. . . . How many more lakes have to die before we get the message?"[1]

Although the problem has been with us for many years, it was curiously unperceived by the public, governments, and even most scientists until quite recently. By the 1960s Scandinavian scientists had figured out that sulfur emissions from other countries were killing fish in their own rivers and lakes, but the rest of Europe showed no eagerness to acknowledge the new threat. Only after the Swedish presentation on the subject at the 1972 Stockholm Conference did the problem begin to receive sustained international attention.

In the eastern portions of North America highly acid rainfall was already a fact of life by the 1950s, but for two decades this appalling development was largely ignored. Not until the late 1970s did both the United States and Canada initiate the systematic monitoring of the chemistry of their rains.

Because it reacts with carbon dioxide in the atmosphere to form carbonic acid, rainfall is normally acidic. "Pure" rain usually has a pH of 5.6–5.7 (a pH of 7.0 is neutral; the lower the pH, the more acidic the rain). The slight acidity of natural rainfall is beneficial, since it helps water dissolve soil minerals and make them available to plant and animal life. But as the acidity increases beyond the natural level due to human actions, destructive impacts appear.

Today the average raindrop falling in most of the eastern United States, some regions of the American West, southeastern Canada, and most of Western Europe has a pH of between 4.0 and 5.0. (Since the pH scale is logarithmic, a drop in pH from 6.0 to 4.0 involves a hundredfold increase in acidity.) Highly acidic rain has been recorded near an industrial area of Brazil as well.[2]

Some individual storms are far worse than average. The town of Wheeling, West Virginia, may hold the record for the most acidic rainfall ever monitored; during one 1978 storm unofficial pH readings dipped below 2.0—more acidic than lemon juice. Thus did Wheeling eclipse Pitlochry, Scotland, which had achieved worldwide notoriety for a 1974 storm with a pH of 2.4, itself more sour than vinegar.

Two types of acid have increased in rain: sulfuric acid, created in the atmosphere from sulfur oxides emitted mainly by coal-burning utilities and factories and smelters; and nitric acid, formed from nitrogen oxides released by utilities, factories, and vehicles as they burn fossil fuels of all sorts. Up to now sulfuric acid is believed to have posed the greatest problem in Europe and eastern North America, while nitric acid is more significant in the American West. The mix seems to be changing over time, with nitric acid gaining importance, perhaps because technologies for the control of nitrous oxide are much less advanced than those for holding down sulfur emissions. But projected increases in coal use may well lead to further increases in sulfuric acids in the rain.

In Europe, average sulfur concentrations in rainfall increased by 50 percent between the mid-1950s and early 1970s. The greatest increases were in Central and South-central Europe, where concentrations jumped 100 percent, and in southern Scandinavia, where they rose 50–100 percent during that period. The amount of sulfuric acid in European rain has tended to level off since the late 1960s, possibly a coincidental benefit of efforts to reduce urban air pollution. Nitric acid levels, on the other hand, continue to climb.

Whether the severity and extent of acid rain in the eastern U.S. and Canada are now increasing is unclear. Total U.S. sulfur emissions declined in the 1970s as air-pollution laws were applied. Maintaining that downward trend will be difficult in the face of expanded coal burning and industry resistance to major expenditures on sulfur-control technologies.

Power plants alone account for more than 80 percent of all sulfur emissions in the eastern United States, and more than 60 percent in the U.S. as a whole.[3] In many European countries, and the Soviet Union too, more than half of all sulfur pollution comes from power plants. Hence acid rain and policies on the choice of energy sources are inextricably intertwined, a fact governments have not been eager to acknowledge as they cope with the energy crisis.

Even as progress has been made against sulfur, nitrous oxide pollution has soared. Total nitrous oxide emissions in the United States have tripled over the last twenty-five years, and according to the Office of Technology Assessment, will rise another 20–35 percent by the end of the century if better control technologies are not developed. In addition to underscoring the need to find better ways to reduce nitrous oxide output from factories and power plants, acid rain provides additional reasons for cleaning up automobile exhausts. Vehicles produce about two-fifths of U.S. nitrous oxide emissions.[4]

Emission levels of pollutants do not correspond directly with downwind rainfall purity. Much air pollution remains localized, and much falls to earth without being transformed into acid. Dust in the air can neutralize acids, while humidity and solar intensity affect the speed at which gases are transformed into acids. Also, our understanding of pollutant movements and chemical changes in the atmosphere is too unsophisticated to allow accurate calculations of the level of acids that will fall in one place as a result of pollution belched out in another.

That the problem transcends national boundaries is undeniable. Roughly half the sulfur in eastern Canada's rain originates in the United States. The exchange of pollutants is two-way, but Canada receives two to four times the sulfur and eleven times the nitrous oxides that it sends to its southern neighbor. As a result acid rain is invariably one of the top items on the agenda when the national leaders of the United States and Canada meet for diplomatic talks. In Europe, Sweden and Norway are the chief losers; more than three-fourths of the acids that plague their southern zones come from other countries.[5] Acid rain is certain to cause increasingly bitter international disputes in the years ahead.

The construction of tall smokestacks to disperse traditional air pollution has exacerbated the acid rain problem. Scattering pollutants to the winds does not make them disappear. More than 200 smokestacks in the United States range in height from 400 to 1200 feet. Canada's Sudbury smelters have a stack a quarter-mile high. Great Britain's dramatic progress against local air pollution, which relies heavily on dispersing pollutants with tall smokestacks, has been partly at the expense of biological resources in southern Scandinavia.

Acid rain's most negative impacts have been on life in rivers and lakes. When the acidity of waters begins to rise, fish reproduction is impaired and calcium in fish skeletons becomes depleted, causing malformed "humpback" fish. Acidic waters also unlock aluminum from surrounding soils, which then builds up on fish gills. As water pH falls below 5.5, smaller species of crustaceans, plankton, molluscs, and flies begin to disappear. At a pH of 5.0 the decomposition of organic matter, the foundation of the aquatic food chain, is undermined. Below a pH of 4.5 all fish are dead and the only remaining life is a mat of algae, moss, and fungus. Lacking organic matter, the water of an acidified lake assumes the crystal clarity of a swimming pool— a deceptive beauty indeed.

At least 5000 of Sweden's lakes are seriously ill, and the government spends $40 million a year pouring lime into some in order to counter acidity. All the lakes in a 13,000-square-kilometer area of southern Norway are damaged, and rising acidity in Scandinavian rivers has caused precipitous declines in salmon and trout numbers since the mid-1960s. Five of Norway's famous salmon rivers have completely lost their claim to fame.[6]

In the Adirondack Mountains of upstate New York, officially declared "forever wild" since 1892, more than half the lakes are in critical condition, more than 200 of them devoid of fish. As trout began to disappear in the 1950s, blame was initially laid on predatory perch—until they too started dying off. As in Scandinavia, some lakes in the Adirondacks are being treated with lime. But this procedure is too expensive for widespread use. Thousands more water bodies elsewhere in the United States, including lakes in the famed Boundary Waters area in northern Minnesota, have registered ominous rises in acidity.[7]

Fish have disappeared completely from at least 140 Canadian lakes, mainly in Ontario, and life has been altered in thousands more. Scientists fear that as many as 48,000 of Canada's lakes could become fishless over the next decade.[8]

Even if acid levels in rain stay constant, the damages will soar over time as the natural buffering capacity of soils and waters is gradually exhausted. Thus, examining prospects in both Europe and North America, the recent U.S. National Academy of Sciences study says that "at current rates of emission of sulfur and nitrogen oxides, the number of affected lakes can be expected to more than double by 1990, and to include larger and deeper lakes."[9]

Circumstantial evidence links acid rain to reduced forest productivity. Under certain soil conditions, increased acidity can initially accelerate tree growth as extra nutrients are released. But that effect is temporary; eventually critical nutrients are leached away. At the same time acidic waters may transfer aluminum from soils to roots, causing a phenomenon known as die-back—trees with dry, brittle crowns and branches that look like victims of drought. Studies in Germany, Sweden, and Canada have correlated die-back with rainfall acidity. Humus tends to decompose less rapidly in acidic soils, reducing the nutrients available to vegetation. Also, experimental evidence suggests that the survival rate of seedlings is cut by acidity.[10]

The growth rate of a forest can be influenced by many factors, making airtight proof of acid rain's role nearly impossible. No significant drop in forest productivity has been definitely linked to acid rain; major research on the subject is under way in Scandinavia, Central Europe, and North America.[11]

The possible impacts on agricultural crops are not well understood, but do not appear to have been great so far. Many farmers in the worst-hit areas are accustomed to conditioning their soils and may thus be offsetting potential damages. Laboratory studies have shown mixed results. Certain root and leafy crops were harmed, grain crops were little affected, and certain legumes, fruits, and other crops were stimulated by acidic waters.[12] Whether continuing acidic rainfall will have effects on agricultural soils is unknown.

Through its corrosive effects on buildings, roofing materials, monuments, metals, and automobile paints, acid rain is exacting an enormous economic toll. In Poland's industrial heartland, acids have so corroded the railway tracks that trains cannot go more than forty miles an hour. Even buried pipelines and power cables can be harmed.

Materials damages attributable to acid rain in the United States alone probably amount to billions of dollars. Some losses are priceless. The Gothic buildings of Cracow, Poland, which UNESCO has declared part of the world's cultural heritage, are losing their unique architectural embellishments to corrosion. The faces of stone statues have crumbled and the gold roof of a sixteenth-century chapel was partly dissolved by the acidic rain. Local architects are considering stripping Cracow's buildings of their more important ornaments and storing them away to protect them from the rain. In this case locally generated pollutants are the primary culprits.[13] But serious deterioration of buildings is occurring even in Ottawa, Canada, which is essentially nonindustrial but receives rainfall with a pH of 4.5.

Acid rain might threaten human health through its role in accentuating heavy-metal problems, although no health impacts have been proven. The same air pollution that causes acid rain often contains mercury, lead, cadmium, zinc, or other metals, which can travel far before raining back down on earth. Also, acidic water can dissolve heavy metals found in the soils around water bodies, making them potentially available to humans. Mercury poses special dangers. Acid water converts inorganic mercury, whether arriving as pollution or found naturally in waters and soils, into its more toxic form of methylmercury. Perhaps in part because of acid rain, lake fish in areas of the United States, Canada, and Sweden contain rising mercury concentrations and could endanger those who eat them.[14]

Drinking water in portions of the Adirondacks and southern Scandinavia contains unsafe levels of various heavy metals; acid rain is suspected as the reason. Residents in the Adirondacks have been advised not to install copper pipes because of the risk of copper's dissolving into the water. They also are told to flush out their household pipes each morning to remove toxic metals leached from the pipes.[15]

Investigation of the direct and indirect economic costs of acid rain is still in its infancy. One 1978 study, conducted for the U.S. government by Thomas Crocker, estimated that acid rain causes $5 billion in damages each year in the states east of the Mississippi River plus Minnesota: $2 billion in materials damages, $1.75 billion in reduced forest output, $1.0 billion in crop losses, and $0.25 billion arising from damages to aquatic life. Various critics charge that these numbers are too high or too low. The New England River Basin Commission estimates that in the New England region plus the Adirondack Mountains of New York, acid rain annually causes $20–$50 million in sport-fishing losses, $100–$200 million in materials damages, and $45–$400 million in forest-product losses.[16] But all estimates are speculative.

The Canadian government has recently initiated a broad program of research on the economic effects of acid rain, including analyses of the losses in commercial salmon fisheries, sport fishing, tourism, and forestry. For example, eastern Canada produces forest products worth $4 billion a year. Dr. Peter Rennie of the Canadian Forestry Service argues that current trends may lead to a 20 percent loss in timber productivity over a twenty-year period, with a lesser rate of loss continuing after that.[17] In both North America and Europe more precise accounting of the full damages caused by acid rain will be essential if governments are to develop the political spine to confront the problem more energetically.

The notion that countries have a responsibility for environmental impacts beyond their borders was accepted in a general way at the 1972 Stockholm Conference, but this area of international law remains underdeveloped. Acid rain, inescapably transnational in scope and too devastating to ignore, is forcing new attention to the issue. In 1979, after years of urging by the Scandinavians, the members of the United Nations Economic Commission for Europe (the ECE, which includes Canada and the United States as well as the countries of both Eastern and Western Europe) signed a "Convention on Transboundary Air Pollution." Although it lacks any enforcement measures or mandatory timetables for action, this treaty does constitute formal political recognition of the international aspects of air pollution and acid rain. The cooperative monitoring and research activities it supported are helping to clear the factual air, and countries have pledged to work toward the reduction of air pollution.

By signing the convention countries have also agreed to exchange information on major policy changes or development plans that "would be likely to cause significant changes in long-range transboundary pollution." Implementation of this provision might have a useful deterrent effect on a country considering energy or pollution-control decisions that will add to the collective acid rain problem. However, the practical force of such pressures is sorely limited, as the Canadians have discovered to their chagrin in ensuing years. Several recent U.S. decisions concerning coal-burning practices and changes in air-pollution laws have displayed little concern for ultimate impacts in Canada, not to mention in acid-plagued areas of the United States.

Apart from their participation in the ECE Convention, the United States and Canada have initiated a bilateral process of research and consultation. In 1978 a coordinated research program got under way. In 1980 the two nations signed an agreement broadening the scope of cooperative research and committing both to the pursuance of domestic air-pollution controls and reductions in the sources of acid rain. Advance notice about proposed policy changes entailing risks of transboundary pollution is mandated, and most significant, the agreement includes a commitment to the future negotiation of a bilateral treaty on air pollution.

In North America, as in Europe, the development of treaties with real bite still seems far off. The costs of acid rain are portrayed as being too diffuse and uncertain; the costs of more stringent pollution control are immediate and real. Perhaps more important, many of the costs of acid rain are not borne by those who cause the problem and who benefit from delayed action. And who speaks for the biosphere?

Although it is one of the more obnoxious components of photochemical smog, ozone, an unstable form of oxygen containing three instead of two atoms per molecule, is extremely rare throughout most of the atmosphere. In the stratosphere, however—the zone sixteen to fifty kilometers above the earth's low latitudes and eight to fifty kilometers above the high latitudes—ozone is less rare, appearing in proportions of a few parts per million. Slight as it is, this concentration of ozone is essential to life on earth. The stratospheric ozone forms a protective shield that absorbs much of the sun's ultraviolet radiation—radiation that, if allowed to reach earth, would promote skin cancer, increase sunburning, and possibly disturb plant and animal life and the climate.

Stratospheric ozone is in constant flux. As the action of sunlight on oxygen creates new ozone molecules, natural agents cause the destruction of others. The natural level of ozone in a given spot may fluctuate over time by about 5 percent above and below the average.

Humans are upsetting the normal ozone balance by adding to the stratosphere new agents able to initiate the process of ozone destruction. Once in the stratosphere, these man-made catalysts can remain for many years or even decades, destroying ozone all the while.

The main culprits appear to be a group of substances called chlorofluorocarbons (CFCs), also known as freons. These have been widely used as propellants in aerosol cans, as refrigerants, as solvents, and in the making of polyurethane foam and other products. Initial fears for the ozone layer were expressed during the debates about supersonic aircraft in 1971 and at the Stockholm Conference. Subsequent research indicated that exhausts from such flights are at most a minor threat to the ozone layer. But the 1974 hypothesis that the chlorine in CFCs would destroy ozone in the stratosphere has gained scientific credence.

Uncertainty and disagreement do exist about the extent of ozone reduction a given level of CFC pollution will cause, and about the resulting impacts on people and the biosphere. Moreover, responses to the problem must at present be based on theory rather than observed facts, since an ozone decline significantly greater than natural fluctuations has not yet occurred.

To promote consistent and cooperative responses in this atmosphere of uncertainty, the United Nations Environment Programme created a unique new institution. The Coordinating Committee on the Ozone Layer was established at a March 1977 intergovernmental meeting in Washington, D.C. It includes representatives of interested governments, several U.N. agencies, nongovernmental scientific organizations, and private industry. At its annual meetings the committee summarizes the latest scientific findings about threats to the ozone and their impacts, building consensus among groups with divergent interests and perspectives. It also identifies research priorities. Although the main actions to control CFC emissions have been taken by individual governments and the European Economic Community, this U.N.-sponsored committee plays a useful role by giving all parties a common set of assumptions.[18]

At its October 1981 meeting the Coordinating Committee concluded that, according to the latest models, continued releases of CFCs at recent rates would eventually reduce stratospheric ozone by 5–10 percent. Ongoing research, while bolstering the basic theory about CFC impacts, has indicated a lower level of eventual ozone decline than was once feared. As recently as 1979 a major study by the U.S. National Academy of Sciences predicted an ozone reduction of 11–16 percent.[19]

Even a 5–10 percent decline is worth worrying about and trying to prevent. The most direct effect on humans would be an increase in skin cancer rates among lighter skinned people. Nonmelanoma skin cancer is the most common form of cancer; in the United States alone it strikes several hundred thousand people a year. Seldom fatal, it nevertheless accounts for about 1600 deaths in the United States annually, and often causes disfigurement, pain, and high expense. Its incidence correlates with exposure to the sun's ultraviolet rays. A 10 percent decline in stratospheric ozone would probably cause hundreds of thousands of extra cases worldwide each year.

More worrisome is the possible rise in the incidence of melanoma, a less frequent but more deadly form of skin cancer. In the United States in 1979, 13,600 cases of melanoma were recorded and 4000 people died from it. Although the contribution of ultraviolet rays to melanoma is more complex than with other skin cancers, a relationship is believed to exist. Melanoma rates have been rising in any case along with the popularity of suntanning, a social trend that may cause far more skin cancers than any changes in the ozone layer. But chances are that ozone depletion would cause thousands of additional melanoma deaths annually in North America, Europe, and Australia.

Many scientists argue that increased ultraviolet radiation would damage many plants and some aquatic species, but the magnitude of the effects is unknown. Evidence indicates that yields of several important crops, including corn, rice, and wheat, would decline. Studies also show that the eggs or larvae of some marine species, including crabs and shrimp, might be damaged by a rise in ultraviolet rays.

An increase in CFCs in the stratosphere would probably influence the climate in several ways. The CFCs themselves would contribute to the earth-warming "greenhouse effect" for which rising carbon dioxide is mainly responsible (see below). At the same time a fall in the ozone concentration would slightly warm the atmosphere too. While the predicted warming effects of these two phenomena are small, they would be in addition to the larger effects of a carbon dioxide–induced warming. Finally, recent evidence suggests that by altering the distribution of ozone around the planet, CFC pollution could cause temperature and climatic changes.

The ozone problem cannot be solved without strong actions by the countries of North America, Western Europe, and Japan, which together account for four-fifths of world CFC production. And responses have been forthcoming. Only four years after the hypothesis about the impact of CFCs had been published, the United States banned the use of CFCs in aerosol cans. Canada, Sweden, and Norway adopted similar policies. Although some European governments have been skeptical about the case for controls, in 1980 the European Community halted growth in its industrial capacity to produce CFCs and planned to reduce aerosol use to at least 30 percent below the 1976 level. Japan too has imposed controls on CFC production.

These various measures, plus the unfavorable publicity that aerosols have received, have had an impact. World CFC production dropped by 17 percent between 1974 and 1979. The use of CFCs in aerosols, which accounted for the bulk of CFC consumption, was cut in half. Eliminating aerosol uses has generally turned out to be rather easy; substitutes exist and many uses are truly nonessential.

Reducing CFC use in refrigeration, in the making of certain foams, and in certain other goods has proven more difficult. Inexpensive substitutes are often lacking and industries have successfully resisted the imposition of restrictions. Thus nonaerosol consumption of CFCs has been growing at the rapid clip of 7 percent a year, which will produce a doubling in ten years.

If recent trends go unchecked, total global production of CFCs will start rising again, probably ensuring serious depletion of the ozone layer. Furthermore, there is nothing to stop CFC production and consumption from rising in non-Western countries, many of which have paid little attention to the scientific debates about ozone depletion. To counter these possibilities, Sweden has called for the negotiation of an international convention to reduce CFC releases. The idea has been endorsed by the UNEP Governing Council and preliminary talks about a treaty began in early 1982.

Cooperative international action is the only sure way to avoid the health and ecological damages of stratospheric ozone depletion. Wide agreement on a meaningful treaty would set a good precedent for addressing environmental challenges to come.

The human-caused buildup of atmospheric carbon dioxide (CO_2) is the quintessential global environmental issue. A continuation of recent trends will probably have momentous impacts on world climate and thus on world society. A few countries, the more industrialized ones, have so far accounted disproportionately for the rise in CO_2, but all countries will contribute to the problem over time. In any case the resulting climatic changes will not be allocated according to any earthly idea of justice. No nation acting alone can prevent an increase in atmospheric CO_2.

Unlike the case with acid rain, the ill-effects of which are partly apparent already, the impacts of a CO_2 buildup can only be inferred. A scientific consensus holds that a significant global temperature change will occur if the CO_2 level doubles. But the precise consequences for climatic patterns, and the resulting social and economic dislocations, cannot be predicted with certainty. Matters of earth-shaking importance must be decided on the basis of theory rather than observation. If we wait to see what changes a doubled or tripled CO_2 level will cause, it will be too late to do anything but try to live with them. Humanity has unwittingly embarked upon a dangerous experiment on a planetary scale.

The CO_2 issue highlights the need for global monitoring of environmental trends and for concerted scientific research to help us predict the likely consequences of our behavior. It also challenges the world community's capacity to cooperate for the common good. We now have fifty years' warning of worldwide stresses that may result from decisions taken in the next decade.

Confronting the CO_2 problem is painful because it adds unwelcome new twists to an already tangled world energy picture. When fossil fuels are burned, the carbon they contain is released to the atmosphere; no feasible technology can prevent this. Likewise, when trees are burned or rot, the carbon they have locked up through photosynthesis is returned to the air whence it came. In turn growing vegetation absorbs carbon dioxide.

Before the Industrial Revolution gathered steam in the mid-nineteenth century, the concentration of CO_2 in the earth's atmosphere was about 260–300 parts per million (ppm). By 1982 the concentration was close to 340 ppm. In theory enough coal, oil, and natural gas has been burned over the last 150 years to boost the atmospheric CO_2 level by roughly twice the measured rise. Thus some "sinks"—mainly the oceans, it is believed—are absorbing part of the human-released carbon from the air.

The role of the earth's living matter in the current carbon budget has been a matter of dispute. Forests, and especially the massive trees of the tropical rain forests, hold a lot of carbon. Humus, the organic matter in topsoil, stores even more carbon worldwide than trees and shrubs do.

Forests are being cleared in large areas, but trees and other vegetation are regrowing in others. Some scientists argue that on a global basis vegetation and humus are now net absorbers of carbon; others argue that deforestation and soil degradation are adding significant net amounts of carbon to the atmosphere. On balance it appears probable that devegatation has been an insignificant contributor compared to fossil-fuel burning up to now. However, widespread destruction of the remaining tropical rain forests could result in a major further release of carbon, and hence should be a matter of worldwide concern.

Natural factors cause global temperature fluctuations, and no observed weather trends can be specifically linked to the CO_2 rise as yet.[20] What has scientists worried is the impact of continuing exponential growth in fossil-fuel use. Until quite recently energy planners tended to assume that global consumption of fossil fuels would climb by several percent a year for the indefinite future. That would lead to a multiplication in atmospheric CO_2 levels over the next century and probably cause rapid shifts in climate.

Soaring energy prices and slowed economic growth over the last several years have provided some breathing space. Projections of future energy consumption and growth have been lowered. But the CO_2 problem still menaces. In the 1970s, even after the 1973 oil crisis, global use of fossil fuels grew by about 2.5 percent a year. If continued, such growth would boost atmospheric CO_2 to double its original level by the middle of the coming century.[21]

Because of a combination of political factors and physical limits, it appears unlikely that world oil use will rise much above recent annual levels, and it may well decline. The real issue in terms of the CO_2 problem is coal. Whether burned directly or after transformation into synthetic liquid fuels, enough coal is economically accessible to multiply the CO_2 level in the atmosphere and wreak havoc on earth. Marked shifts in national energy-use patterns do not come about quickly or cheaply. Many scientists fear that societies, through their investments in equipment and infrastructure over the coming years, will commit themselves to decades of dependence on energy sources whose use guarantees climatic disruptions.

What would be the impact of a doubling of CO_2 over the preindustrial level? Scientists generally agree that because of the "greenhouse effect" the earth and its surrounding air will be warmed. Atmospheric CO_2 allows solar heat to reach the earth's surface but inhibits its dissipation back into space. According to the most widely accepted theory, a doubling of CO_2 would cause the average global temperature to rise by about $3°C$ ($+$ $1.5°C$). The warming would be slightly less in equatorial zones but markedly greater in polar regions, especially near the North Pole, where a warming of $7°-10°C$ might occur. Such global temperature changes would surpass the natural fluctuations that have occurred over the last several thousand years.[22]

Such a warming would alter global patterns of wind, rainfall, and oceanic circulation, all of which are influenced by regional temperature differentials. Unfortunately, however, scientists lack the knowledge to forecast with any precision just how the climate will change.

The world would not receive less total rain; on the contrary, higher temperatures mean more evaporation and more precipitation. But the rains would be redistributed geographically, and the weather could become more variable than has been customary. Comparisons of warmer with cooler years in this century show that small temperature changes make a climatic difference. In the warmer years rainfall tends to decline over much of the United States, Europe, the Soviet Union, and Japan, and to increase over India and the Middle East. Whether a greater and longer lasting warming would produce the same results is uncertain. However, it seems probable that the high-rainfall zones in temperate regions, which support today's most productive agriculture, would move toward the poles. Thus, for example, the North American "cornbelt" would shift northward, reducing output in the United States and increasing potential output in Canada, but also requiring use of soils that are less fertile on average.[23]

Significant climate changes are bound to be socially traumatic. In the abstract, increased agricultural potential in one region may offset lost potential in another. But farming systems are deeply intermeshed with local cultural and political patterns and depend on supporting infrastructure—roads, equipment, marketing systems, research and education efforts—that cannot be moved from country to country and cannot be created overnight. Because of the impediments to rapid cultural and economic adjustment, there could be far more losers than winners overall.

A CO_2-induced climate change might cause jarring redistributions in wealth, and thus international political conflict. The poorest countries, where efforts to introduce new farming techniques in recent decades have often foundered, would have far more difficulty than the rich countries in adapting to climatic change. Thus the gap between rich and poor might well widen even if some less-developed areas were to begin receiving more rain. And if rainfall in just a few of today's marginal, semiarid areas in Africa and Asia, which barely sustain hundreds of millions of the world's poorest people as it is, were suddenly to decline, famines and refugee problems of unparalleled extent would result.

Changes in climate would also affect natural ecosystems, rendering some richer and impoverishing others. The composition of species in some areas would be altered. Sensitive to changes in ocean temperatures and currents, some marine ecosystems, possibly including productive fisheries, would be disrupted. On land, the patterns of freshwater availability for irrigation might change.[24]

Perhaps the most bizarre result of a global warming would be an eventual rise in sea level. A warming of just 2°C is believed enough to cause the disintegration of the gigantic West Antarctic ice sheet, which alone would boost average sea level by at least five meters, flooding many cities and farmlands and driving tens of millions of people to higher ground. Many scientists guess that this process would take centuries to unfold. But some argue that the ice sheet could break up within a few decades of a warming, which would pose a challenge of quite a different order.

All in all the list of probable consequences of a global warming is not pleasant to contemplate. The degree of social disruption these various events would cause would depend on the speed with which the changes occurred and the extent to which societies were able to anticipate and prepare for them. Uncommon acts of prudence and international cooperation would be essential if adjustments to unfolding changes were to be eased. And the disruptions will probably occur in an era when the world's population is double its current level and social stresses relating to environment, resources, and economic inequality are even more acute than today.

Still, the impacts of a CO_2 buildup are decades away and cannot be quantified. Drastic efforts to cut global fossil-fuel use immediately could cause huge economic losses and political strains. So what is to be done in the next few years?

One obvious response to the CO_2 issue is to accelerate cooperative research in order both to improve understanding of the problem and to build global consensus on its implications. The better we understand the intricacies of the carbon cycle, the better we can design appropriate energy and forest policies. The better we can foresee changes in climate, the better we can prepare for them.

An ambitious global research program has been initiated under U.N. auspices, drawing creatively on the world's scientific talent. Under the umbrella of its World Climate Programme, the World Meteorological Organization is coordinating the monitoring of CO_2 trends and analysis of their probable climatic effects. The United Nations Environment Programme is sponsoring related work on the social impacts of climatic change. Much of the actual research on these topics is carried out under the aegis of the International Council of Scientific Unions, a worldwide nongovernmental association of scientists.

Essential as better scientific knowledge is, the response to the CO_2 challenge must involve more than research. Human knowledge about the carbon budget and climate change will never be perfect; we already know enough to warrant serious concern. The urgent need for research cannot be used as an excuse for irresponsibly ignoring the consequences of today's decisions. Waiting another decade or two to begin factoring the CO_2 implications into energy policy quite likely amounts to imposing great hardship on a future generation.

Knowledge of the CO_2 issue should alter the way societies think about energy policy. For the time being they need to nurture a diversity of possible energy sources rather than—as some advocate because of the size of the resource—making all-out commitments to coal and coal-based synthetic fuels as the chief global sources of power for the next several decades. Coal, and the remaining oil and gas reserves, certainly have key roles to play in the global transition to a new energy order. But plans for their wider use in the near future must take account of the probable need to stabilize and then reduce fossil-fuel burning early in the next century. Investments that would for practical purposes commit societies to rising fossil-fuel use for a longer period must be avoided. In the meantime feasible energy alternatives and energy conservation must be vigorously pursued.

Consideration of a host of other environmental and economic concerns points in the same policy directions as the CO_2 challenge does. Restrictions on the burning of fossil fuels in the North are needed to combat acid rain and urban air pollution. The sustainable management of tropical forest areas is important for reasons far more immediate than avoidance of carbon releases. The rapid expansion of one possible energy alternative, nuclear power, is hampered by unresolved problems of radioactive waste disposal, nuclear weapons proliferation, and lack of public confidence.

Sound economics as well as environmental considerations point to the supreme importance of increased efficiency of energy use in all countries. Especially since the 1979 world oil-price rises, the industrial countries have begun to break the historically tight link between growth in economies and in energy consumption. They are gradually cutting the massive fuel wastage built into current transportation, housing, and industrial patterns, and are paying attention to the energy efficiency of new investments. Clearly, future economic growth will require far less energy than previously forecast.

Less-developed countries too are discovering the economic wisdom of improved energy efficiency. Just as in the West, many Third World factories unnecessarily waste oil or electricity, for example. But for countries at the early stages of development, rapid continuing growth in energy consumption will nevertheless be necessary if economic growth is not to be squelched.

Together with the apparent leveling off of world oil production, the CO_2 issue raises questions of equity between North and South. Energy is integral to development and is most so in periods of rapid urban growth and industrialization. Today's poor, oil-importing countries face tremendous disadvantages in this respect compared to the situation earlier faced by countries that achieved development in the era of plentiful, dirt-cheap oil. To the extent that oil remains a cheaper and more convenient fuel than available alternatives, poorer countries deserve access to whatever oil they need, as richer countries cut their use of dwindling oil supplies and break the ground for new energy sources.

The United States, Europe, and the Soviet Union among them account for three-fourths of all the fossil fuels burned to date, hence three-fourths of the CO_2 released. Near-term increases in oil, gas, and coal use in the Third World, which starts from a small base, cannot be begrudged by those alarmed about the CO_2 buildup.

Over time, a global transition to energy sources that are less polluting and more sustainable seems inevitable. Many renewable energy technologies show promise and are sure to play significant roles in the next century. Some are ready for wider application today, but governments have been strangely reluctant to grant renewables the same subsidies they have lavished on the oil and nuclear industries.

The introduction of renewable technologies can be hastened by appropriate national and international actions. Public policies to provide strategic financial incentives and to fill gaps in research, information-sharing, education, and technical training can lay the groundwork for faster adoption of new energy technologies. The outlines of desirable national and international policies were laid out by the 1981 United Nations Conference on New and Renewable Sources of Energy, in Nairobi. Unfortunately, though, weary and unimaginative Western governments proved unwilling to create practical mechanisms for transforming the agreed policies into reality.

Some warning of the earth by the "greenhouse effect" is now inevitable.[25] The goal can only be to hold the CO_2 rise as low as feasible. Some have proposed, for example, an international goal of stabilizing atmospheric CO_2 at just 50 percent above the preindustrial level. This would have substantially less momentous impact than the oft-discussed doubling. It could be accomplished if the global rate of growth in fossil-fuel consumption were to decline steadily to zero over the next twenty-five years, and then the consumption level were to fall to two-thirds of today's over the next hundred years after that.[26] Any number of scenarios involving different rates of growth and decline in fossil-fuel use can be imagined that similarly prevent a doubling of CO_2. The point is to get the world's governments to face squarely the connections between CO_2 and energy policy, and quickly.

8 CROPLANDS AND WASTELANDS

CHRONIC AND WIDESPREAD, the unchecked degradation of croplands reveals much about human society. Soil destruction has contributed to the fall of past civilizations, yet this lesson of history is seldom acknowledged and usually unheeded. Today's cropland losses impair the well-being of the living as well as of generations to come. Yet in this matter as in others societies seem incapable of acts of foresight.

Betraying ecological illiteracy, most people are unaware of their dependence on a thin sheet of topsoil. Yet in many countries the productivity of croplands does more to determine economic health than does the rate of industrial investment or of minerals exploitation. As Lester Brown writes, "civilization can survive the exhaustion of oil reserves, but not the continuing wholesale loss of topsoil."[1]

Although cropland losses and impairment are nothing new, in the late twentieth century these trends appear to be reaching ominous dimensions. As a result of population increases, rising global demand for agricultural products, and unequal access to land and jobs, hundreds of millions of the world's poor try to farm lands that are not suited to this purpose or that require special protective measures. Meanwhile even prime farmlands in both rich and poor countries are badly managed; they are seldom protected from urban sprawl and often farmed in ways that undermine future productivity.

World agricultural productivity has, to be sure, risen dramatically over recent decades. In all continents save Africa food production has risen faster than population growth. Nearly everywhere the potential exists for substantial further gains in crop yields despite the land losses and degradation occurring. But regional or global production figures provide little solace to those on marginal lands who see the basis of their livelihoods wash away. And declines in the quality of cropland inevitably mean higher costs for producing a given amount of food. As the natural productivity of the land is diminished, future requirements for investment in land and water development and fertilization rise. Today's market signals do not fully reflect the long-term economic and social costs of cropland degradation.

Many resource specialists have begun to view cropland degradation as one of the great environmental challenges of the era. Consider the following statement from the United Nations Food and Agriculture Organization (FAO), a body not normally given to alarmist statements about agricultural resources:

The world has at present 1.5 billion hectares of arable land under cultivation. It is also estimated that 5–7 million hectares of this are being completely lost for agricultural production every year through soil degradation. Against this background it has to be considered that the population in developing countries, where most of the soil loss is taking place, will double in the next 20–30 years and agricultural production will need to be increased by 60 percent over the same period to feed the increased population.

It is expected that most of this increase will have to come from more intensive production on existing cultivated land, large areas of which are already subject to degradation, and it is planned to bring 200 million hectares of new land into production by the year 2000. However, it appears that this amount would only just compensate for the amount of soil lost over the same period if land degradation were allowed to proceed unchecked.[2]

In addition to the soil degradation of which the FAO statement speaks, which takes such forms as erosion and, on irrigated lands, waterlogging and salinity, the intentional conversion of cropland to nonfarm uses takes a great toll. In the United States, the world's breadbasket country, about one million acres (0.4 million hectares) of cropland are paved over, built on, or permanently flooded each year.[3] This number may seem small in comparison with the estimated potential U.S. cropland base of 540 million acres. But the land lost to shopping centers, airports, and the like includes a disproportionate share of the flattest and more fertile fields, while newly developed croplands often require expensive investments and tend to be inherently less productive.

Projections of future commercial demands on U.S. agriculture indicate that most of the potential cropland is likely to be needed by the year 2000. As the 1981 report of the National Agricultural Lands Study warns: "The cumulative loss of cropland, in conjunction with other stresses on the U.S. agricultural system such as the growing demand for exports and rising energy costs, could seriously increase the economic and environmental costs of producing food and fiber in the United States during the next 20 years."[4] The study's authors rightfully compare the problem of farmland protection today with the difficulties faced by those preaching energy conservation a decade ago.

Farmland conversion is by no means confined to developed countries. Historically, most cities were founded amid prime agricultural lands. As the cities of the Third World expand, highly productive fields are forever lost. Projections of urban growth in the developing countries raise the spectre of massive cropland losses at a time when increased food output will be vital.

Particularly on better quality farmlands, soil erosion's drain on productivity is often insidious and unnoticed. Water and wind erosion gradually thin the topsoil, robbing it of valuable nutrients and organic matter. Where agriculture is modernized, the losses to erosion can usually be masked by heavy use of chemical fertilizers. But the costs are nonetheless real. At a time when the prices of fossil fuels (from which nitrogen fertilizer is manufactured) are soaring, they cannot be lightly dismissed.

Recent surveys of U.S. farms reveal that erosion is high enough to reduce long-term productivity on 141 million acres—one-third of the area now cropped. Maintained for fifty years, recent trends would reduce output by fifty to seventy-five million tons of grain a year, which equals half of 1980 U.S. grain exports.[5] Recent technological and market developments have sharpened the erosion threat. Modern machinery and chemicals permit planting of erosion-causing row crops such as corn and soybeans without the rotations and fallows that preserved soils in the past. Economic pressures and booming world markets encourage farmers to maximize production even at the expense of long-term soil quality.

Erosion in the Third World is poorly documented but, available studies suggest, of mammoth and rising proportions. In the tropics rain tends to come in violent downpours that rip away topsoil when it is left vulnerable. The greatest erosion occurs on marginal lands—

hillsides and arid zones where farming is a precarious business. Gaping man-made gulleys blight the hills of much of Asia, Africa, and Latin America. In dry zones, desperate farmers plant areas that should be left in pasture; the topsoil is airborne with the first windstorm. As populations rise in the absence of technological progress, the fallow cycles that traditionally conserved the land are squeezed. Soil nutrients and organic matter disappear, crops fail, and the soil washes or blows away.[6]

In both rich and poor countries the impairment or total destruction of irrigated soils is rampant and especially costly. Waterlogging and soil salinity, resulting from mismanagement of water applications and inadequate drainage, plague every single country with a significant irrigated area.

Rangelands too are degraded almost everywhere. In the United States more than half the privately owned rangelands are, because of overgrazing and related erosion, producing forage at half their potential or less. In many regions, especially in the Third World, pastures are declining to desert-like barrenness. The ability of such areas to support human life is often permanently damaged.

In the end the protection of agricultural lands from erosion or conversion must be linked to broader efforts to use all lands for maximum benefit while protecting them for the future. B. B. Vohra, a leading Indian civil servant, has written eloquently of the costs to his country of past and present land-use patterns. The spread of irrigation, improved crop varieties, and fertilizer use have helped India achieve major increases in agricultural output. Yet present and future production potentials are undercut by damage to the land. Currently, Vohra notes, at least 61 percent of the country's agricultural lands and at least 72 percent of the nonagricultural lands are degraded to some degree. Because of past abuse huge areas of India, a country with no land to waste, are today lying useless. Laments Vohra:

No wonder we are so desperately short of food, fruits, fibres, fuel-wood, timber, animal products and indeed everything that the land produces. . . . No wonder destitution and unemployment stalk the country. It is high time we realised the state we are in, for what we are witnessing is the unchecked erosion—literal as well as figurative—of our resource base even as the demands on it from a steadily increasing population and steadily increasing expectations of a better life are rising rapidly. Our situation can indeed be compared to that of a leaking boat into which more and more people keep climbing even while, unknown to its occupants, the hole in its bottom goes on increasing in size.[7]

Soil degradation is an especially elusive problem for national governments and international agencies. Even where its dimensions and implications are recognized, effective measures to reverse the negative trends are rare. Unlike the case with such other environmental threats as ocean dumping or the release of ozone-destroying chemicals to the air, soils cannot be protected by national fiat or international treaty.

Soil degradation results from the actions of millions of individual farmers each responding to particular economic incentives. Farming techniques that hold erosion to tolerable levels are usually available but farmers may not know about them or may not be able to afford them. Tenant farmers have no strong reason to protect the land in any case. Government policies to change incentives and promote the adoption of conserving technologies are essential, but difficult to design and pursue. The protection of prime farmland from conversion too is often beyond the practical reach of national governments because land rights are so bound by complex laws and traditions.

Much of the severe degradation of the Third World's marginal lands is rooted in trends the individual farmer can do little about. When economic development patterns and population growth force legions to farm lands that ought to be left in pasture or forest, efforts to disseminate antierosion technologies may well be futile. The remedies lie outside the scope of on-farm technologies.

While recognizing these constraints, the United Nations is trying to improve soils protection worldwide through various means. UNEP and FAO are jointly promoting a "world soils policy" that lays out principles for responsible national policies. They have completed worldwide maps of soils potentials and degradation, support improved data-gathering, and publicize critical problems and possible responses.

In recent years the international community has made a special effort to confront land degradation in the world's drier zones. A set of arid-land trends known collectively as "desertification" imperils many of the world's poorest people, and became the subject of an unusual world conference in 1977. That meeting and its follow-up provide a useful case study of the constraints on, and opportunities for, international actions to ease the critical natural resource problems of the Third World. The remainder of this chapter examines the matter of desertification and the role of the world community in combatting it.

Surely one of the more unpredictable events in the United Nations over the last decade was the convening of the United Nations Conference on Desertification in Nairobi, Kenya, in 1977. That a global conference, attended by senior diplomats as well as technical experts, would be held on such a seemingly esoteric subject would have been unthinkable a few years earlier, when even the word "desertification" was unknown to all but specialists.

The catalyst for this event was well-publicized human suffering in the Sahel, the huge region just south of the Sahara where years of drought culminated in widespread crop failures and livestock deaths in 1972 and 1973. Even as they rushed in famine relief, development experts began to realize that forces much deeper than a drop in rainfall were undermining the region's well-being. The development patterns of recent decades, they began to see, were out of kilter with the zone's ecological limits, causing a degeneration of the natural resource base and a rising vulnerability to drought.

As awareness of the Sahel's problems spread, those concerned about resource degradation in other semiarid parts of the world also began to get a hearing. Ecologically unsound development, it became clear, was jeopardizing the livelihoods of scores of millions of people living in the world's drier zones—and was whittling down the potential economic contributions of huge areas in developed and developing countries alike. The tragedy of the Sahel pushed to the forefront of global attention a set of complex, enduring problems whose breadth had largely been ignored before.

One-third of the earth's land surface is arid or semiarid. Where rainfall is near zero and other water resources are lacking, the land is usually devoid of humans. But many semiarid lands can be surprisingly productive, and skillful herdsmen and farmers can eke a living from quite hostile desert environments. A fortunate few derive wealth from oil and other minerals below their desert sands. All told, close to 700 million people live in arid or semiarid zones. Some 62 million of these, estimates Egyptian ecologist Mohammed Kassas, live directly off lands that are turning to waste because of soil erosion, vegetation change, salt encrustation, and dune formation.[8]

Recent studies have revealed the enormous scale of the economic losses and human suffering associated with desertification. The U.N. conference considered three major categories of dryland problems. The first, rangeland degradation, usually involves severe erosion and a conversion of vegetation from nutritious perennial grasses to weeds that even goats cannot eat—the results of overgrazing and depletion of tree cover for fuel and building materials. In the second, rain-fed croplands lose productivity as topsoil, nutrients, and organic matter disappear—often because of a decline in the soil-restoring fallow period, or after plowing without suitable erosion controls. Third, yields on irrigated fields fall as inexpert water applications and inadequate drainage lead to rising salinity, alkalinity, or waterlogging.

The actual losses can only be surmised. Scientists contributing to the preparations for the 1977 U.N. conference estimated that roughly six million hectares of formerly productive land were going out of production each year because of desertification in its various forms. Since then Dr. Harold Dregne of Texas Tech University has made a pioneering effort to measure the losses more comprehensively, estimating the area of agricultural land deteriorating to the point where it yields zero or negative net economic returns. Each year, he calculates, about twenty million hectares, an area the size of Senegal, decline to this point—half a million hectares of irrigated land, eighteen million hectares of rangeland, and two million of rain-fed cropland.[9]

The quality of life for some of the world's most excruciatingly poor people—in semiarid Central Africa and in India's huge "drought-prone" areas—is getting worse as their land degenerates. Something similar happened temporarily in the midwestern United States during the Dust Bowl of the 1930s; in *The Grapes of Wrath* John Steinbeck chronicled the desperate migration of thousands to a new life in California. But tens of millions in the Third World today have no California to head for when the soils that sustain them blow away.

Examining the extent of past and present desertification, Dregne estimates that the potential value of annual production foregone on damaged lands is over $26 billion, comparable to the 1979 GNP of Thailand or Colombia. This then is the invisible cost of desertification to the world economy.

While some areas of rangeland and cropland have been destroyed beyond the point of economically feasible restoration, most of the desertified areas could be profitably rehabilitated. Many semiarid lands show remarkable resilience, as is demonstrated by the oft-noted resurgence of greenery when overgrazed wastelands are protected by a fence. Land restoration requires changes in the economic pressures and farming practices that produced the damage in the first place, and effective management of recovery programs. It also takes money. The United Nations estimates that at least $48 billion would be needed in developing countries over twenty years—an average of $2.4 billion a year—in order to rehabilitate all their damaged irrigated lands, half their afflicted rangelands, and 70 percent of their impaired rain-fed croplands, and to stabilize sand dunes covering some two million hectares.

Current global expenditures (including both international aid and local government funds) devoted to the fight against desertification in developing countries are probably less than one-fourth of that amount. In theory significant increases in such funding will pay off handsomely. But in practice the money needed has not been forthcoming. Why? For one reason, many of the largest expenditures are needed in the poorest countries, which cannot possibly tackle these problems without external financial and technical aid. And international assistance faces severe limits because of donor-country political reasons unrelated to the opportunities for cost-effective investments.

Second, the economic returns on land rehabilitation and protection activities are often spread over a long time and are low compared to those of alternative investments. Governments get most political credit for projects with quick, flashy returns, and bankers using conventional discounting methods have little interest in moderate returns thirty years down the road. Thus in the Sudan, for instance, further development of irrigated acreage along the Nile will virtually always look more financially attractive than programs to stabilize rain-fed farming. (That millions of people may be uprooted and the fertility of a huge chunk of the country badly impaired as a result of the neglect of rain-fed agriculture may suggest that blind adherence to conventional economic analysis has its drawbacks.) Likewise, investments in export crops always look more attractive in a region like the Sahel than efforts to intensify production of rain-fed food crops in a sustainable manner. Hence the scandalous situation in which, even in the postfamine years of the late 1970s, no more than 4 percent of aid to the Sahelian region was devoted to improved production of the rain-fed crops that provide 95 percent of the region's grain output.[10]

A major obstacle to greater investment against desertification is the difficulty of spending money productively. Occasionally outside funds and off-the-shelf technologies can be used simply to fix a dune or install drainpipes below irrigated fields—and with good results. But desertification problems cannot usually be isolated from the complex web of local political, social, and economic forces. It is one thing to pay people to plant some trees and quite another to gain public cooperation and control over animals in order to protect planted seedlings. Researchers can develop new seeds and rotation patterns for food crops, but where agricultural extension services are nonexistent, government institutions are wholly oriented toward export crops, and marketing policies depress grain prices for the benefit of urban residents, rural land use is unlikely to be transformed. In short, desertification is seldom a technical problem that can be solved with an injection of knowledge and money alone. It is a socioeconomic and a developmental problem linked to basic patterns of national life. As always, solutions require money. But they also require difficult political, cultural, and bureaucratic reforms.

Natural climatic changes can lead to the genuine expansion and contraction of deserts. But misuse of the land, too, can make it appear that the desert's edge is marching forward. Depletion of trees and grasses permits sand dunes to blow over fields, or the outright transformation of pastures into sandy or stony wastelands. Many of the horror stories about the relentless southward drive of the Sahara in Africa, and the Rajasthan Desert's march toward New Delhi, have been greatly exaggerated. Still, huge expanses along the edges of these and other deserts have been laid barren. Aerial photos taken in northern Sudan in 1975 were compared with maps from 1958; in seventeen years the line at which scrub vegetation gives way to treeless desert had shifted southward by ninety to one hundred kilometers.[11]

By far the greatest losses to desertification have little to do with the "spread" of true deserts. On-site misuse of range or farmland reduces patches to desert-like conditions, or causes less visible changes in the qualities of soils and vegetation that render them less useful to humans. The proper metaphor is a pox with spreading pustules, not an advancing army.

Agricultural trends well below the desert's edge in Sudan's northern Kordofan Province provide a good example of the real desertification problem. Livestock numbers in the province multiplied sixfold between 1957 and the mid-1970s, putting unbearable pressures on grasses and shrubbery. Travelers stepping down from their camels or Jeeps discover that what appears to be lush ground is no more than a tangle of thorny weeds that are inedible to livestock. As the population grows without a simultaneous transformation of agricultural technologies, the traditional cropping cycle—sound and sustainable when followed properly—is breaking down, resulting in both crop-yield reductions and the outright loss of arable lands.

In the past, patches of land covered with *Acacia senegal,* a soil-renewing tree that also produces gum-arabic and excellent fuelwood, were cleared and planted with millet, sorghum, maize, sesame, and other crops for from four to ten years. The depleted land was then left idle until the *Acacia* scrub reinvaded it; after eight years or so the trees could be tapped for gum-arabic, a valuable cash crop, for six to ten years. Finally, as the trees began to die, they were burned and the cycle began anew. Jon Tinker describes the recent evolution of this system:

This ecologically balanced cycle of gum gardens, fire, grain crops, and fallow is now breaking down, the 1968–73 drought having in many areas given it the *coup de grâce.* Under pressure of a growing population, the cultivation period is extended by several years and the soil becomes too impoverished to recover. Overgrazing in the fallow period prevents the establishment of seedlings. Gum trees are lopped for firewood. More and more widely, *Acacia senegal* no longer returns after the fallow, but is replaced by non-gum-producing scrub. . . . And without the gum to harvest for cash, the farmers must repeatedly replant their subsistence crops until the land becomes useless sand.[12]

Two thousand miles to the west, on the Mossi Plateau of Upper Volta, degeneration of the land likewise provides a harbinger of things to come elsewhere. Here as in many areas experiencing ecological decline superficial appearances can mislead. Except where severe gully erosion blights the view, lightly wooded, usually grassy landscapes punctuated by millet fields are common.

But the grasses are mainly of inedible species. Most of the trees are disfigured; only those species that provide food, fodder, fertilizer, medicines, rope, or other essential products have been left standing, and closer inspection reveals regeneration of these valuable species to be spotty at best because seedlings are nibbled by goats or uprooted during cultivation.

The "open spaces" turn out to be fully used. Nearly every bit of uncropped land is either lying fallow as part of someone's crop cycle, or has been abandoned because the soil is useless. "The soils are tired," say villagers throughout the region. With yields dropping, they must clear ever-larger areas to grow enough food to survive. Young adults are lucky if they can get farming rights on steep hillsides or on less fertile lands. Fields are cropped repeatedly with no fertilizers to replenish their nutrients, no manure to help rebuild the thin topsoil. This is the way the wasteland spreads, not with a bang but a whimper.

As in many parts of the Sahel, rains on the Mossi Plateau since the 1968–1973 drought have generally not returned to the levels common in the decades that preceded it. But almost as important, the effective use of available water has plummeted. Rain tends to visit the Sahel in just a few torrential downpours. Storm waters rush off denuded land, skimming off soil as they are lost forever to local use. (The force of the region's rains can scarcely be imagined during the dry season; the Sahelian landscape is littered with broken dams, built in self-help projects in the early 1970s and washed out in the next rainstorm.)

In the context of the agrarian stagnation and extreme underdevelopment that prevails in Upper Volta, population growth catalyzes destruction of the resource base. Since the country has one of the world's highest death rates, its population is growing more slowly than in most Third World countries; the natural increase is believed to be around 2 percent annually. But in the Mossi Plateau—given prevailing technologies—any growth in human numbers causes environmental stress. Agricultural experts reckon that under present farming methods a maximum of only about thirty people per square kilometer can be fed without soil damage. Ecologist Robert Winterbottom calculates that natural vegetation growth in the region can sustainably provide firewood to about twenty-five people per square kilometer. Today the population density has reached fifty per square kilometer in many portions of the plateau, and surpasses a hundred in some.[13]

Life for many is a form of chronic disaster, with only migration to forestall more overt social and ecological distress. Mossi people are moving to the still-fertile, less densely populated south and west of Upper Volta—where land-use conflicts are erupting between newcomers and the original inhabitants and the same cycle of degradation looms in the future. A high portion of the country's young men have left to work in menial jobs in the economically vibrant Ivory Coast. The typical village is simultaneously overpopulated relative to current technologies and depopulated of the individuals most likely to innovate and reverse the downward spiral.

Simply blaming the ills on population growth, and expecting contraception to cure them, is neither accurate nor realistic. The sorry state of affairs is the culmination of centuries of colonial and postcolonial development patterns that have failed to create a sustainable way for the majority to improve their lives. Where close to half all children die and adult literacy is below 5 percent, expecting the wide and effective use of family planning in the absence of other radical changes is hardly rational.

A better future is possible for the Mossi Plateau and other endangered areas, but it will depend on progress on many fronts at once. Farming systems that combine food production, forestry, and animal husbandry—systems that preserve soil fertility as they boost output, all with minimal reliance on imported fertilizers—are feasible but inadequately studied. Simple antierosion and water-conserving works on fields could raise crop yields dramatically. A comprehensive approach to development is essential, including provision of primary health care, household water supplies, elementary education, agricultural improvements, forestry, and family planning. National commitments to improving the exploited role of women must also be part of the solution; as the main farmworkers and as potential childbearers women need the opportunity to innovate that is now denied them.

Sound development in the poor, rural societies suffering most from desertification must entail new forms of social organization in countless small, dispersed villages, and among hard-to-reach nomadic groups. Implementation of a thousand small projects is harder than building a large irrigated estate or a factory; it requires reforms in the structures and attitudes of government bureaucracies as well as an overriding shift in national priorities toward equitable rural development—unavoidably at the expense of local elites.

In the Sahel and many other regions the colonial quest for raw materials and the postcolonial quest for foreign exchange caused a near-total emphasis on export crops like cotton and peanuts. Certainly cash crops can play a constructive role in development, but too often the priority granted them by public policies has resulted in food shortages in times of drought, a vulnerability to declining international terms of trade, and ecological damage as the food-crop area is squeezed. Perhaps the most serious consequence of the export-crop bias has been the associated neglect of research and infrastructure in support of agricultural systems for peasant farmers.

Political scientist Michael F. Lofchie describes the situation in much of Africa: "Decades of over-concentration on export cultivation have left the continent's food-producing regions badly undersupplied with infrastructure, deprived of government services, desperately short of capital for development, and technologically pre-feudal. As a result, any attempt to improve Africa's food-producing capability will need to concern itself with a fundamental structural transformation of the rural economy."[14]

But, as Lofchie goes on to note, to shift governmental priorities toward food crops and extend the benefits of the development process to more people involves more than technical decisions: "Policies which have the potential to undermine the established economic primacy of the export sector would run directly counter to the large and powerful array of social groups which have a stake in the profitability of the export economy."

One of the most controversial aspects of desertification has been the role of nomads. In the early 1970s, immediately after the Sahelian drought, many observers laid blame on the nomads and their herds of cattle, camels, sheep, and goats for causing the spread of the desert. Drastically cutting herds was often seen as the critical challenge. In reality the story is more complicated. Most nomadic groups, it turns out, have historically had prudent systems of grazing control, designed to take maximum advantage of available grasses without serious destruction. But over the last quarter-century in particular, the spread of settled farming has compressed nomads into smaller areas with less reliable rainfall, and together with the demarcation of national borders, has drastically limited their freedom to move about in response to changing pasture conditions. New boreholes have often disrupted traditional patterns of range-sharing among tribal groups, resulting in severe overgrazing around wells. And improved veterinary services have enabled herd sizes to grow without simultaneous improvement of grazing controls.[15]

Livestock numbers and movements do need better control, but the flexbility and ecological knowledge of nomadism must be built upon rather than replaced. Those "experts" trying to develop workable range-management strategies—and this is a field best known for its failures—must also be sure to ask the right questions. Right, that is, from the point of view of herders as well as of governments. Officials, mindful of export earnings, ask how meat production and sales can be maximized without degrading the pastures. But the nomadic family may have other primary goals. How big does the herd need to be in order to ensure that large numbers will survive the next drought? And how many animals are necessary for meeting the social obligations imposed by marriages and other customs? The successful strategy will take account of rather than ignore the aspirations of the population that is supposedly being helped; pastoralists themselves must be involved in the design and implementation of range-improvement schemes. It may well be that only they can make productive, sustainable use of the life-defying desert fringes.

All the many political, economic, and cultural concerns discussed in the preceding pages are part of the desertification problem. Case studies from other parts of the world reveal similarly complex pictures. The term "desertification" provides a useful conceptual entree into these webs, forcing particular attention to their ecological aspects. But "desertification" has limitations as a conceptual umbrella for the full range of actions needed to enhance human life in arid and semiarid lands. Halting the desert's spread is often not as simple as it once seemed to many, and this has complicated the recent antidesertification efforts of the international community.[16]

Although the passage of nearly five years hardly permits a final assessment of the impact of the United Nations Conference on Desertification, certain things are already clear. The conference—especially because of its excellent documentation—was successful in raising awareness about desertification among governments in the affected countries and among international aid agencies. Considering both groups' histories of ignorance or indifference, this was no mean feat. The analytical papers and case studies commissioned by the United Nations, together with the national reports submitted by many countries, did much to draw the attention of policymakers to the disastrous trends unfolding beneath their noses, and helped spotlight the political and social roots of land-use trends.

The record of the conference in stimulating countervailing policies and institutions is less encouraging. Any hopes that a massive, immediate global response to the problems so well outlined in Nairobi would be coordinated by the United Nations were quickly dashed. The pledging conferences convened by UNEP to solicit donor support for specific projects have not become a significant mobilizer of additional aid. Meanwhile the U.N.'s Special Account to Combat Desertification, set up by the conference to attract funds that the United Nations would dispense directly, has remained a dry well, having received a derisory $5000 as of late 1981. UNEP's Desertification Branch, inadequately staffed and struggling to keep up with U.N. paperwork and preparations for meetings, serves neither as action-stimulator nor as an effective information source. Few national governments have even tried to write, let alone implement, the suggested national plans of action.[17]

This is not to say that nothing has been done to fight desertification in the last few years. On the contrary—and in part because of the awareness sparked by the Nairobi conference—relevant new activities are under way in nearly all the afflicted areas. In arid-zone countries ecological rehabilitation has overnight become a catchword among development experts, and national political leaders give speeches on the dangers of deforestation and soil erosion. And external aid to, for example, the countries of the Sahel doubled between 1975 and 1979, with an increasing (though still grossly inadequate) share of it devoted to the improvement of dryland farming, grazing management, and forestry.

Positive as these trends may be, the degradation of productive lands apparently continues nearly unabated. The money and talent devoted to "antidesertification" activities are far from adequate, yet much of the existing investment is poorly used. Both the quantity and the quality of land-regeneration activities must rise in the coming years if further human suffering is to be minimized. The United Nations does have a useful role to play in this endeavor, although it is still groping toward the definition of that role.

In assessing why action after the Nairobi conference has been so disappointing, blame enough exists for all parties. The United Nations tried to set up a new funding mechanism without the requisite political support, and should hardly have been surprised when large sums did not appear. Yet had the political climate been different and potential donors (OPEC and the Eastern bloc as well as the usual Western donors) been willing to put some real eggs in the U.N. basket, a useful institution might well have emerged. Likewise, the weakness of current U.N. antidesertification planning is no measure of what might have been; it is too easy to point to the inefficacy of an organism that has been deliberately starved.

Some of the conference proposals—such as for transnational green belts above and below the Sahara—seem with hindsight to have been politically naïve and insensitive to the practical constraints. Still, one person's naïveté is another's vision. The same may be said of UNEP Executive Director Mostafa K. Tolba's unsuccessful quest for new "automatic" methods of international financing for desertification control (such as an international tax on desert minerals). The world is not worse off for such ideas' having been put on the table. Indeed the Nairobi conference was the first intergovernmental meeting formally to endorse the concept of automatic international taxation, an idea whose time may someday come.

Ultimately, the main responsibility for the slow progress against desertification rests not with the United Nations but with the governments of the afflicted countries. Some countries, especially in Africa, are so poor and lacking in trained people that outside assistance is crucial if disaster is to be forestalled. Nowhere, however, can outside aid substitute for a local political commitment to the required economic and bureaucratic reforms.

An examination of postdrought development trends in the Sahel, the birthplace of global concern about desertification, helps reveal both the limits and the opportunities facing the United Nations in its efforts to follow up on the Nairobi conference. The Sahelian countries have their own regional planning organization, CILSS (the French acronym for Permanent Interstate Committee for Drought Control in the Sahel). The main Western aid donors have in turn formed a coordinating and analytical body called the Club du Sahel. The Club and CILSS have tried, with limited success, to fit all the new programs into a coherent strategy. Their planning efforts got started before the 1977 Nairobi conference, and have proceeded largely independently of U.N. efforts to promote the conference Action Plan.

Among other things the Club/CILSS studies have dramatized the relative neglect of forestry and rural development in national development programs. During the five years from 1975 through 1979, forestry activities, while on the rise, received a mere 1 percent of the more than $6 billion provided to the region in foreign aid. Projects to improve rain-fed grain crops have received only 3 or 4 percent of total aid. These meager numbers represent progress compared with the 1960s, when aid to forestry was negligible and virtually all assistance to rain-fed agriculture was aimed at cotton and peanuts. But it is clear that even today neither the region's governments (whose own priorities heavily influence the pattern of foreign aid) nor the donors (who nevertheless hold great leverage over spending patterns) are adequately confronting the long-term trends that, according to their own analyses, imperil the Sahel's development chances.

What have been the results of the large postfamine aid flows, and newly energized development efforts, in the Sahel? In a frank 1980 report, the Club du Sahel and CILSS assessed the results of the previous five years' development experience. Some of the key conclusions:

Rain-fed cereals production, which provides the foundation for feeding the Sahel, has continued to develop by extending areas cultivated [instead of] through intensification of production. . . . Also, yields are getting lower which is a sign that at least in certain regions land is over-exploited.

Areas irrigated under good water control have hardly increased: despite efforts made, the new irrigated projects developed barely compensate for losses due to the deterioration of old projects.

Overall cereals production—rain-fed and irrigated—remains quite vulnerable to drought and is far from satisfying needs. . . . recourse to food imports and food aid has become a permanent need.

The intensification of livestock has not really begun and mixed farming, which is an important factor in such intensification, has progressed slowly.

The fisheries potential, both ocean and inland, which is known to be considerable, has not been developed for the benefit of Sahel populations any more than it was four years ago.

Despite the lack of statistics, one can say that deforestation in the Sahel is continuing and it is to be feared that it is accelerating; efforts made in reforestation are not equal to the needs.[18]

Straining to find some good news, the report observes that despite the severe economic and social after-effects of the great drought (and continued poor rainfall since), the region has survived without major catastrophe—for which outside assistance and new programs undoubtedly deserve some credit. Most important, "the period 1975–80 was a time for gaining a progressive and deep understanding of real problems. . . . the idea has been progressively understood that the drought was only one factor among others" accounting for the plight of the Sahel. Policymakers in the region are now far more aware than they once were, for example, of the need to support peasant food cultivators, and of the urgency of reforestation.

To be fair, spectacular improvements could not have occurred in such a brief period. Many of the thousands of projects that dot the Sahelian landscape—village woodlots here, improved soil conservation there, wood-saving cooking stoves here, a small dam there—are in fact achieving positive results, and many more are teaching lessons of future utility. Still, current programs and policies in the region do not yet add up to a response that will create a sustainable and more prosperous future for the majority of the people. It would be an underestimation of both human and biological resilience to say that a critical point of no return is near, beyond which the situation is hopeless. But if the obvious lessons of the last decade are not soon translated into practice in the field, the social and economic costs of putting development on a workable footing will constantly rise—and vulnerability to the inevitable next drought will rise as well.

What, then, could be a constructive U.N. contribution in the Sahel and other regions struggling against desertification? Considering the diversity of the problems, and their grounding in local cultures and politics, the role of global institutions is necessarily circumscribed. But it is also clear that national governments, which must be the main implementers of sustainable development, often lack the knowledge and the will to improve matters. Hence the need for the international exchange of ideas and lessons, and the international prodding of political consciences.

In practical terms, UNEP's Desertification Branch could cultivate a much stronger role as an analytical center and as a clearinghouse for information on policies and trends. It could help identify gaps in knowledge about desertification and spread the word about successful approaches. It could encourage other institutions to engage in the sort of sector planning and critical analyses being attempted by the Club du Sahel and CILSS for the Sahelian region, and could synthesize the findings into regional and global assessments. This means being seen as building on rather than competing with others' efforts in this field. Finally, rather than repeating its largely fruitless efforts to mobilize funding for a broad array of "antidesertification" development projects, many of which can be considered just as well through usual foreign aid channels, UNEP could now concentrate on mobilizing support for a few projects of a special nature—those, such as ecological monitoring, that would fill critical knowledge gaps, or that involve unique approaches and will expand intellectual frontiers.

The United Nations can also continue to help poorer countries analyze their desertification problems and design appropriate policies and projects. For many African countries this is the function of the U.N. Sudano-Sahelian Office; UNEP itself works directly with countries elsewhere. Donor governments have many different motives for offering aid, recipient governments many different motives for accepting it. Skillful reporting by an international body can help all parties keep their professed long-term goals in sight.

Desertification is not some mysterious force operating independently of socioeconomic trends. Too much dwelling on antidesertification spending targets, and on antidesertification action plans, can be misleading. The degradation of croplands or of rangelands often results from the activities of desperately poor people, forced to undercut their own futures in order to survive through tomorrow. Hence desertification can only be tackled in the context of a sound overall development strategy. Nor can the normal clash of interest groups be ignored while confronting the seemingly technical problems of desertification. Successful desertification control, like all successful rural development, often involves giving those who are presently powerless the means to solve their problems, and this in turn is often threatening to commercial and bureaucratic interests.

Desertification is a symptom of development gone awry. Direct actions to combat the symptoms are certainly necessary—but deeper political and economic reforms are essential if there are to be lasting benefits.

9 DEFORESTING AND REFORESTING THE EARTH

OUR DEPENDENCE ON TREES is easy to forget. In the rural Third World the importance of forests—the source of essential cooking fuel, building materials, and foods—is obvious enough. But economic advancement does not reduce a society's reliance on forest products. As countries develop, wood remains a basic raw material for construction, furniture, railroad ties, power poles, cellophane, rayon, plastics, and much else besides.[1]

Transformed into paper, wood serves as an essential tool for communications, commerce, education, and government. Soon wood may also be processed into liquid fuels and a wide array of petrochemical substitutes. Forests provide natural havens of inestimable value, while trees anywhere provide shade and beauty.

Forests also perform irreplaceable ecological services. They assist in the global cycling of water, oxygen, carbon, and nitrogen. They lend stability to hydrological systems, often reducing the severity of floods and permitting the recharging of springs, streams, and underground waters. Trees keep soil from washing off mountainsides and sand from blowing off deserts; they keep sediment out of rivers and reservoirs and help hold topsoil on agricultural fields. Forests house countless plant and animal species of current or potential value to humans.

Until recently writings about the "basic needs" of the world's poor generally ignored the fundamental importance of forests to human well-being. Describing conditions in central India, forester R. Chakravarti writes: "It is often said that the three basic human needs are food, clothing and shelter. One cannot think of food and shelter without wood, which is a more basic need. In fact it may be truthfully said of an average villager that he is still in the 'wood age.' "

Cultivation in many underdeveloped areas still relies mainly on wooden plows, and farm produce is transported in wooden carts. Houses are bult of wood and mud or bamboo and thatch. Wood is required for a host of other purposes such as fencing, furniture, implements, and handicrafts. Above all, continues Chakravarti, "wood, a marvelous, God-given means of storing solar energy, is also required to cook food with."[2]

Forests are often evaluated by economists in terms of their ability to provide a dead product, wood. But for many of those residing in and around them forests are a living resource. In many regions tree leaves and forest grasses sustain cattle, which in turn pull plows and carts and supply milk and fertilizer. Leaves, fruits, nuts, honey, and wild animals provide a significant share of the food supply of hundreds of millions of people. Traditional medicines and useful barks are taken from woodlands. Commercially valuable products such as mushrooms, drugs, gums, and resins are extracted from forests as well.

The global pattern of forest-product use and distribution mirrors the skewed distribution of economic wealth and development. Eighty percent of the wood used in the Third World is burned for fuel, and most of it never passes through a commercial market. Though developing countries contain three-fourths of the world's people and more than half its forests, they account for just 14 percent of global consumption of "industrial wood"—marketed logs, sawn wood, panel products such as plywood and fiberboard, paper, and other products. Annual per capita paper use in developing countries is less than one-fortieth that in North America. In fact each year the average American consumes about as much wood in the form of paper as the average resident in many Third World countries burns as cooking fuel.[3]

About one-third of the world's industrial wood is traded internationally. Four-fifths of the trade originates and ends in developed countries, with North America and the Soviet Union having a surplus and Japan and Western Europe a deficit. Many poorer tropical countries export timber, but like most other developing nations they import much of their paper and manufactured wood products. Southeast

Asia exports a large volume of timber to Japan in particular, while African tropical logs go mainly to Western Europe.

Even as the demand for industrial wood soars, a large proportion of humanity will continue to rely on firewood for cooking and home heating. Close to half the world's people now cook with wood, crop residues, or dried dung, and close to half of all the wood cut each year worldwide is burned for fuel. More than one billion people live in areas where the collection of wood already outpaces new growth, depleting the resource. If the pace of planting is not stepped up, hundreds of millions will face mounting economic hardships and will be forced to wreak great havoc on their surrounding environments.[4]

Acute scarcities of firewood and timber already plague wide areas of Africa, Asia, and Latin America. But a continuation of the last quarter-century's trends of deforestation, inadequate forest renewal, and growth in wood demand would have worldwide repercussions. The amount of exploitable timber available per person in the world is falling; in the words of the U.S. government's *Global 2000* study, we face a "transition from a period of global forest wealth to a period of global forest poverty."[5] Real prices of commercial wood products are certain to rise, choking off projected consumption increases, fueling inflation, and denying low-income people everywhere many of the benefits that forest products provide.

To some extent market forces automatically help offset timber scarcity. Higher prices will induce technological innovation, new investments, the substitution of alternative materials, conservation, and tree planting. But market forces alone will not provide an acceptable solution. In a world of extreme income disparities, the adjustments of the market take a heavy toll among the underclass, many of whom will have no good substitute for writing paper in school or for firewood on the hearth. Even in more affluent countries rising wood prices will impose social burdens.

As the understanding of forests' importance grows, so does the need for better information about their extent. In much of the world data on forest trends have generally been unreliable or altogether lacking. But recently a large number of surveys have been initiated, many of them making use of satellite photography, and the quality of forest data is improving fast.

Discussions of forest trends are plagued by definitional problems. How many trees, how close together, make a forest? At what point does selective logging become deforestation? If the clearing of a slash-and-burn farmer will be left for natural regrowth, has deforestation occurred? Even statistics on tree planting can be confusing. A eucalyptus plantation established on former cropland should not be lumped together with a restored hillside forest of mixed native species. And "reforestation" often means clearing standing forests to make room for tree plantations.

According to a world survey conducted in the early 1970s by Reidar Persson, about one-fifth of the earth's land is covered by closed forests (where tree crowns cover 20 percent or more of the ground when viewed from above). Roughly another 12 percent of the land is covered by open woodlands (where scattered trees provide a crown cover of 5–19 percent).[6] Forests are not, of course, distributed uniformly among continents or countries. North America, the Soviet Union, Northern Europe, and the humid tropical belt across Central Africa, South America, and Southeast Asia are rich in forest. Most of Africa and Asia and parts of Central and South America are forest-poor.

In North America and Europe the forest area is roughly stable; in fact the modernization of agriculture over the last half-century has allowed a considerable reversion of farm to forest. In these regions the challenge in the years ahead is less one of preserving forest lands than of balancing competing environmental, recreational, and industrial demands and of choosing appropriate timber-management techniques.

Among less-developed countries, China and South Korea stand out for having substantially increased their forested areas in recent times. Throughout most of Africa, Asia, and Latin America, the forest area is shrinking, and usually not according to any rational plan. Areas that were densely settled long ago—such as the Middle East, parts of North Africa, the Andean region of South America, and most of China and South Asia—lost the bulk of their forests in ages past, though the depletion of tree cover generally continues. But many developing countries in other areas are now experiencing unprecedented forest destruction.

Many of the most severe human impacts of the decline in tree cover are unfolding in drier, lightly wooded areas of the Third World where devegetation helps create desertlike conditions and acute fuelwood shortages. But what most people think of as deforestation—the conversion of closed forests to other uses or to scrubland—today occurs mainly in the humid tropics.

As of the mid-1970s, according to a U.N. study, tropical moist forests covered about 935 million hectares, and had been reduced from their natural area by 40 percent. Estimates of the rate at which tropical forests are disappearing have varied considerably. The differing estimates reflect both the inadequacies in the data and different definitions of deforestation. The natural balance of large areas is being disrupted by logging even where permanent clearance does not occur.[7]

An assessment of the world's tropical forest resources has just been carried out by the FAO under the auspices of UNEP's Global Environmental Monitoring System. Drawing on the latest surveys and distinguishing among types of forests, their commercial potentials, and types of human impacts, this U.N. assessment represents a giant step in the documentation of global forest trends. For Latin America the annual rate of deforestation in the late 1970s was found to be about 4.2 million hectares a year. In Africa the annual decline in closed forest was about 1.3 million hectares. Forest clearing in Asia was estimated at about 1.8 million hectares annually. Thus the global decline in tropical forest area was estimated to be 7.3 million hectares a year, or 14 hectares a minute.[8]

Such regional and global estimates of cleared forests understate the gravity of the forest problem. In Africa, for example, an additional 2.3 million hectares of open woodlands is cleared each year, and the vegetation of vast further areas of woodland is declining with severe consequences for land and people. Also, the survival of extensive forests in one region provides little comfort to residents of areas experiencing wholesale forest destruction. The dense forests of West Africa and a few other areas in the continent (especially Madagascar, Rwanda, and Burundi) are disappearing fast, while rain forests in parts of Central Africa are little touched as yet. The Ivory Coast has lost 70 percent of the forest with which it began the twentieth century; there and in Nigeria some 10 percent of the accessible closed forest was cleared *each year* in the second half of the 1970s. The U.N. assessment of Africa concludes: "In the long run there is a real ecological threat to the whole continent."

To the surprise and relief of many, recent satellite photos of Brazil's Amazonian rain forest revealed that only 2 percent of the area had been cleared as of the mid-1970s. Thus there is still time to put the management of this unique resource—a tropical forest of 280 million hectares, more than three times the size of France—on a sustainable footing. But the same photos revealed extensive and ill-planned clearance along the southern fringes of the rain forest, along roads and around towns, and in a large eastern zone. Also, while photos from later years are only now being compared with those from the mid-1970s, preliminary indications are that annual clearance has recently been well above the one million hectares a year that had commonly been assumed.[9] Still, relative to their endowments the countries that occupy the upper tributaries of the Amazon system—Peru, Colombia, Ecuador, Venezuela—are probably losing forests at a much faster pace than is Brazil. Clearance for grazing and farming is rapid in Central America too, where little rain forest save that in national parks may survive the next two decades.[10]

The formerly dominant timber exporters of Southeast Asia are fast approaching their days of reckoning for past forestry sins. In late 1977, while pressing for the adoption of a new forestry policy, the deputy premier of Malaysia shocked his compatriots by projecting that Peninsular Malaysia's once-lush forests would be severely depleted in just twelve years. He predicted that by 1990 the rate of timber production would not be adequate to meet domestic, let alone foreign, demand. Stringent new logging controls are being imposed in Thailand following the National Forestry Department's estimate that the country's forests will be virtually gone in twenty-five years if present logging and farming practices continue. Thailand has a special problem with poachers of valuable tropical hardwoods; in some recent years thirty or more forest guards have been killed in gun battles.[11]

Recent satellite pictures of the Philippines, traditionally a major timber exporter, indicate that forests now cover only 30 percent of the country, though the government feels a forest cover of 46 percent is desirable for economic and environmental reasons. If existing logging patterns prevail, a consortium of Philippine research organizations has concluded, all original old-growth forests will have been cut down by the year 2000 and projected timber supplies from second-growth forests and plantations will not suffice to meet even domestic needs. Destructive increases in flooding and sedimentation have already been registered.[12] Indonesia, which emerged in the 1970s as the world's leading tropical-timber exporter, retains extensive and rich forests on its outer islands—yet most of them have been slated for logging in the years ahead.

The global story of tropical forest depletion is mixed but on the whole somber. Many areas are undergoing rapid and wasteful destruction, while a few—mainly parts of Amazonia and Central Africa —enjoy a reprieve from the ax for the time being. As forests are razed in the absence of sound land-use plans, priceless biological resources are eliminated, crucial ecological services disrupted, and future economic potentials lost. The statement that all the world's rain forests will be gone by century's end is clearly exaggerated. But a continuation of recent trends will be costly.

The spread of agriculture, firewood collection, and unregulated timber harvesting are the principal immediate causes of forest losses. But behind these lurk more basic failures. Usually, uncontrolled deforestation is a symptom of a society's inability to get a grip on other fundamental development problems: agricultural stagnation, grossly unequal land tenure, rising unemployment, rapid population growth, and the incapacity to regulate private enterprise to protect the public interest.

The spread of farming in one form or another is by far the major cause of outright forest loss today, as it has been throughout most of human history. Although its extent is often exaggerated, some potentially arable land yet remains under forest in parts of Africa, Latin America, and Southeast Asia. Given the population increases in store for these regions, the conversion of much of this land to agriculture over the coming decades will be necessary.

However, the spread of agriculture is often characterized more by chaos and ecological destruction than by rationality, even when it is "planned" by governments. Politicians always find it easier to hand out unoccupied land than to redistribute proven farmland, however unequal the ownership of the latter may be. Even where national forest resources are glaringly deficient, as in India, governments often succumb to public pressures to turn forest lands over to cultivators.

In the tropical rain forests, where little is known about soil conditions and potentials, both legal and illegal colonists are trying to carve farms out of the jungle. Much tropical land colonization, as U.N. analysts have observed, "is indiscriminate . . . an ill-advised use of the land. It is merely a process of trial and error. Very often the chosen forest land cannot support permanent agriculture. When soil fertility is lost, cultivation is abandoned and the land is often grazed. The bare soil will frequently return to forest, unless, as is often the case, it is first destroyed by erosion."[13] By now even the most ecologically illiterate economic planners realize what biologists have long said: the apparent fertility of lush jungle soils is often illusory.

In South America, for example, the colonization of tropical forests has generally preceded the completion of land-use surveys that would tell where farming is feasible and where forests must be left to protect the ecological balance. Thus in Ecuador, where overpopulation and unequal land tenure are driving peasants down both sides of the Andes, the government has little idea how many migrants are entering the rain forest, let alone where they should go. The process is euphemistically called "semidirected colonization," meaning that when the government discovers a new concentration of aspiring farmers in the jungle, it struggles to provide essential roads, clinics, agricultural advice, and other support.

When, with much fanfare, it began building the Trans-Amazon Highway in 1970, the Brazilian government dreamed of mass colonization of its huge, largely empty Amazon Basin. Hopes were expressed that the opening of new farmlands would relieve the notorious poverty and social conflicts of Brazil's Northeast and meet the country's burgeoning food demands. But within a few years, as crops failed, roads washed away, new communities disintegrated, and the public expense of colonization soared, the dreams faded. Official support for peasant colonization of the Amazon was dropped in favor of the encouragement of large-scale cattle ranches and other agro-industries.

Today, although colonists invariably accompany new roads and enterprises throughout the region, migration into Amazonia is concentrated in the state of Rondonia, which occupies the southwestern corner of the rain forest. Soils there have proved to be far more fertile than in most of the Amazon Basin and a new road allows popular access. The influx of tens of thousands of families into Rondonia has outpaced the government's capacities for control and support. Land tenure is chaotic, land-use planning only a hope, and native Indian tribes are endangered.

In their review of development prospects in Brazilian Amazonia, Robert Skillings and Nils Tcheyen of the World Bank observe that "If as much as 10 percent of the soils of the Amazon region . . . were rich enough to be suitable for settlement—and this proportion is probably too high—it would accommodate only around 350,000 families on 100 hectare lots. And the figure would be lower if, as should be the case, some land with good soil is left as biological reserve." Experience has proven that, apart from some floodplain lands, most of the areas where farming is feasible are best suited for tree crops (such as cocoa, rubber, and oil palm) rather than grains. The events of the 1970s, together with emerging research findings, should put to rest once and for all the myths that the Amazon Basin will feed a hungry world or provide an escape valve for Latin American population growth.[14]

The great danger is that spontaneous migration to Amazonia will, to quote Skillings and Tcheyen, "overflow into places for which it is not suited, with very serious environmental and social results." Policy changes elsewhere in Brazil—land reforms, increased incomes and employment for the bottom half, and a slowdown in population growth—are necessary if costly destruction of the Amazon forest is to be avoided.

Much of the blame for tropical forest destruction is often laid on the shoulders of shifting cultivators—those who slash and burn a clearing in the forest, grow crops for a few years until soil fertility dissipates, and then move on to clear a new patch. However, while itinerant farmers are indeed major agents of deforestation, it is important to differentiate among the various sorts of shifting cultivators and the soundness of their methods.

Traditional systems of shifting cultivation entail lengthy fallow periods during which soil fertility is restored and trees regrow on the cultivated plots. Today many traditional peoples in the Amazon Basin, Central Africa, and Southeast Asia are still practicing shifting cultivation in harmony with nature. It is when such farmers get hemmed in by logging companies, the spread of plantations, or other incursions of modern society that they can become enemies of the forest. In addition, as human numbers in a given region rise and the free forest area about them shrinks, fallow cycles are shortened to the point where trees have no chance to regrow.

Many of the "shifting cultivators" causing the greatest forest destruction today are not traditional practitioners of this art at all. They are rootless, landless people struggling to make what living they can amid unfamiliar ecological conditions. In Indonesia, for instance, many of those who have migrated from crowded Java to the outer islands have found continuous cultivation of the land unworkable, either because the soils are not appropriate or because promised technical assistance has not materialized. Many migrants have become new shifting cultivators who damage the timber and wildlife resources of the areas over which they spread. In Venezuela, which has a high rate of unemployment and rising numbers of landless peasants, 30,000 families, most of them practicing shifting cultivation, are living within national parks, forest reserves, and other supposedly protected areas. An influx of shifting cultivators in the watershed above the Panama Canal is, by causing increased siltation of a crucial reservoir, jeopardizing both the canal's future utility and Panama City's water supply. This has prompted a major new U.S.-Panamanian program of reforestation and improved land management.[15]

In Central and South America large areas of tropical forest have been cleared to create grazing lands, a transition that is sometimes unsustainable and frequently of dubious social value. The Brazilian government has granted huge concessions in the Amazon region to both domestic and foreign corporations to raise cattle. Large tax incentives have attracted investors to grazing enterprises that would otherwise be uneconomical and will probably be short-lived.[16] Finally cognizant of the tremendous economic and ecological losses involved, the Brazilian government recently stopped granting new tax benefits for the creation of pastures in the dense rain forest, although agreements signed earlier are still being honored and clearing for this purpose continues.

Large landowners in Venezuela too are transforming forest into pasture, while in Central America virgin forest is giving way to pastures created by ranchers anxious to cash in on the lucrative beef-export market to the United States. Pointing to massive soil erosion on denuded slopes and to the widespread deterioration of soil structure, ecologist Joseph Tosi has estimated that more than half the pastureland in Costa Rica is not suited to grazing. Ironically, even as Costa Rica's cattle production has soared, its domestic per capita beef consumption has fallen by half in the last fifteen years. The economic returns from the expanding cattle industry are not widely shared even in this country, with the most liberal political system in Central America.[17]

Outside the humid tropical zones the last extensive forests in many Third World countries are on the steep slopes and more remote reaches of mountains. Agriculture nearly everywhere has traditionally been concentrated on the plains and valley floors, and with good reason, for severe erosion and other ecological calamities often occur when slopes are left unprotected by vegetation. Yet today, pushed by the lack of access to land or jobs, cultivators are moving up mountainsides in many parts of Africa, Asia, and Latin America, clearing forests as they go.

Frequently a precarious and futile business, mountainside farming and the associated deforestation can also affect the welfare of those in farms and cities downstream by increasing flooding and the siltation of rivers, reservoirs, and harbors. Citizens in dozens of countries —Colombia, India, Indonesia, Nepal, Nigeria, Pakistan, the Philippines, and Tanzania, among others—are today learning the same lesson that a surge in the severity of alpine torrents taught Europeans a few centuries back: humans strip mountainsides of trees at great risk to their own well-being.

Firewood collection can contribute to the depletion of tree cover, especially in areas that were only lightly wooded to begin with. Where the balance between tree growth and human numbers permits, peasants can make do with dead wood and scraps from trees cut for other purposes. Dense forests can produce a lot of burnable material without any live trees being felled. In some areas, such as Java, home gardens supply a good share of family firewood needs.

Elsewhere, however, the gradual thinning of woodlands is a common result of the daily foraging of villagers. In Madhya Pradesh, which holds more forest than any other Indian state, a recent survey revealed that the annual cutting of firewood and small timber exceeded new growth in twenty-six of forty-five districts. If current trends persist, sixteen of these deficit districts will be virtually bereft of trees within twenty years; more than half the state will be devoid of trees within fifty years.[18]

The outright destruction of living trees to meet fuel needs occurs most commonly around cities and towns, where commercial markets for firewood and charcoal exist. Well-organized syndicates bring fuel by truck, camel, and donkey cart into cities like Ouagadougou in Upper Volta and Niamey in Niger, damaging the landscape in a widening circle. In Sudan, forest rangers have accosted armed crews as they fill trucks with illegally cut wood that will be converted into charcoal for sale in the cities; shootouts reminiscent of the American Wild West have occurred.

Rising firewood prices can tempt desperate individuals as well as greedy big-time entrepreneurs into cutting live trees. Near Bhopal, the capital of Madhya Pradesh State, the forest department has granted people the right to collect headloads of dead wood in the forest reserves for personal use. Yet throughout these reserves are signs that "dead wood" is being actively manufactured: trees with their bark girdled and trees axed outright. Live trees become "personal" headloads of dead wood that then find their way into city markets; as a consequence nearby forest reserves are gradually being reduced to scrubland. On the outskirts of Bara, a town in semiarid central Sudan, live hundreds of former nomads who lost their herds to drought and now eke out a living selling wood and charcoal. Much of the wood they sell is illegally cut from dwindling stands of valuable gum-arabic trees in the region. Describing their destructive activities to Norwegian geographer Turi Hammer, the wood sellers were surprisingly frank: "We take trees belonging to other people. We cut them when they are too young. We never pay any tax. . . . We must live from something. What else can we do?"[19]

Logging in humid tropical forests—much of which has been done by multinational corporations—usually involves not clear-cutting but the "creaming" of the forest's small proportion of commercially valued species. However, the process of cutting and removing selected trees amid dense foliage and on delicate soils usually causes far more destruction of vegetation and wildlife than the bare statistics of extracted timber would suggest. One Indonesian study revealed that logging operations damaged or destroyed about 40 percent of the trees left behind.[20]

Even when practiced responsibly, logging in many tropical forest areas leads to the permanent loss of forests. Wherever loggers build roads and settlements, other people follow. With or without government approval, cultivators move along new logging roads and into cut-over areas, hoping to put down roots. The clearings and smoke plumes of slash-and-burn cultivation are normal sights around new roads throughout the humid tropics. When these farms fail, they are sometimes replaced by cattle pastures or by useless, tenacious grasses.

Even when it is not followed by cultivation, logging can leave the forest permanently bereft of the more valuable species. Much of West Africa is logged out for commercial purposes, even where forests still stand. In East Kalimantan, the main homeland of Indonesia's lucrative timber boom, logging firms are supposed to follow a "select-fell" system in which only larger trees of the desired species are cut, and then only from areas in which a set number of smaller specimens can be left to replenish the stock. In theory such a system would permit the logging of a given area every thirty-five years without depletion. But a 1977 study of the operations of nine different companies revealed that "none was leaving the required 25 select crop trees per hectare and, indeed, on much of the area there were not sufficient trees at the start to comply with the regulation."[21]

The notion that these areas will be ready for another valuable harvest in thirty-five years thus appears to be wishful thinking at best, or a convenient lie at worst. Of East Kalimantan's seventeen million hectares of forest, thirteen million have been earmarked for logging by the more than one hundred licensed companies at work there.

Even selective logging sometimes destroys resources of great daily value to people living in or around the forest, while the profits and consumer benefits of the operation are mainly enjoyed by people in faraway capital cities or foreign lands. When evaluating the economics of timber operations governments can easily overlook the multitude of products and services the forest renders to local people; in some cases their combined value may rival or surpass the value of the forest as timber. But most of the nontimber benefits do not accrue to those who hold power over the destiny of the forests.

In the Himalayan hills of the Indian state of Uttar Pradesh, a grassroots people's movement has arisen to defend what it sees as the local residents' interests against timber operations. Logging in the area by outside contactors has jeopardized ecological stability and reduced local peoples' opportunity to profit from sound forest exploitation. Members of the Chipko movement, as it is known, have halted objectionable logging activities by hugging trees about to be sawed. More recently they have worked with villages in tree planting and conservation education.

As the availability of traditionally marketed tropical species declines, technologies for the use of all species and sizes of trees are emerging. In such operations, which already exist in the South Pacific, most of the wood is ground into chips for later reconstitution as particle board or paper. The land is clear-cut and may either be replanted with trees, converted to agriculture, or simply abandoned to scrub growth.

A combination of all-species use and fast-growing tree plantations has its attractions. The output of wood and fiber from a relatively small area can be multiplied, taking the pressure off virgin forest lands. But if not followed by careful fertilization and replanting, all-species use can be much more harmful than traditional logging has been. Also, the long-term viability of plantations on many rain forest soils remains uncertain.

As it considers opening large portions of the Amazon Basin for timber exploitation, the Brazilian government hopes to enforce a system of selective logging that allows for natural regeneration of prime species. At the same time it is closely watching the results of the intensive tree plantations established on the huge private holdings of D. K. Ludwig at Jari, in the northern Amazonian region of Brazil. There, after some initial growth and pest problems, tree plantations for the production of pulp seem so far to be workable but of dubious profitability. And whether yields can be maintained for several harvestings on the same soils will only be revealed by experience. (The Ludwig operation was sold to Brazilian investors in early 1982.)

In Brazil and elsewhere, both approaches to tropical forest exploitation—natural regeneration and intensive plantations—have theoretical merit and both deserve a trial. But neither approach is of proven sustainability. Historically, most tropical timber has been mined like a nonrenewable resource.

The economic benefits of tropical logging have often been captured mainly by richer processing and importing countries and by wealthy elites within the timber-exporting countries. Over the last decade the major timber-producing countries of Southeast Asia have restricted the export of uncut logs in order to encourage investments in local sawmills and processing facilities. This is an important step in the right direction. Still, far more can be done to increase the local employment and economic benefits derived from tropical forests while protecting their future ecological and economic values. A recent U.N. report notes that Finland and the Congo have roughly comparable forest estates.[22] Yet in 1979 Finland exported forest products worth 115 times those of the Congo.

The companies cutting down tropical trees seldom take responsibility for replanting the lands they harvest. A wood-chip operation in Papua, New Guinea, pays a royalty of $48 per hectare cleared, and has avoided paying any further taxes to the country. The cost to the government of replanting denuded areas is $450 per hectare, nearly ten times the royalty received. As a result, notes Prof. Dennis Richardson, "less than 10 percent of the area cut-over annually is being replanted or cleared for agriculture. The avowed objective of this project was 'to develop the forest resources of the Madang Timber Area'; the phrase has a hollow ring."[23]

Third World governments borrow international aid money to finance replanting of lands that were stripped of trees for private profit and foreign consumption. Looking at forestry patterns in Southeast Asia and the Pacific, Richardson writes: "There can surely be no justification for poor countries borrowing scarce capital at concessionary interest rates to subsidize the provision of raw material for Japan." He goes on to observe that Japan is doing an excellent job of building up its domestic forest resources even as it imports hardwoods from countries where harvests greatly exceed new growth.

Worldwide efforts are long overdue to make the companies and consumers who benefit most from logging bear a greater share of the costs of forest renewal. Simultaneously, forest industries need to be reconstructed to increase the benefits to poorer timber-exporting countries, and to the poor within those countries. Some concerned Westerners have proposed drastic cuts in consumption of tropical timber products in order to help save Third World forests. But if methods for the sound management of tropical forestry can be developed and enforced, the world could have its wood and the forests too.

What are the consequences of uncontrolled deforestation and forest-product scarcity? Curiously, although substantial literature exists on the gains possible through the exploitation of timber resources, virtually none exists on the consequences of a failure to put forestry on a sustainable footing. A better understanding of the price of inaction might cause many national planners to alter their forestry policies.

One outcome of a nation's forestry shortcomings can be a rising dependence on imported forest products. Already most Third World countries are net importers of forest products, particularly paper (the production of which requires both wood-fiber and manufacturing plants).

Trade-deficit figures do not come close to capturing the negative impacts of tree scarcity, some of which are acutely felt by low-income citizens even in timber-exporting countries. For one thing the major forest products used by most Third World residents never enter the market economy; when fruits or firewood become scarce, people either do without or they switch to noncommercial alternatives rather than to imported goods. For another, foreign exchange shortages and high prices can hold a nation's wood and paper consumption well below the levels at which basic needs are satisfied.

Thus in Pakistan, to provide an extreme case, the use of industrial timber is only about half what one would expect even considering the country's pitiful income level. Between 1965 and 1975 per capita income rose by 27 percent; according to experience elsewhere a comparable increase in forest-product consumption should have occurred, but none did. World Bank analysts point out that "although consumption and supply are obviously in balance, there is a considerable shortage of industrial wood in the country. This shortage is manifesting itself in a number of ways including sharply increasing prices, and substitution in a variety of end-uses such as concrete railway sleepers, steel transmission poles and steel furniture."[24]

To what extent is wood scarcity one of the driving forces of inflation? Mesmerized by their own analytical tools, modern economists often pay little heed to the natural systems on which human activity is based. Yet an inadequate supply of forest products is already an inflationary force worldwide, and appears certain to be even more of one in the coming decades.

The deepening timber shortage in Pakistan has been accompanied by astonishing rises in the price of domestic lumber. In the Rawalpindi market, one popular species that sold for fifteen rupees a cubic foot in 1967 sold for forty-five rupees in 1973 and eighty rupees in 1976. A simple board then cost twice as much in Pakistan as in the United States, though the income of the average American was forty-six times that of the average Pakistani.

The pressure of demand on timber supplies has even promoted inflation in the United States, with all its forest wealth. Between the 1870s and the 1950s the real price of forest products multiplied two and one half times.[25] In the 1970s wood prices surged anew, contributing to spectacular rises in the costs of construction and housing.

The social impact of timber scarcity on housing is especially pernicious in poor countries. Even if Third World governments were to make a serious effort to meet the housing problem, adequate wood supplies would not be available in many cases. For example, the Indian state of Gujarat's ambitious plan to construct huts for landless laborers in the late 1970s was derailed by the paucity of raw materials. The program called for 25 million wood poles, but only 400,000 of these became available each year; and only 4 million bamboo stalks were produced a year although 765 million were needed.[26]

Soaring firewood prices are another inflation source. Almost everywhere commercial firewood markets exist, prices have multiplied over the last decade. In one town in Upper Volta, a donkey cartload of wood that sold for 350 Central African francs in 1970 cost 1000 francs in 1975 and 1750 francs in 1979.[27] In parts of West Africa and Central America urban families spend one-fourth of their income on wood or charcoal for cooking. As market prices have outpaced the purchasing power of the urban poor, many state governments in India have had to establish special firewood depots that sell low-priced fuel to the poorest groups. Subsidized firewood has joined subsidized food as a measure necessary to prevent starvation in India.

Firewood scarcity exacts other less visible burdens too, especially on women.[28] Many users do not buy wood with money but with their own time and labor. Gathering firewood—which is often regulated to women and children—can become a real economic and personal drain. In central Tanzania 250–300 days of work are required to provide the annual firewood needs of a household. In parts of India one member of each family must spend two days gathering a week's worth of wood. In smaller towns and rural areas of Upper Volta women commonly spend four to six hours, three times a week, walking miles from home to gather firewood.

As fuel becomes harder to find people may cut back on essentials. In bitterly cold mountain areas families must do without the warmth of a nighttime fire and suffer the resulting discomfort and ill health. The nutritional impact of firewood scarcity has not been well investigated, but in areas of West Africa and Latin America people have recently been forced to give up one of their traditional hot meals a day. Peasants in Nepal and Haiti have reportedly cut back on their consumption of those vegetables that require cooking.

With firewood unavailable, rural people switch not to fossil fuels, which are always expensive and often unavailable, but to crop residues and dried cow dung. The resulting diversion of organic matter and nutrients from field to fireplace carries its own negative economic effects. According to the FAO, some 400 million tons of cow dung are annually burned in Asia, the Near East, and Africa. Each ton burned means a loss of about fifty kilograms of potential grain output.

Rising prices and outright shortages of paper have been yet another forest-related source of inflation and hidden hardships. Recent global surges in paper prices are the result of boom-and-bust cycles in the pulp-and-paper industry rather than of a shortage of wood for pulping. Still, the paper industry requires huge amounts of wood. Breaking the Third World's costly dependence on paper imports will require the creation of forests as well as the building of the small-scale factories now being boosted by some international agencies.

The environmental consequences of unwise deforestation are seldom expressed in economic terms, but many of them directly influence economic output as well as human welfare in the broader sense. Decades of research have proved that the deforestation of watersheds, especially around smaller rivers and streams, can increase the severity of flooding, reduce streamflows and dry up springs during dry seasons, and increase the load of sediment entering waterways. Yet most efforts to combat such problems have entailed engineering measures —dams, embankments, dredging—that address symptoms but not their causes.

The exact contribution of deforestation to flood trends is probably impossible to pinpoint, but as flooding worsens in country after country, new attention is being given to the protection of watersheds. In the fall of 1978 India suffered some of the worst flooding in its history. Following two days of concentrated rainfall, 66,000 villages were inundated, more than 2000 people drowned, and 40,000 cattle were swept away. Two states, West Bengal and Uttar Pradesh, lost a total of $750 million in crops. Many Indian officials are beginning to wonder whether their chronic flood problems can be ameliorated without a restoration of forest cover in the increasingly denuded hills of northern India and Nepal. According to the country's National Commission on Floods, the area annually afflicted by floods now averages forty million hectares, compared to twenty-five million hectares three decades ago. Perhaps more important, rising numbers of people live in flood-prone areas. Indian expenditures to offset flood damages averaged $250 million a year between 1953 and 1978.[29]

The costs of accelerated reservoir sedimentation are not hard to understand. Studies of seventeen major reservoirs in India reveal them to be silting up at three times the expected rate, apparently because of the deforestation of upstream areas. So valuable is water in arid Pakistan that the expensive new Tarbela Dam was built with full knowledge that the heavy silt load of the Indus would render it virtually useless in fifty years. Because of severe erosion linked to deforestation, the Ambuklao Dam in the Philippines has an expected economic life of just thirty-two years. Numerous reservoirs in Kenya have filled with sediment in fifteen or twenty years, grossly reducing their ability to support power generation, provide irrigation water, and control floods. Deforestation has also made necessary the costly dredging of irrigation canals in Kenya, Indonesia, and many other countries.[30]

Some of the costs of deforestation are by nature incalculable. Should the clearing and disruption of tropical forests continue at recent rates, thousands of plant and animal species, many of them not yet named, will become extinct. The full ecological and economic repercussions of such unprecedented biological losses cannot be predicted.

Scientists studying the rising level of carbon dioxide in the atmosphere have added a new reason for concern about the loss of tropical forests. A vast amount of carbon is stored in the extensive forests of the tropics, particularly in the massive older trees of virgin forests. The release of that carbon through deforestation and burning could add significantly to the atmosphere's carbon dioxide, helping cause global climatic shifts. Issues like species extinction and climatic changes make the fate of the world's forests a matter of consequence to people everywhere.

Forestry planning must incorporate both a long-term horizon and a humane social vision. One of the most positive developments in the global environmental scene over the last decade has been the new recognition of the importance of forestry among aid agencies and Third World governments. But the sources of deforestation are deep.

Meeting the forestry challenge requires radical changes in the roles of foresters and national forest agencies. Their traditional mandates have been to protect and manage the exploitation of forest reserves. Good foresters have always been concerned as well with protecting environmentally crucial forest areas and with sustaining the long-term output of the forests in their care. But even these desirable traits are not enough. Today foresters need to move outside the forests and help people meet their basic forest needs.

Firewood scarcity is often most serious in areas far removed from designated forests. The increase in tree planting required just to meet projected fuel needs, let alone wood for other uses, is awesome; according to World Bank calculations, the rate of firewood planting (now perhaps 500,000 hectares a year in the Third World, excluding China) must jump fivefold if enormous ecological and economic costs are to be avoided.

But simply increasing the area planted with trees will not necessarily do justice to social and environmental concerns. With forestry, as with all development activities, who does the producing and who gets the benefits are as crucial as what gets produced. The management of a village woodlot can be designed in ways that help or hurt the rural poor.

As an alternative to large plantations, integrating trees and wood production into small-farm systems holds great potential in both semiarid and humid areas. Spatially dispersed forestry practiced by many farmers can often provide far greater environmental benefits than a woodlot concentrated in one place.

Another major need is for the improved management of natural woodlands in order to increase their output of useful products. Recent "reforestation" schemes in semiarid West Africa have sometimes been a mixed blessing, entailing the clearing of rich and diverse woodlands to make room for plantations of fast-growing exotic species. The multitude of nonwood products that local people glean from the forest are thus lost—and the productivity of exotic plantations in the Sahel has often turned out to be far lower than expected. Little research has been done on the indigenous species of the Sahel and on how the production of wood and other values might be boosted without destroying the forest. In a similar vein the replacement of native forests with teak plantations in the Indian state of Bihar has undercut the livelihoods of tribal people who depend on the forest for many essentials. In this case the people have fought back; hundreds of arrests and twenty-five deaths have resulted from this conflict since 1978.[31]

Desirable approaches to forestry differ from place to place. But probably no country lacks the physical resources to meet its most urgent rural forestry needs. Villages virtually everywhere have unused or misused lands on which fast-growing woodlots can be planted. Individual farmers are often willing and able to grow more trees in and around their fields when given the means to do so. In watersheds, the raising of crops, trees, and livestock can be integrated in new ways that protect soils as they provide extra benefits for people. Agroforestry systems can give shifting cultivators a stable, productive life. Idle lands along roads and canals and around fields can be planted to trees that produce food, fodder, timber, traditional medicines, and industrial raw materials as well as a more hospitable environment. Cheap, efficient cooking stoves can be disseminated that cut family wood-fuel needs in half.

To an outsider, prompting rural communities to grow some badly needed trees may not seem like such a tall order. But as the experience of countries such as China and South Korea that have already implemented participatory forestry on a wide scale demonstrates, actually doing so requires changes in the attitudes and activities of governments and aid agencies, and reforms in villagers' social organization and land use.

Foresters, like development planners generally, are used to running things from above. What contact they have had with villagers has usually been in their roles as policemen, denying destitute people access to protected lands and wood.

Yet experience has shown that tree-planting cannot be imposed from above and carried out in the face of a hostile population. New forms of land use impinge upon the daily activities of everyone. When the local people are not active supporters, saplings have a way of disappearing overnight. With fodder usually as scarce as firewood, uncontrolled goats or cattle can quickly ruin a new plantation. Community involvement then is not just an ideologically appealing goal; it is a practical necessity if rural forest needs are to be met. Popular participation is important for economic reasons too, for in most countries the costs of the needed plantings and upkeep would be prohibitive if local residents did not pitch in generously with their labor.

Community forestry, as the new approach is known, has begun to catch on over the last decade. U.N. agencies have begun promoting the concept, and the world's major aid institution, the World Bank, announced in 1978 a marked shift in its forestry program, with emphases on fuelwood and small-scale activities replacing the former preoccupation with large-scale industrial timber. Having lent nothing for firewood projects in the early 1970s, the World Bank now expects to loan $1 billion for this purpose in the first five years of the 1980s. Other aid agencies have shown new interest in people-oriented forestry as well.

Many Third World governments have finally begun to pay heed to forestry needs. Once a bureaucratic backwater, forestry is emerging as an exciting and prestigious profession. Some states in India are creating whole new branches of their forestry departments to pursue "social forestry"; there and in many other countries, a new generation of foresters with new skills and attitudes is being trained.

Whether the issue is the maintenance of timber output, the protection of ecological stability, or the growing of fuel, a host of workable forestry technologies are known and await wider implementation. But essential as they are, forestry measures alone will not be enough to solve the deforestation problem. Many of the underlying sources of deforestation originate outside the scope of forestry per se. In order to halt the destructive spread of cultivation, national development patterns must provide the destroyers with alternative ways to feed themselves; in particular, crop yields and employment must be boosted on the lands best suited to farming. Sound forestry policies can contribute to these efforts, but broader decisions on investment priorities, land tenure, and the choice of technologies will be even more critical. Woodland depletion by firewood gatherers can be greatly mitigated by tree planting, but broader attention to rural energy needs, alternative energy sources, and national energy priorities is also necessary. Underlying all the sources of deforestation to varying degrees is, of course, human population growth. A vast amount of tree planting is essential over the coming decades, but its benefits will be undercut if the deeper roots of deforestation are not eradicated.

10 BIOLOGICAL DIVERSITY AND ECONOMIC DEVELOPMENT

TALK OF "ENDANGERED SPECIES" evokes images of tigers under seige in Asia and cheetahs losing ground in Africa, of whales hunted to scarcity in the Antarctic and whooping cranes clinging to life in North America. It may also bring to mind recent positive preservation developments: whaling quotas, restrictions on trade in rare-animal pelts, DDT bans, and international "save the tiger" campaigns.

Even as such salvaging operations finally get under way, many leading biologists have begun sounding the alarm about an unsolved, unsung species problem of vaster proportions and wider implications. At risk, they say, are not just hundreds of familiar and appealing birds and mammals. Examination of the survival prospects of all forms of plant and animal life—including obscure ferns, shrubs, insects, and molluscs, as well as elephants and wolves—indicates that huge numbers of them have little future. Thousands—some scientists say hundreds of thousands—of unique, irreplaceable life forms may vanish by the century's end.[1] Such a multitude of species losses would constitute an irreversible alteration in the nature of the biosphere even before we understand its workings—an evolutionary Rubicon whose crossing *Homo sapiens* would do well to avoid.

Estimates of the number of plant and animal species living on earth range from three million to more than ten million. Yet to date only about one and one-half million species have been recorded in the scientific literature; about most of these, little more is known than their appearance and location. It is possible that several million insects and plants—along with far fewer members of other animal classes—await discovery, mainly in the tropics. If current patterns of human activity continue, many species will vanish before their existence, much less their biological importance or economic utility, is established.[2]

Currently, the International Union for Conservation of Nature and Natural Resources (IUCN) estimates that an average of one species or subspecies of higher animal is lost each year. Overall, roughly 1000 birds and mammals are now thought to be in jeopardy. Although endangered animals receive the greatest public attention, plant extinctions are often more significant ecologically. According to Peter H. Raven, director of the Missouri Botanical Garden, a disappearing plant can take with it ten to thirty dependent species such as insects, higher animals, and even other plants. Estimates of the past and current rates of plant extinctions are not available, but the IUCN's Threatened Plants Committee finds about 10 percent (20,000–30,000) of the world's flowering plants to be "dangerously rare or under threat."[3]

These estimates of species at risk understate the true problem, for they deal only with known and higher life forms. It seems probable that many unnamed species are disappearing in scientifically uncharted tropical areas. In his book *The Sinking Ark,* Norman Myers surmises on the basis of extrapolation that, right now, at least one species might be disappearing each day in tropical forests alone. Even outside the tropics, many small, obscure organisms such as worms, mites, beetles, and herbs may be disappearing without our knowledge.[4]

The ways in which humans destroy other species are legion. The excessive hunting or collecting of animals for food, profit, or recreation is a time-honored means of extermination. Indeed considerable evidence suggests that the demise of the large Pleistocene mammals of North America, including the woolly mammoths, horses, camels, and mastodons, was caused by Stone Age hunters who filtered across the Bering Strait more than 11,000 years ago. Today hunters and collectors remain significant threats to many mammals, birds, reptiles, and fishes. Hunters shoot endangered animals for their hides, heads, or tusks, and even some unscrupulous zoo suppliers imperil rare species.[5]

The lure of spectacular profits continues to drive the trade in endangered species and derivative products. Despite countervailing laws and treaties, consumers remain willing to fuel a scandalous global business. A Bengal tiger coat sells for $95,000 in Tokyo, a coat made from South American ocelots for $40,000 in West Germany. A single orchid or Amazonian parrot can fetch $5000.[6]

Rhinoceros horns are used in medicines in Asia, where powdered horn can be worth its weight in gold. The young men of Yemen, many of whom earn big money working in Arabian oil fields, are willing to pay high sums for the rhino-horn dagger handles that certify their manhood. Ninety percent of Kenya's rhinos have been killed since 1970, and the World Wildlife Fund has launched an emergency campaign to save African rhinos.

Japan's chapter of Friends of the Earth, noting that wildlife products represent the ultimate in chic fashion, compiled in 1981 a shopping list for Tokyo's best dressed woman, each of the products then being available at the city's major department stores: tortoise-shell glasses ($4140); imported lizard-skin shoes ($1750); crocodile handbag, belt, keyholder, and wallet ($7275); vicuna scarf ($250); peccary gloves ($140); ostrich watchband ($140); and ivory and tortoise-shell accessories ($2000). Add in a fur coat of African leopard for $50,000, and a woman could be fashionably clothed for less than $70,000.[7]

Wildlife losses to hunters and collectors are deliberate, so theoretically could be controlled through well-enforced national and international regulations. And progress is being made against the global trade in endangered species. More difficult to combat are the inadvertent losses that result from the pursuit of goals unrelated to plants and animals per se. The contamination of water and air with toxic chemicals, for example, presents a diffused but genuine threat to nature. Publicity about the effects of DDT on falcon eggs helped spur severe restrictions on the use of chlorinated hydrocarbons in North America and Europe. Yet persistent pesticides are increasingly and often profligately applied to Third World croplands.

By far the biggest single cause of extinctions over the next few decades will be the destruction of habitats. As both populations and economies grow, and human settlements sprawl, undisturbed natural areas shrink. Wildlife breeding zones, migration routes, and browsing and hunting domains are paved, inundated with water, grazed, or plowed. Forest lands are denuded by farmers or timber companies and then given over to cattle, crops, or nonnative tree species. Plant species unique to a small locality can be erased from the earth by a single bulldozer, as can the animals that feed on them; predators dependent on a complex food web may disappear once the wild area around them is compressed below a critical minimum size.

The problem of habitat destruction exists on every continent, but it is particularly serious in the humid tropics, which is where the major species losses are predicted. Viewed in terms of biological diversity, the moist tropical forests of Africa, Asia, and Latin America hold an importance far beyond the land area they occupy. Suffused with exceptional amounts of light, warmth, and moisture, the tropical rain forests house a remarkable variety of ecosystems and species.[8]

Probably far fewer than half the species of the humid tropics have been seen or catalogued by scientists. Even in Africa, the best explored of the three tropical regions, an average of more than 200 new plant species is still collected every year. Large areas of South America remain *terra incognita* to scientists. Botanists who collected 239 plant specimens on one recent expedition along the Panama-Colombia border found one in every five to be a new species. As Peter Raven observes: "Billions of dollars have been spent on the exploration of the moon, and we now know more about the moon than we do about the rainforests of, say, western Colombia. The moon will be there far longer than these forests."[9]

Strong pressures are building to exploit the remaining virgin territories of the tropics. Many tropical forests lie within countries that, though biologically affluent, are economically poor, and whose governments are not inclined to value abstract, long-term ecological goals above immediate economic gains. Moreover, in many tropical countries, including some where significant numbers of people have relatively high incomes, land-tenure patterns are inequitable, population growth rates are high, and prevailing development patterns are not providing nearly enough jobs.

The consequences of poverty, inequality, and rapid population growth are land-hungry people desperately trying to carve a living out of the forest, and foreign exchange–hungry governments eager to promote rapid logging. Even affluent people in faraway lands, who demand wood and agricultural products, add to the pressures on tropical ecosystems.

Rising numbers of people, virtually all of them seeking ever more material goods, will put massive pressures on wildlife habitats everywhere. But large numbers of extinctions will result directly from the efforts of the Third World's economically dispossessed to eke out a living from the land.

Slowing the loss of species must therefore entail much more than the ratification of international treaties, the passage of national conservation laws, and the policing of national park boundaries—essential as all these steps are. The future shape of the biosphere will depend in good measure on the shape of political and economic policies affecting employment, land tenure, income distribution, and population growth.

The extermination of a species seldom poses such an obvious threat to humans as other kinds of environmental deterioration such as air pollution and the spread of deserts. Yet for many reasons a decline in the diversity of life forms should worry everyone. The impending large-scale loss of species is without precedent and will result from the disruption of complex ecological systems. Not surprisingly, no means exist for quantifying the costs. But the biological impoverishment of the earth will certainly mean the economic as well as esthetic impoverishment of humans.

Probably the most immediate threat to human welfare arises from the shrinkage of the plant gene pools available to agricultural scientists and farmers—a critical, if largely separable, aspect of the more general problem. While the global spread of modern agricultural methods and hybrid seeds has brought needed increases in food production, it has also entailed the substitution of relatively few seed varieties for the wide array of strains traditionally planted. At the same time, forest clearance and the spread of cultivation wipe out the wild relatives of domestic crops that still exist in some regions.[10]

Switching to more productive strains is often desirable. Unaccompanied by adequate seed collection, however, such "progress" can involve the extinction of unique crop varieties that are closely adapted to the local environment and highly resistant to local pests. A half-century back, 80 percent of the wheat grown in Greece consisted of native breeds; today more than 95 percent of the old strains have virtually disappeared, replaced by the products of modern plant science. The spread through the Middle East and Asia of new high-yielding wheat and rice varieties since the mid-1960s has inadvertently caused a drastic shrinkage of the gene pools in such traditional centers of crop diversity as Turkey, Iraq, Afghanistan, Pakistan, and India.[11]

Future agricultural progress is undermined as the diversity of genes on which plant breeders can draw declines. A locally evolved strain in some remote corner of the earth may hold the genetic key to an important agricultural breakthrough. Thus in 1973 Purdue University scientists trying to develop high-protein sorghum examined more than 9000 varieties from all over the world before they discovered in the fields of Ethiopian peasants two obscure strains with the qualities they sought.[12] Who knows what other irreplaceable plant resources have quietly vanished?

Since pests, diseases, production technologies, and agricultural goals all tend to change over time, the sustaining of agriculture depends not only on major breeding breakthroughs but also on the routine development of fresh crop strains that incorporate newly needed traits. Yet countless locally evolved varieties, some undoubtedly with properties of huge value, are being obliterated. As British biologist J. G. Hawkes observes, the genetic diversity borne of some 10,000 years of local adaptation of ancient domestic crops such as wheat, barley, lentils, peas, maize, potatoes, and others "is now being swept away." What were once considered to be "inexhaustible gene pools are now beginning to dry up; indeed, in some cases the diversity for certain crops, such as wheat and barley in southwest Asia, African rice in west tropical Africa, and fruit trees in southwest and southeast Asia has almost completely disappeared." Likewise, the wild relatives of many commercial crops are disappearing just as their use in plant breeding is accelerating.[13]

Planting large areas to genetically uniform crops involves serious risks. The more homogeneous the fields, the higher their vulnerability to large-scale losses from pests, diseases, and weather abnormalities.

The Irish potato famine of the 1840s provides the classic example of the dangers of monocultures; the decimation by corn blight of 15 percent of the U.S. corn crop in 1970 and repeated insect devastations of Southeast Asian rice crops over the last decade have underscored the continuing folly of agriculture's reliance on a narrow genetic base.[14]

The preservation of diverse crop strains is in theory one of the more manageable aspects of biological impoverishment. Huge numbers of seeds can, with proper care, be stored in seed banks and made available to breeders as the need arises. In response to the alarms sounded by Australian plant geneticist Otto H. Frankel and others, a start toward halting the erosion of the earth's crop genetic resources has in fact been made in recent years. An International Board for Plant Genetic Resources (IBPGR), headquartered in Rome and funded by governments and U.N. agencies, is promoting a variety of regional seed-collection, storage, and documentation schemes. Still, the global effort remains inadequate. Lamenting the continuing disappearance of primitive crop varieties and the deficiencies of current seed-collecting programs, J. T. Williams, executive secretary of the IBPGR, says that "for many crops we are facing a crisis situation."[15]

The presence of diverse germ plasm in seed banks does not necessarily mean that adequately diverse varieties will be planted in farm fields. Among other things the increased patenting of seed varieties and the increased marketing of seeds by multinational companies appear likely to hold down the variability of seeds in actual use.

The future of productive forestry, like that of agriculture, is undercut as the genetic resources vanish on which tree breeders and planters can draw. Unlike agriculture, most forestry still depends on trees growing in the wild. As expanding demands for lumber, firewood, and paper press against the shrinking forests, the areas planted to well-selected species will have to increase rapidly. Yet land clearing, timber harvesting, and the spread of homogeneous tree plantations are all contributing to the disappearance of tree varieties of potential value to foresters. As with food crops, the collection of the seeds of tree species and varieties is essential. Given the length of time it takes to grow a tree and test its qualities, however, seed collections cannot provide anywhere near the research benefits that living forests can.

In an age of plastics and moon shots, few people appreciate the extent to which humans remain dependent on natural products and processes. Although their harvest is seldom recorded in economic statistics, wild plants and animals are essential to the lives of many people in Africa, Asia, and Latin America; this consideration alone justifies serious concern about the degradation of natural areas. But in even the most technologically advanced societies, plants and animals serve a variety of crucial industrial, medical, and other purposes. Numerous industrial gums, oils, dyes, and pesticides come from natural sources, and many additional uses for wild species are constantly being discovered.

Some species of proven economic value are under acute pressure, but perhaps the greatest social costs of species destruction will stem from future opportunities unknowingly lost. Only a small fraction of the earth's plant species have been screened for medically useful ingredients. Nearly all the food humans eat comes from only about twenty crops, but thousands of plants are edible and some will undoubtedly prove useful in meeting human food needs.

No one can confidently say that products of comparable significance to rubber (which following its discovery in South America became one of the world's most important commodities) or quinine (derived from Amazonian cinchona bark, and for the 300 years up to World War I the only effective remedy for malaria) remain to be discovered. But no one can confidently say they do not, either.

Medical researchers' interest in plant-derived or plant-inspired drugs has intensified over the last few decades. The mid-twentieth-century discovery of a series of "wonder drugs" from natural sources (some of which had been used for centuries by traditional folk healers) has "sparked a revolution," says Harvard botanist Richard Evans Shultes. "It crystallized the realization that the plant kingdom represents a virtually untapped reservoir of new chemical compounds, many extraordinarily biodynamic, some providing novel bases on which the synthetic chemist may build even more interesting structures." According to one study, more than 40 percent of the modern pharmacopoeia originated in nature rather than in chemists' laboratories.[16]

Realizing that, as one observer put it, "the humblest bacterium can synthesize, in the course of its brief existence, more organic compounds than can all the world's chemists combined," scientists are stepping up their investigations both of ancient folk medicines and of hitherto unused plants with intriguing chemical properties. The plant kingdom is receiving special attention from cancer researchers, who hope to find tumor-inhibiting agents in nature that can provide prototypes for synthetic anticancer chemicals. Tens of thousands of plant species have been screened for this purpose and a number have shown promise, but the search has really only just begun—and it is being undermined by the extermination of unexamined species.

One plant-derived class of compounds of particular medical value is the alkaloids. These biologically active chemicals include narcotics such as morphine and nicotine; hallucinogens such as LSD and mescaline; poisons such as that in Socrates' hemlock; and a host of medicines used as painkillers, antimalarials, cardiac and respiratory stimulants, pupil dilators, muscle relaxants, local anesthetics, tumor inhibitors, and antileukemic drugs. Once extracted from plants, many alkaloids have served as models for synthesis by chemists; some, however, are still obtained solely from natural sources. A tropical periwinkle plant, for example, provides a chemical used to fight leukemia; the plant is becoming rare because its high commercial value has prompted overcollection. Curare, a muscle relaxant widely used by anesthesiologists in the operating room, is still distilled from vines in Upper Amazonian jungles by Indians, who have long poisoned their arrow tips and blowgun darts with the concentrated extract. Alkaloid-bearing plants appear twice as frequently in a given area of the tropics as in temperate zones, so the loss of potentially valuable compounds is inevitable as tropical habitat destruction spreads.[17]

Marine creatures, too, are now receiving special scrutiny. After examining chemicals from more than 2000 sea plants and animals, biologists recently discovered a powerful antiviral and anticancer agent in the bodies of sea squirts. Says Dr. William McClure of the University of California at Los Angeles: "I think there will be a lot more good drugs coming from sea creatures in the future. It's logical —there are thousands of living creatures which must protect themselves against disease and the environment much as any land creature does. So they are full of biologically active agents."[18]

Recent advances in biological technologies such as genetic engineering are opening up hitherto unimagined possible uses for the genetic material in plants and animals. The application of microbiology to agriculture, for example, may well bring revolutionary improvements in crops, with yields, pest and drought resistance, protein content, and fertilizer needs tailored for maximum benefit. The two great limiting factors in this field, writes Dr. Winston J. Brill in *Scientific American,* are the small financial commitment to basic research in agriculture and "the loss of irreplaceable genetic resources from the total gene pool." He adds: "The accelerated destruction of the gene pool is doubly ironic. It is caused primarily by the clearing of land in the tropical rain forest for farming. Moreover, it is happening at the dawn of an age in which such genetic wealth, until now a relatively inaccessible trust fund, is becoming a currency with high immediate value."[19]

The extermination of a unique, unstudied organism or ecosystem involves an irreversible loss to science. Basic knowledge about living systems and ecological interrelationships, of which a great deal remains to be gleaned, is no mere academic concern; it underlies our understanding of how the world works and what our place in it is. Lost scientific opportunities, like lost economic opportunities, are by nature incalculable. We cannot know how long our understanding of evolution would have been set back, for instance, had the unique fauna of the Galapagos Islands been destroyed before the young Charles Darwin visited the islands on H.M.S. *Beagle* in 1835.

Beyond particular economic or scientific losses caused by the destruction of particular species lies a more basic threat: the disruption of ecosystems on which human well-being depends. No matter how sophisticated modern technologies may seem, human livelihoods are ultimately grounded in biological processes, enmeshed in ecological webs so intricate that the consequences of destabilization cannot often be foreseen.

One common result of ecosystem damage, for example, is an increase in the prevalence of small, hardy, fast-reproducing plants and animals of the sorts usually considered weeds or pests. Cockroaches and crabgrass will thrive in a world of rampant natural degradation. In their book *Extinction,* Paul and Anne Ehrlich write: "It seems certain that over 95 percent of the organisms capable of competing seriously with humanity for food or of doing us harm by transmitting disease are now controlled gratis by other species in natural ecosystems."[20]

No one could claim that all existing species are ecologically essential to human culture. But scientists cannot yet say where the critical threshholds lie, at what level of species extermination the web of life will be seriously disrupted. Identifying and protecting those species whose ecological functions are especially important to society are crucial tasks facing both scientists and governments. In the meantime prudence dictates giving existing organisms as much benefit of the doubt as possible.

The array of economic, scientific, and ecological arguments for conservation together build a powerful utilitarian case for alarm over current trends. Still, many situations are bound to arise in which human activities threaten species of little if any provable material importance. Conservationists need not give up such struggles, but if their credibility is to be preserved, they must be frank about their motivations and realistic in their assessments of the probable costs of extinction. No one needs to apologize for being concerned about the unprecedented biological losses we face.

In the long run, philosophical considerations may prove as potent as economic considerations as a force for species preservation. Biologist David W. Ehrenfeld, noting that "practical" arguments on behalf of a species sometimes fail to hold water, calls for an explicitly *noneconomic* approach to the issue: "Long-standing existence in nature is deemed to carry with it the unimpeachable right to continued existence. Existence is the only criterion of value. . . ." Ehrenfeld dubs this ethical justification for preservation the "Noah Principle," after its first known executor. Faced with an endangered-species problem of unparalleled dimensions, Noah took into his ark "everything that creepeth upon the earth." No animal was excluded because it lacked economic value—although Noah apparently did not appreciate the biological importance of plants.[21]

Otto Frankel has urged the worldwide adoption of an "evolutionary ethic"—a determination to "try to keep evolutionary options open so far as we can" without forcing "undue deprivations on those least able to bear them."[22] The alternative to living by such a creed is destroying many of those habitats and species that do not seem immediately useful; humans would appoint themselves as the ultimate arbiters of evolution and determine its future course on the basis of short-term considerations and a great deal of ignorance.

The descent from the airy summit of evolutionary ethics to the everyday human landscape of the tropical world is a jarring one. Sad but true, to be rich in birds, insects, trees, and fungi is not necessarily to be rich in food and consumer goods. Far from it: many tropical countries are burgeoning with the destitute. Alongside biological wealth live hundreds of millions of people who get by on no more than a few hundred dollars a year, who watch three or four of every ten babies die by age five, whose opportunities for a better life are choked off by rigid structures of political and economic privilege, and whose numbers are likely to double over the next quarter-century. Their deprivation will corrode the foundations of even the best designed preservation structures.

For governments of countries at every income level, immediate economic gains hold greater political appeal than any long-term, unquantifiable values that might be sacrificed as a result of their pursuit. When nations are poor, the temptation to choose short-term material benefits regardless of future ecological costs often proves irresistible. Beseiged by restless legions of the jobless and the landless, governments are naturally inclined to transform remaining pristine areas into agricultural settlements—and in fact often lack the ability to prevent such transformations even when they want to.

Despite the countervailing pressures, a few tropical countries—including Colombia, Cameroon, Costa Rica, Peru, Thailand, and Venezuela—have already established sizable natural reserves. Brazil plans to set aside as much as 11 percent of its Amazonian area in national parks or biological reserves.[23] Leaders in wildlife-rich Kenya and Tanzania have also initiated farsighted conservation policies. Assisted by private international conservation organizations and U.N. agencies, other Third World countries have taken first steps toward the preservation of their biological heritages by designating limited areas for protection.

It would be wrong to assume that poor people, and leaders of poor countries, do not care about wildlife and natural areas. Most rural residents of the Third World are more openly dependent—spiritually and economically—on nature than are the most ardent Western conservationists. When questioned, villagers in places like the Sahel or India often express deep concern about the decline in birds, animals, and forests about them, and not only for material reasons. Increasingly, national leaders see local wildlife as part of a unique national endowment. In as impoverished and new a nation as Mozambique, the ruling party in 1977 declared: "Our country's plant and animal life is extremely rich, and this wealth is the heritage of the entire population. . . . The policy of the party and the activity of the state are directed toward ensuring ecological balance, protecting and developing animal and forest reserves, and guaranteeing the survival and restocking of the different plant and animal species."[24] The intergovernmental organization of drought-stricken states in the West African Sahelian zone (CILSS), when listing priorities for development projects and foreign aid, has consistently included wildlife conservation. Yet no donor country has been bold enough to back up financially the regional leadership's acknowledgment that nature preservation has a place alongside the improvement of agriculture and industry in the struggle to improve the Sahel's dismal quality of life.

Still, in the long run, and even in countries with excellent conservation laws and ample nature reserves, the protection of large natural areas will be feasible only if the deeper socioeconomic forces that imperil them are dispelled. Even the famous American conservationist Aldo Leopold once admitted that "wild things . . . had little human value until mechanization assured us of a good breakfast." As long as large numbers are denied the means to make a decent living, the nature reserves will be in jeopardy. Illustrating this point as he stressed his own commitment to the preservation of African wildlife, Chief Gatsha Buthelezi, political leader of the KwaZulu "homeland" in South Africa, has said, "More and more of my people . . . see my enthusiasm for the wilderness getting less and less relevant to the major issue of their survival."[25]

Current socioeconomic trends endanger the spectacular wildlife of the East African savannas—the zebras, elephants, and lions that symbolize Africa's biological richness to many. While great international attention has been accorded the threats posed by ivory and skin poachers, a far greater, more insidious threat to African wildlife is the continuous loss of habitat to human settlements. The large game parks of Kenya and Tanzania do not cover sufficient areas by themselves to prevent the depletion of many species, yet humans are closing in around their boundaries. And more ominous, "the national parks are surrounded by a hostile population which has little sympathy for the park system or for conservation efforts," writes Kenyan ecologist Walter J. Lusigi.[26]

Beyond handwringing about the population explosion, many conservationists distraught over Third World species losses have in the past paid little attention to the socioeconomic structures and human plights underlying current nature destruction. The integration of concerns for human progress with concerns for nature preservation in the World Conservation Strategy—jointly produced in 1980 by the IUCN, World Wildlife Fund, and UNEP—indicated a major advance in the thinking of the traditional conservation groups. And it has been well received in the Third World; many countries are now developing national conservation strategies.

Accustomed to perceiving species-protection battles in North America and Europe as battles against mindless development, many conservationists may find it hard to devote attention and energy to the Third World battle for rapid economic development—albeit development of an ecologically sustainable, socially sensitive sort. But unless national and international economic systems provide many more people with land or jobs, the dispossessed will naturally covet and molest "legally protected" lands, trees, and animals. Similarly, if rapid population growth in tropical countries is not soon slowed, human pressures to exploit virgin territories will overwhelm even the most stalwart conservation efforts. Success in bringing down birth rates, however, is also linked to more general social progress. Clearly, the struggle to save species and unique ecosystems cannot be divorced from the broader struggle to achieve a social order in which the basic needs of all are met.

Considering the geography of imperiled species and of human poverty, some level of further species extinctions is inevitable. Today's urgent tasks are the setting of global preservation priorities and the marshaling of resources to ensure that the more critical species and ecosystems are protected. Biologist Thomas Lovejoy observes that "limited resources of manpower and money are in fact forcing us into employing on a planetary scale an environmental form of triage, the practice evolved by Allied forces in World War I of sorting the wounded into three groups: those likely to die despite medical care, those so lightly injured as to probably recover without care, and the remainder on whom medical resources were concentrated."[27] Galling as it sounds to anyone steeped in the mysteries of biology, consciously writing off some life forms in order to save many more may be the best among unpleasant alternatives.

To recognize the inevitability of further human-caused extinctions is not to sanction their blithe acceptance. Given the extent of our scientific ignorance, practical as well as ethical reasons exist for a presumption of value for every species, however obscure. Richer countries can afford virtually to halt exterminations within their borders without imposing serious hardships on anyone.

It is in the Third World, where massive disruptions of wild habitats are unavoidable, that the most difficult choices must be made. Scientists and governments need somehow to identify the endangered areas and species of greatest importance to humanity and then do what is necessary to preserve them.

Although scientists have long recognized the need for a broader concern with habitat preservation, most protection efforts in the past have been pursued on a species-by-species basis. Considerable resources and worldwide public attention have been devoted exclusively to the salvation of, for example, the tiger or the bald eagle. In regions where few animals are in jeopardy, or with species of great esthetic, economic, or ecological importance, such an approach may still make sense. Campaigns centered on a well-known animal can generate sizable public donations and interest, and can lead to conservation policies that in turn help preserve the domains of countless species with less popular appeal.

Plants or animals endangered by hunters, collectors, or fur and ivory traders can only be protected on a species-by-species basis. Improper exploitation of wildlife within countries must, in the first place, be controlled by national governments. However, the Convention on International Trade in Endangered Species of Wild Fauna and Flora (CITES), which came into effect in 1975, is beginning to be a powerful tool against harmful hunting and collecting. The convention, now signed by about seventy countries, prohibits or regulates trade in live specimens and product derivatives of listed plants and animals. Unfortunately, many countries whose participation matters have not yet ratified the convention. The delinquent nations include prominent species importers such as Austria, Belgium, the Netherlands, Singapore, Spain, and Yemen, and species exporters such as Mexico, Sudan, and Thailand.[28] Also, enforcement of the convention, which can depend on the ability of customs officers to identify individual wildlife species, is generally weak.

While a special conservation focus on important individual species should continue, the inadequacy of that approach must be recognized. Worldwide, the number of jeopardized species is simply too great for the standard protection methods to be applied effectively. The major threat to most species today—the destruction of habitats supporting large numbers of interdependent species—cannot be analyzed or halted using a species-by-species approach. The overriding conservation need of the next few decades is the protection of a representative cross section of the world's ecosystems.

A start toward the creation of the needed ecological protectorates has been made under U.N. auspices. As of late 1981, 210 areas in fifty-five countries had been recognized by UNESCO as part of its global network of Biosphere Reserves. These areas, which are managed by individual countries, are intended to include a representative array of the world's biotic communities, including both untouched and modified zones. The reserves will help protect biological diversity while providing scientists with opportunities for basic research and comparisons of environmental trends among regions. The Biosphere Reserves system is being developed in conjunction with a broader global program of applied ecological research under the Man and Biosphere Program.

While an encouraging development, the Biosphere Reserve system is incomplete. Only about half the world's "biogeographical provinces," or ecosystem types, are included so far, and the quality of reserve management varies widely. The coverage of arid lands, lowland tropical forests, coastal zones and wetlands, marine areas and islands, and grasslands is especially inadequate.[29] Hamstrung by a lack of resources, the UNESCO coordinating unit (only two professionals working half-time on Biosphere Reserves) has had only a few hundred thousand dollars to spend on the program. More international funds are critically needed to help developing countries select and manage appropriate reserves. Funds are also essential to support experiments on ways to maximize direct human benefits from reserves and surrounding buffer zones. Ultimately, it is of course the responsibility of each country to set aside protected areas—and far larger areas than will be registered with UNESCO.

Scientific ignorance about the land area needed to save most or all the species of a given tropical ecosystem is a problem. In an ambitious and pioneering experiment, the World Wildlife Fund–U.S. and Brazil's National Institute for Amazonian Research are documenting the survival of species over time in protected Amazon forest enclaves of varied sizes. Essential information about the minimum critical size of ecosystem reserves will be produced.

Nature reserves cannot be successfully managed in isolation from local society. They must be planned within the context of broader regional development. In many cases reserves can be demarcated in areas that ought to be set aside anyway for other good reasons, such as watershed management, recreation, or the protection of indigenous tribal cultures.

To the extent compatible with biological goals, economic uses such as selective forestry, game cropping, or tourism can be allowed; where more pristine conditions are necessary, unused zones can be surrounded by exploited buffer areas. Ecologically sound uses of forests by native peoples can often be allowed to continue without sacrificing conservation goals. The use of nature reserves by nearby school systems can be encouraged, perhaps thereby helping schools to perpetuate rather than eradicate the extensive botanical and zoological knowledge of traditional tropical cultures.

Because so much responsibility for preserving the earth's genetic heritage falls to poorer countries, the possibility must be considered of distributing the costs of conservation fairly among nations. If the world's extant species and gene pools are the priceless heritage of all humanity, then people everywhere need to share the burdens of conservation according to their ability to do so. Not only do people in developed countries share the long-term benefits of tropical conservation, but they also, because of their penchant for consuming tropical agricultural and forest products, share responsibility for tropical ecosystem destruction.

Calling for the internationalization of conservation costs is of course easier than devising realistic measures for doing so. Means for assisting countries with the direct expenses of nature protection—research, training, land purchases, administration of parks and preserves—are not hard to identify. Already a variety of private organizations are helping countries with research and the development of conservation infrastructure. United Nations and bilateral aid agencies have occasionally supported wildlife and forest conservation projects. But biological diversity has not yet become a customary concern of major aid agencies.

Effective measures for offsetting the broader development potentials lost when large, usable areas are set aside are more difficult to imagine. International tourism can sometimes help parks pay their way, but its contribution is likely to be significant in only a few regions that enjoy spectacular scenery or wildlife. Usually, moreover, the economic benefits of tourism are captured by too few local people to compensate the majority for lost opportunities.

In the end the only workable answer lies in the wider arenas of economic progress and reform. If international aid and trade policies, and local social policies, can promote broad-based development without destroying the natural environment in the process, then the need for international conservation aid will gradually disappear. Equitable economic progress will provide alternative livelihoods for people who might otherwise endanger nature reserves. It will also allow people to take a farsighted view of the importance of biological diversity. Only a local public that cares—and that can afford to act on behalf of its concern—can save a nation's biological heritage.

III. Conditions for Progress

11 THE CONSERVATION OF HUMANITY

THIS BOOK, a survey of global environmental trends, yields good and bad news. On the positive side, public understanding of environmental imperatives has increased over the last decade, and needed new institutions have evolved. On the other hand, many of the social, economic, and technological forces that underly environmental difficulties have scarcely been checked.

Appreciation of the material and spiritual importance of a healthy natural environment has spread. Perhaps the most dramatic intellectual shifts are occurring in the Third World, where understanding of the ecological underpinnings of human life—largely lost in the postwar dreams of industrialization—is on the rise. The new interest in environmental quality complements recent shifts in thought among development theorists, many of whom now stress the need to address the basic needs of the poor directly rather than hope that the benefits of growth will trickle down to them. Improving the lot of the underclass and protecting environmental quality can be mutually supportive goals.

Both internationally and within nations, the new appreciation of our bonds with nature has spawned new institutions and policies— new U.N. and governmental agencies, new laws, altered aid programs, new international treaties. Yet for the most part responses remain inadequate to the needs.

In the words of the U.N.'s *World Environment 1972–1982:* "The ratio of words to action is weighted too heavily towards the former. And despite the evidence that people's perception of environmental problems has improved, it is less clear that many groups have adapted their lifestyles in response."

Many "environmental" trends are overt manifestations of other deeper currents. Hence specific environmental-control measures, while crucial, do not guarantee that degradation will be halted. The benefits of installing antipollution devices on cars can easily be lost as auto use soars; a protected forest will not remain inviolate if nearby people have no jobs or fuel.

More than anything else, the stone wall of inopportunity facing the poorest billion or so people ensures the continuing degradation of natural resources in large parts of the world. The slowed economic growth of the 1980s means that any potential downward trickle of benefits has slowed to a drip. Even the sometimes dazzling growth of the last quarter-century left a huge underclass with little chance to better their lives. An unknown but significant number are worse off than before. In the absence of wider economic and social reforms, efforts to protect wildlife and forests, to manage watersheds and arid lands, to clean up urban shantytowns and waterways, will never be fully successful.

Nor are birth rates apt to fall quickly among people with so little reason to have hope for the future. Despite the dramatic slowdowns in population growth in developed countries, China, and a few other places, the world demographic outlook remains menacing. Not only are human numbers projected to more than double in little over a century, but the increases will also be concentrated in some of the poorest regions.

What will happen to the African landscape if the population there quadruples? What will conditions become in Latin American cities, already reeling from immigration, if the continent's numbers triple? Where will the extra 3.5 billion people projected for Asia—an increase equal to the entire world population of the late 1960s—find food, fuel, and shelter? The earth undoubtedly possesses the technical potential to sustain the projected increases. But realizing it will require improbable degrees of social organization and global cooperation, all the more so if climatic patterns start changing. The natural environment, and thus the quality of human life, will suffer grievously as societies struggle to cope with multiplying numbers.

Energy choices have major implications for the environment. The seemingly unlimited availability of low-cost oil and gas up to the early

1970s fueled the automobile explosion, but also held down coal burning. Urban air benefited greatly, and acid rain did not spread as rapidly as it might have. Renewed reliance on coal by utilities and factories seems likely to undo recent gains against air pollution and to acidify the rain over wider areas. Major commitments to coal and coal-based synthetic fuels probably also amount to acceptance of human-caused climate changes in the middle of the coming century —changes which are bound to cause hardship for the underclass at least. Another major energy alternative, nuclear power, carries its own unresolved problems of safety, waste disposal, and weapons proliferation.

In parts of the Third World soaring oil prices have exacerbated the scarcity of fuelwood. Kerosene, traditionally the main wood substitute, has been pulled farther out of reach of the poor. Villagers in a few places have actually been forced backward in history as the high price or unavailability of kerosene requires them to switch back to wood for cooking their meals and warming their homes. Whether tree-planting programs and alternative energy sources can be provided quickly enough to avoid massive landscape damage and social hardship remains to be seen.

The increased use of renewable energy sources should reduce energy-related environmental damage. Governments have not yet granted renewables the same research support and subsidies they give other energy forms, especially nuclear power, thereby missing a chance to hasten their availability. Still, biomass production and large-scale hydropower development can cause significant damage to land and people if not properly managed. Increasing the efficiency of energy use remains the most environmentally benign response to the energy challenge, one not yet fully exploited anywhere.

In the absence of more stringent pollution-control regulations, and of stronger efforts to recycle materials and conserve resources, economic growth itself will inevitably mean increased degradation. The Organization for Economic Cooperation and Development (OECD) recently warned that existing environmental controls in the developed countries would be inadequate to prevent increases in pollution even with the slower than expected economic growth of the early 1980s: "Total pollution emissions in a number of sectors, assuming present quality standards and technology, could rise 30 percent or more between 1978 and 1985. . . . If environmental measures were to be relaxed, deterioration would be greater. In the face of growth, even slow growth, only strengthened measures will maintain and gradually improve environmental quality."[1]

Unfortunately, a weakening of environmental regulations is now being urged by some politicians and businessmen as a response to economic difficulties. A broader public understanding of the economics of environmental protection, the society-wide costs and benefits involved, is essential if good ecology is to be good politics.

Most of the world's critical environmental problems are rooted in local or national conditions, and must be confronted primarily at these levels. Still, global environmental policies and institutions are also necessary. International measures are not only needed to address the truly global threats, but also to aid countries in confronting internal problems of worldwide concern.

Events in the decade since the Stockholm Conference have not diminished the case for having an international environmental agency. In an era when human modifications of the biosphere can occur on nature's own scale, the monitoring of environmental trends and assessment of their significance is vital to the security of every country. With potential transnational threats to the climate, the oceans, and human health provoking international controversy, a global arbiter able to coax scientific consensus on the facts is essential —and then someone needs to keep reminding governments about long-term or subtle environmental threats they may prefer to ignore. An international actor can often help spur cooperative actions to meet common threats, protect sources, and encourage the development of needed international law agreements.

An agency is needed to facilitate the flow among countries of information and lessons of experience on environmental issues. Global public education about natural resource problems and their meaning for society must be promoted. Developing countries, which face unprecedented and dangerous pressures on natural resources, need assistance in planning for growth that is ecologically sustainable and in coping with the hazards of modern technologies. Finally, some mechanism is needed to coordinate actions affecting environmental trends of the many agencies of the U.N. system as a whole.

The United Nations Environment Programme (UNEP), the main institutional creation of the Stockholm Conference, has, with varying degrees of effectiveness, undertaken activities in each of these areas. In some, progress has been achieved:

- The Regional Seas program has brought together countries in several regions to confront shared problems of pollution and coastal degradation that had hitherto been beyond the reach of international negotiations.

- The UNEP-sponsored Coordinating Committee on the Ozone Layer has helped build international consensus on the dimensions of the threat to the stratospheric ozone layer and its implications. Bringing together representatives of private industry, governments, and international agencies, the committee has set an excellent precedent for the analysis of other global threats.

- Through the Global Environmental Monitoring System (GEMS), UNEP has promoted development of needed monitoring programs by other U.N. agencies and scientific organizations. Drawing the results together into meaningful assessments has proceeded more slowly.

- The International Register of Potentially Toxic Chemicals maintains a data bank on chemicals on which governments can draw, and endeavors to spread information about newly discovered hazards and governments' regulatory decisions.

- In cooperation with the International Institute for Environment and Development, UNEP has extracted from multilateral development banks promises to adopt new environmental-impact-study procedures when making loans in the Third World, although in many cases these have not yet become working procedures.

- As the major initial funder, UNEP shares responsibility for the increasingly successful implementation of the 1973 Convention on International Trade in Endangered Species of Fauna and Flora (CITES).

- A computerized network for the transfer of environmental information (INFOTERRA) has been set up, with eighty countries participating, although this service has been underused.

- UNEP has provided funds to numerous private groups around the world for pioneering analytical work on the relationship between environment and development, for public education, and for the improvement of media coverage of environmental topics.

If programs such as these do not add up to a remade world, they nonetheless indicate that some action is under way. And several other U.N. agencies with larger budgets and more operational mandates are addressing critical global environmental issues within their sectors. Still, the scale and momentum of many environmental threats—such as natural resource degradation in the Third World, toxic chemical pollution, and possible atmospheric disruptions—far outweigh the hesitant efforts of the international community at cooperative research and solutions.

Obviously the world is not ready to hand over significant power to a global environmental authority, and UNEP's successes or failures should not be judged against such a standard. But a rising number of less ambitious programs could accumulate into a significant global response.

Sound information about environmental trends, combined with public concern and pressures, could expand the limits of political possibility. Governments are—for understandable if not always admirable reasons—unwilling to take costly measures on the basis of scanty data and disputed predictions. Hence the importance of pushing ahead with development of the Global Environmental Monitoring System, of accelerating the analysis of particular threats, and of communicating the results more widely.

The evolving GEMS program has established a high scientific standard and clarified the complex choices involved in the documentation of environmental trends. But, in part because of the inherent constraints, "the world community has not yet achieved one of the major goals of the Stockholm Conference—the compilation, through a global program of monitoring, research and evaluation, of an authoritative picture of the state of the world environment," to quote UNEP's own 1982 report on environmental trends. That report suggests adding a new element in future years: "even an imperfect series of environmental statistics, drawing together what we have (and, through its manifest inadequacies, providing a stimulus to better observation) would be an improvement on the present situation."

One can imagine a more aggressive UNEP's sponsoring evaluations of a host of critical problems, working to build consensus on their dimensions and policy implementations. The process of research and analysis could be linked more closely to the development of global action plans, of new treaties or concepts in international law, of codes of conduct on responsible governmental and corporate policies, and the like.

Both in terms of subjects to cover and functions to perform, UNEP has an impossibly full platter, particularly since it has less than $30 million a year to spend. The organization's failure to define a manageable set of priorities is a commonly voiced criticism. Yet imposing realistic limits is not easy. In terms of subject matter the Third World has from the beginning insisted that major emphasis be placed on issues of environmentally sound development such as human settlements and desertification. The developed countries have accepted this emphasis but have also insisted, quite properly, that issues of global concern such as monitoring, pollution, and atmospheric threats be addressed as well.

No simple blueprint for paring down UNEP makes sense. As the main coordinator and promoter of environmental action for the United Nations, UNEP must keep its fingers in many pies. The choice of emphases must be guided as much by where the pragmatic opportunities to make a difference lie as by abstract consideration of roles. UNEP's leaders must display sharp political judgment, remaining alert for half-open doors through which UNEP can push even as it continues to highlight the full range of environmental problems.

International needs are far broader than anything the U.N. system can undertake. Many treaties or policy commitments required for the management of transboundary problems (pollution of shared rivers, cross-border pollution, acid rain) can best be pursued by countries bilaterally or regionally.

Whatever determines the economic prospects of the absolute poor will have a greater impact on the future stability of the biosphere than any specific environmental programs will. Those who care about the environment must also care about reforming national and international economic orders to give the underclass a better deal.

The poorer countries desperately need financial and technical aid to help them confront the interlocking cycles of poverty, resource degradation, and rapid population growth. Enormous sums are required if clean water is to be provided to a higher proportion of humanity, if woodlots are to be planted on the necessary scale, if small-farm food production is to be multiplied as it must, and if family planning services are to be made available to all now lacking access. Third World countries also need help to develop the technical capacity to regulate pollution, the handling of toxic chemicals, and occupational safety.

Virtually all Third World countries are now undergoing wrenching technological and social transformations that pose huge ecological dangers. With so many people subsisting on the bare margins of life, these countries cannot afford to repeat all the ecological errors of the developed countries, nor to provoke the severe ecological backlashes that are peculiar to tropical conditions. Building institutions for environmental analysis and regulation, and for improved natural resource management, is no less important in poor than in rich countries.

Books like this one invariably are said to be long on problems and short on solutions. Such charges often reflect a misunderstanding of the nature of the responses called for by the troubled relationship between human society and nature. In a general way we can describe institutions that are needed and approaches that have succeeded or failed somewhere. But overgeneralization about answers, especially on a worldwide basis, is not only futile; it can also be counterproductive, diverting attention from the true needs, which are specific to a place and a time.

The writer Shirley Hazzard made the point well in her 1973 book on the United Nations, *Defeat of an Ideal:*

Nothing could be more indicative of our modern predicament than the simplistic call for "solutions"—a cry that derives more from advertising slogans and political campaigning than from an understanding of human affairs, and which is put forward to repel complexities, as if the contemplation of a difficulty played no part in its resolution. Grave and intricate maladies that have accreted over generations will not be disposed of in a set of glib recommendations, or in the reiteration of exhausted abstractions. It is in fact far easier to propose the eternal "concrete measures" than to reckon with the fluidity of time and events in which these must be usefully employed.[2]

An easing of environmental, resource, and development challenges depends not on one-time solutions, but rather on the initiation of appropriate processes of change. First must come the perception that a problem exists, and then an understanding of its relation to other aspects of life and to social goals.

Of course, broad approaches of proven value can usefully be identified and duplicated. To give one example, tree-planting programs that involve public participation in their planning and in sharing their benefits have worked well in such politically different places as China and South Korea, while programs imposed from above have usually failed. These lessons can be drawn upon by those undertaking forestry anywhere. But success stories rarely provide replicable models. Rather, they suggest attitudes and approaches that can be starting points for successful action attuned to local conditions.

Public pressures and in some cases public participation in planning have been driving forces behind most of the environmental gains of the last two decades. Especially in developed countries, nongovernmental organizations have pushed governments to curb pollution and preserve natural areas. It was the exceptional interest displayed by private groups that made the Stockholm Conference such an exciting and significant meeting.

More than is the case with many matters of public policy, meeting environmental threats benefits from public organization and involvement. Sound environmental policies usually require acceptance of a longer term perspective than either political leaders or businessmen are accustomed to. Also, the signals of an unregulated marketplace often ignore important ecological consequences of business activity. Citizen action—to identify and publicize issues, to press for responsible government policies, and to work directly on environmental improvements—can help offset the myopic tendencies of government and industry.

Over the last decade nongovernmental organizations, ranging from peasant groups literally fighting for their livelihoods to city-based nature clubs, have increased in number and importance in parts of the Third World. Unfortunately such groups often face governmental indifference or hostility. Sometimes, of course, this is the case in Western countries too. But the concerns and energies of ordinary people are essential resources in the struggle to create a more livable environment.

Technological change, the seeming source of many environmental problems, is sometimes also touted as the key to their solution. Potential research breakthroughs that could make a difference can certainly be identified. Cheaper solar power, cheaper and more effective ways to remove poisons from smokestacks and tailpipes, safer and more reliable contraceptives, hardier and faster growing trees—the list could go on. New biotechnologies, applying genetic engineering techniques to agriculture and forestry, seem to hold exceptional promise.

Still, few serious challenges will be resolved through technological progress alone. Appropriate social organization is usually the primary need. Higher yielding crops can contribute to the battle against hunger but will not automatically mean more food for the hungry; reforms in the distribution of assets, services, or employment are essential for that. Better contraceptives are badly needed. Yet many among the underclass will continue to have little interest in family planning unless their economic prospects improve. The simple, low-cost method for treating the effects of severe diarrhea that was recently developed will save many lives. But unless health-care systems are reorganized, many stricken rural children will not receive even this treatment. And only access to clean water, together with improved sanitary habits, will cut the awesome incidence of diarrhea and other infectious diseases among the children of the underclass.

In this context, global overspending on weapons research and arms appears doubly tragic. Now surpassing $500 billion a year, military spending soaks up resources badly needed in the fight for a more sustainable world order. Vital research frontiers go unexplored while military research budgets soar. And the sheer diversion of capital, talent, and official energy to military matters hampers the ability of societies to undertake the investments and organizational reforms essential to their future ecological security.

The failure of the superpowers to curb a weapons spiral that can benefit neither side sets the grim global tone on this subject. But developing countries too increasingly buy arms at levels far beyond identifiable security requirements, often with the encouragement of developed-country arms salesmen. Among the countries of Sub-Saharan Africa the proportion of total imports devoted to arms rose from 1.3 percent in 1969 to 9.3 percent in 1978, depleting already meagre funds available for productive investments.[3] One can acknowledge legitimate security concerns and still suggest that something is out of whack when the world is incapable of raising $80 million a day to provide clean water to all people, but lays out $1.4 billion a day on weapons.

Over time our understanding is deepening both of the influence human culture has on the biosphere, and of the influence the biosphere has on human culture. The troubled points in this inescapable relationship we have come to call environmental problems.

The biosphere seldom presents human society with imperatives; rather we face choices about what sort of world we want to live in. Responses to environmental threats can be formulated only in relation to broader human goals. The issue is not whether societies can adapt to further environmental degradation, but what the price of doing so will be.

Civilization could undoubtedly survive the extinction of elephants and orchids, but the world would be spiritually as well as economically poorer. Civilization has for centuries accommodated a vast underclass living in extreme poverty and amid extreme environmental degradation. That some 40,000 infants and small children die each day as a result leads many people to work for reform of the global social order.

Environmental choices must be guided by a vision of a desirable human society and of the quality of the natural environment needed to support that vision. In the struggle to create a more decent, a more human world, the environmental factor is gradually receiving its due respect. That may be the real legacy of Stockholm.

NOTES

Chapter 2. The Global Underclass

1. Quote from McNamara's Address to the World Bank Board of Governors, Nairobi, Kenya, Sept. 24, 1973; World Bank, *World Development Report, 1980* (Washington, D.C., Aug. 1980).
2. World Bank, *1980 World Bank Atlas;* Robert S. McNamara, Address to the World Bank Board of Governors, Washington, D.C., Sept. 30, 1980.
3. World Bank, *The Assault on World Poverty* (Baltimore: Johns Hopkins University Press, 1975), p. v.
4. Food and Agriculture Organization (FAO), *Agriculture: Toward 2000* (Rome, July 1979).
5. Ibid.
6. Shlomo Reutlinger and Harold Alderman, "The Prevalence of Calorie Deficient Diets in Developing Countries," World Bank Staff Working Paper No. 374, Washington, D.C., March 1980.
7. The Gambia study and the Chambers quote are both cited in Anil Agarwal et al., *Water, Sanitation, Health—for All?* (London: Earthscan, 1981). See also Robert Chambers et al., "Seasonal Dimensions to Rural Poverty: Analysis and Practical Implications," Institute of Development Studies, University of Sussex, Brighton, England, Feb. 1979.
8. James P. Grant, "The State of the World's Children 1980," UNICEF, New York, 1980; Derrick B. Jellife, "Tropical Problems in Nutrition," *Annals of Internal Medicine* 79 (1973): 701.
9. Grant, "State of the World's Children."
10. Reutlinger and Adelman, "Prevalence of Calorie Deficient Diets."
11. Production trends in U.S. Department of Agriculture, *Global Food Assessment, 1980* (Washington, D.C., July 1980).
12. FAO, Press Release, Rome, July 2, 1981.
13. International Food Policy Research Institute, *Food Needs of Developing Countries: Projections of Production and Consumption to 1990* (Washington, D.C.: IFPRI, Dec. 1977).
14. Reported in the Brandt Commission Report, *North-South: A Program for Survival* (Cambridge, Mass.: MIT Press, 1980).

15. Much of the analysis in this section is drawn from Erik Eckholm, *The Dispossessed of the Earth: Land Reform and Sustainable Development* (Washington, D.C.: Worldwatch Institute, June 1979).

16. Milton J. Esman, *Landlessness and Near-Landlessness in Developing Countries* (Ithaca, N.Y.: Cornell University Center for International Studies, 1978), p. 4.

17. International Labour Office, *Poverty and Landlessness in Rural Asia* (Geneva, 1977).

18. FAO, *Review and Analysis of Agrarian Reform and Rural Development in the Developing Countries Since the Mid-1960s* (Rome, 1979); Asian Development Bank, *Asian Agricultural Survey 1976* (Manila, April 1977).

19. FAO, *Review and Analysis of Agrarian Reform;* World Bank, "Land Reform: Sector Policy Paper," Washington, D.C., May 1975; FAO, "Agrarian Reform and Rural Development in the Region with Reference to the World Conference on Agrarian Reform and Rural Development," 15th FAO Regional Conference for Latin America, Montevideo, Uruguay, Aug. 15–19, 1978; Solon L. Barraclough and Arthur L. Domike, "Agrarian Structure in Seven Latin American Countries," *Land Economics,* Nov. 1966.

20. John M. Cohen, "Land Tenure and Rural Development in Africa," in Robert H. Bates and Michael F. Lofchie, eds., *Agricultural Development in Africa* (New York: Praeger, 1980). See also International Labour Office, *Employment, Incomes and Equality: A Strategy for Increasing Productive Employment in Kenya* (Geneva, 1972).

21. Peter Dorner, *Land Reform and Economic Development* (Baltimore: Penguin Books, 1972); Ram Dayal and Charles Elliott, *Land Tenure, Land Concentration, and Agricultural Output* (Geneva: U.N. Research Institute for Social Development, 1966); Schlomo Eckstein et al., "Land Reform in Latin America: Bolivia, Chile, Mexico, Peru and Venezuela," World Bank Staff Working Paper No. 275, Washington, D.C., April 1978.

22. International Labour Office, *Employment, Incomes and Equality;* Keith Griffin, *The Green Revolution: An Economic Analysis* (Geneva: U.N. Research Institute for Social Development, 1972); Dorner, *Land Reform and Economic Development.*

23. Sylvia Blitzer, Jorge E. Hardoy, and David Satterthwaite, "Habitat—Five Years After," Earthscan Press Briefing Document No. 26, London, June 1981.

24. Ibid.

25. In *Shelter: Need and Response* (Chichester, England: John Wiley and Sons, 1981), Jorge E. Hardoy and David Satterthwaite review the housing, land, and settlement experience of seventeen Third World nations. Self-help housing is discussed in Bruce Stokes, *Helping Ourselves* (New York: W. W. Norton, 1981).

26. Michael P. Todaro with Jerry Stilkind, *City Bias and Rural Neglect: The Dilemma of Urban Development* (New York: Population Council, 1981); Kathleen Newland, *City Limits: Emerging Constraints on Urban Growth* (Washington, D.C.: Worldwatch Institute, Aug. 1980).

27. Survival International is a London-based organization that supports tribal peoples. Its publications, and those of two American organizations—Cultural Survival and

the Anthropology Research Center—are excellent resources on this topic, and provide ample backing for the strong statements in this section.

28. Catherine Caufield, "The Last of the Nambiquara," *New Scientist,* April 7, 1980.
29. From summary of talk given at the World Bank, Feb. 1, 1980.
30. Described in World Bank, Office of Environmental Affairs, *Economic Development and Tribal Peoples: Human Ecologic Considerations* (Washington, D.C., July 1981), an excellent review of the plight of tribal peoples and the related policies desirable for lending agencies.

Chapter 3. The Population Factor

1. Rafael M. Salas, "The State of World Population 1981," New York, U.N. Fund for Population Activities, 1981.
2. Africa's demographic prospects are explored in *People* 8, no. 1 (1981). Most figures in the preceding paragraphs on regional and national growth are from Population Reference Bureau, "1981 World Population Data Sheet," Washington, D.C., 1981.
3. Population Reference Bureau, "1981 World Population Data Sheet."
4. Health aspects of birth control are reviewed in Erik P. Eckholm, *The Picture of Health* (New York: W. W. Norton, 1977), and Kathleen Newland, *The Sisterhood of Man* (New York: W. W. Norton, 1979).
5. Chen Muhua, "Birth Planning in China," *International Family Planning Perspectives,* Sept. 1979.
6. W. Parker Mauldin and Bernard Berelson, "Conditions of Fertility Decline in Developing Countries, 1965–75," *Studies in Family Planning,* May 1978.
7. Frank L. Mott and Susan H. Mott, "Kenya's Record Population Growth: A Dilemma of Development," *Population Bulletin,* Oct. 1980; Ronald Freedman, "Theories of Fertility Decline: A Reappraisal," in Philip M. Hauser, ed., *World Population and Development* (Syracuse, N.Y.: Syracuse University Press, 1979).
8. U.N. Population Division, "Selected Factors Affecting Fertility and Fertility Preferences in Developing Countries: Evidence from the First Fifteen WFS Country Reports," presented to World Fertility Survey Conference, London, July 1980.
9. Charles F. Westoff, "The Unmet Needs for Birth Control in Five Asian Countries," *Family Planning Perspectives,* May/June 1978.
10. Ibid.
11. International Planned Parenthood Federation, "IPPF Survey of Unmet Needs in Family Planning, 1971–76," London, Dec. 1977. The 1980 estimate of women at risk and unprotected by contraception was supplied to the author by the IPPF, June 23, 1981.
12. Indonesian, Korean, and other programs are described in Bruce Stokes, *Helping Ourselves* (New York: W. W. Norton, 1981).
13. Global assistance figures supplied by U.S. Department of State.
14. Brandt Commission Report, *North-South: A Program for Survival* (Cambridge, Mass.: MIT Press, 1980).

15. R. O. Greep et al., *Reproduction and Human Welfare: A Challenge to Research* (Cambridge, Mass.: MIT Press, 1976); Linda Atkinson et al., "Prospects for Improved Contraception," *International Family Planning Perspectives,* June 1980.
16. Chen Muhua, "Birth Planning in China"; Pi-chao Chen, "Three in Ten Chinese Couples with One Child Apply for Certificates Pledging They Will Have No More," *International Family Planning Perspectives,* June 1980; "Birth Planning Propaganda, Incentives and Peer Pressure," *Draper Fund Report,* March 1980; Barry Kramer, "China, in Effort to Slow Population Growth, Is Likely to Impose Harsh Economic Punishment," *Wall Street Journal,* Oct. 3, 1979.

Chapter 4. Health and the Human Environment

1. Dobzhansky quote in René Dubos, *Man Adapting* (New Haven, Conn.: Yale University Press, 1965). See also René Dubos, *Mirage of Health* (New York: Harper and Row, 1959); and Erik P. Eckholm, *The Picture of Health* (New York: W. W. Norton, 1977).
2. Life expectancy and infant mortality figures are from the Population Reference Bureau, "1981 World Population Data Sheet," Washington, D.C., 1981.
3. World Health Organization (WHO), *Sixth Report on the World Health Situation* (Geneva, 1980).
4. Alan Berg, *The Nutrition Factor* (Washington, D.C.: Brookings Institution, 1973); Anil Agarwal et al., *Water, Sanitation, Health—for All?* (London: Earthscan, 1981).
5. WHO, *Sixth Report.*
6. Ibid.
7. Ruth R. Puffer and Carlos W. Serrano, *Patterns of Mortality in Childhood* (Washington, D.C.: Pan American Health Organization, 1973).
8. WHO, *Sixth Report.*
9. Nevin S. Scrimshaw, Carl E. Taylor, and John E. Gordon, *Interactions of Nutrition and Infection* (Geneva: World Health Organization, 1968).
10. Guatemala study reported in Gerald T. Keusch, "Malnutrition and Infection: Deadly Allies," *Natural History,* Nov. 1975. On worms, see Agarwal et al., *Water, Sanitation, Health—for All?*
11. Agarwal et al., *Water, Sanitation, Health—for All?"* provides an excellent summary of available data on water supply and sanitation programs, and of the U.N. Decade.
12. WHO, *Sixth Report.*
13. Ibid.; United Nations Environment Programme, "The State of the Environment, 1978," Nairobi, Kenya, 1978.
14. For further references on schistosomiasis, see Eckholm, *The Picture of Health.*
15. World Bank, "Health Problems and Policies in the Developing Countries," Staff Working Paper No. 412, Washington, D.C., Aug. 1980.
16. American Heart Association, "Heart Facts," New York, 1973.
17. WHO, *Sixth Report.*

18. Michael P. Stern, "The Recent Decline in Ischemic Heart Disease Mortality," *Annals of Internal Medicine,* Oct. 1979; Weldin J. Walker, "Changing United States Life-style and Declining Vascular Mortality: Cause or Coincidence?" *New England Journal of Medicine,* July 21, 1979.

19. U.S. Congress, Office of Technology Assessment, *Assessment of Technologies for Determining Cancer Risks from the Environment* (Washington, D.C.: U.S. Government Printing Office, June 1981), reviews recent literature on the various environmental causes of cancer. See also Eckholm, *The Picture of Health,* for further international references.

20. James F. Fries, "Aging, Natural Death, and the Compression of Morbidity," *New England Journal of Medicine,* July 17, 1980.

Chapter 5. Oceanic Affairs

1. "Marine Fisheries in the New Era of National Jurisdiction," in Food and Agriculture Organization (FAO), *The State of Food and Agriculture,* forthcoming.

2. FAO, "Review of the State of World Fishery Resources," March 1981, like earlier annual reports, reviews the status of fish stocks in each region.

3. The collapse of the anchovy fishery is discussed in John Gulland, "The Harvest of the Sea," in William W. Murdoch, ed., *Resources, Pollution and Society,* 2nd ed. (Sunderland, Mass.: Sinauer Associates, 1975).

4. FAO, *Agriculture: Toward 2000* (Rome, July 1979).

5. For an excellent review of the dynamics of krill and their treatment in the Antarctic Convention, see Barbara Mitchell and Richard Sandbrook, *The Management of the Southern Ocean* (London: International Institute for Environment and Development, 1980).

6. FAO, "Marine Fisheries in the New Era of National Jurisdiction."

7. FAO, "Fisheries Development in the 1980s," Rome, 1981.

8. The history of whaling and efforts to control it are reviewed in R. Michael M'Gonigle, "The 'Economizing' of Ecology: Why Big, Rare Whales Still Die," *Ecology Law Quarterly* 9, no. 119 (1980). This lengthy article also presents an eloquent antiwhaling argument.

9. FAO/UNEP, "Draft Global Plan of Action for the Conservation, Management and Utilization of Marine Mammals," Rome, 1980.

10. Personal communication, John Beddington and Justin Cooke, Aug. 28, 1981.

11. See, for example, FAO, "Review of the State of World Fishery Resources."

12. Personal communication, Dr. Kenneth Sherman, National Oceanic and Atmospheric Administration, Narragansett Laboratory, Sept. 11, 1981.

13. "The Baltic—A Regional Sea Marine Pollution Case Study," *Marine Pollution Bulletin,* June 1981.

14. Council on Environmental Quality (CEQ), *Environmental Quality, 1980* (Washington, D.C., Dec. 1980); FAO, *Assessment of the Effects of Pollution on Fisheries and Aquaculture in Japan* (Rome, Oct. 1976); FAO, *Pollution: An International Problem for Fisheries* (Rome, 1971).

15. "Round the World News," *Marine Pollution Bulletin,* issues of March, May, and Aug. 1979.
16. Glenn Frankel, "Va. Officials Say Kepone Up in Fish," *Washington Post,* Aug. 15, 1981.
17. FAO, *Assessment of the Effects of Pollution.*
18. "Mercury Accumulations in Bombay," *Marine Pollution Bulletin,* Sept. 1979.
19. John Madeley, "Oil Spills: Who Pays?" Earthscan, London, Nov. 1980.
20. CEQ, *Environmental Quality, 1979* (Washington, D.C., Dec. 1979); FAO, *Assessment of the Effects of Pollution;* Okada, Osama, et al., "Fisheries in Asia—People, Problems, and Recommendation," Pacific Asian Resource Center, Tokyo, 1980.
21. IUCN, "First Report on the Global Status of Mangrove Ecosystems," Oct. 1981; Samuel C. Snedaker, "Mangroves: Their Value and Protection," *Nature and Resources,* July-Sept. 1978.
22. Michael Goulding, *The Fishes and the Forest* (Berkeley: University of California Press, 1981).
23. FAO, "Review of the State of World Fishery Resources."
24. Ibid.
25. FAO, *Economic Impact of the Effects of Pollution on the Coastal Fisheries of the Atlantic and Gulf of Mexico Regions of the United States of America* (Rome, Aug. 1977); FAO, *Economic Aspects of Pollution on the Marine and Anadromous Fisheries of the Western United States of America* (Rome, Oct. 1976); U.S. Department of Commerce, *Water Quality and Molluscan Shellfish: An Overview of the Problems and the Nature of Appropriate Federal Laws* (Washington, D.C., March 1977).
26. FAO, *Assessment of the Effects of Pollution.*
27. Consumers' Association of Penang, *Pollution: Kuala Juru's Battle for Survival* (Pulau Pinang, Malaysia, Dec. 1976).
28. Jeremy Bugler, "The Polluted Seas," Earthscan Press Briefing Document No. 7, London, Jan. 1978, describes the Regional Seas Program.
29. "Cleaning Up the Med," *Newsweek,* Sept. 3, 1979.
30. Peter Thacher, "A Master Plan for the Watery Planet," *Uniterra,* Jan./Feb. 1981.

Chapter 6. Pollution: Old and New Dimensions

1. Evidence on the health effects of air pollution is reviewed in Erik P. Eckholm, *The Picture of Health* (New York: W. W. Norton, 1977).
2. OECD, *The State of the Environment in OECD Member Countries* (Paris, 1979). The following uncited data on pollution trends are from this source.
3. See, for example, Lester B. Lave and Gilbert S. Omenn, "Clearing the Air: Reforming the Clean Air Act," Staff Paper, Brookings Institution, Washington, D.C., 1981.
4. EPA, "Trends in the Quality of the Nation's Air—A Report to the People," Washington, D.C., Oct. 1980.
5. G. Akland et al., "Air Quality Surveillance: Trends in Selected Urban Areas," *WHO Chronicle,* April 1980.

6. Warren Hoge, "New Menace in Brazil's 'Valley of Death' Strikes at Unborn," *New York Times,* Sept. 23, 1980.
7. OECD, *State of the Environment.*
8. *World Environment Report,* Jan. 1, 1980, and Feb. 2, 1981; Anil Agarwal et al., *Water, Sanitation, Health—for All?* (London: Earthscan, 1981).
9. OECD, *Environment Policies for the 1980s* (Paris, 1980), p. 12.
10. A. M. Freeman III, "The Benefits of Air and Water Pollution Control: A Review and Synthesis of Recent Estimates," report prepared for the Council on Environmental Quality, Washington, D.C., Dec. 1979; CEQ, *Environmental Quality— 1979* (Washington, D.C., Dec. 1979).
11. General Accounting Office, "Environmental Protection Issues in the 1980s," Washington, D.C., Dec. 30, 1980.
12. OECD, *Environment Policies for the 1980s,* p. 5.
13. Michael G. Royston, *Pollution Prevention Pays* (Oxford: Pergamon Press, 1979); Michael G. Royston, "Making Pollution Prevention Pay," *Harvard Business Review,* Nov.–Dec. 1980.
14. "The Next Decade," *EPA Journal,* Nov./Dec. 1980.
15. Ingo Walter and Judith L. Ugelow, "Environmental Policies in Developing Countries," *Ambio* 8, no. 2–3 (1979).
16. U.S. Congress, Office of Technology Assessment, *Assessment of Technologies for Determining Cancer Risks from the Environment* (Washington, D.C.: U.S. Government Printing Office, June 1981).
17. Toxic Substances Strategy Committee, *Toxic Chemicals and Public Protection* (Washington, D.C., May 1980).
18. Personal interview, Dec. 21, 1981.
19. S. B. Skerfving and J. F. Copplestone, "Poisoning Caused by the Consumption of Organomercury-Dressed Seed in Iraq," *WHO Bulletin* 54 (1976).
20. U.S. Agency for International Development, "Environmental Impact Statement on the AID Pest Management Program," Washington, D.C., May 13, 1977.
21. Erik Eckholm and S. Jacob Scherr, "Double Standards and the Pesticide Trade," *New Scientist,* Feb. 16, 1978.
22. World Health Organization, "Occupational Health Programme," Report by the Director General, Geneva, April 9, 1976.
23. Eckholm and Scherr, "Double Standards and the Pesticide Trade"; Georganne Chapin and Robert Wasserstrom, "Agricultural Production and Malaria Resurgence in Central America and India," *Nature,* Sept. 17, 1981.

Chapter 7. Global Atmospherics

1. U.S. National Academy of Sciences, *Atmosphere-Biosphere Interactions: Toward a Better Understanding of the Ecological Consequences of Fossil Fuel Combustion* (Washington, D.C., 1981); "How Many More Lakes Have to Die?" *Canada Today/D'Aujourd'hui,* Feb. 1981.
2. Gene E. Likens et al., "Acid Rain," *Scientific American,* Oct. 1979; Conrad

Kleveno, U.S. Environmental Protection Agency, personal communication, Sept. 1980.

3. National Wildlife Federation and Environmental Defense Fund, "Acid Rain: A Problem in Need of Immediate Legislative Remedy," Washington, D.C., Sept. 3, 1981; Office of Technology Assessment (OTA), "Staff Draft of Report on the Impacts of Atmospheric Alterations" Washington, D.C., Aug. 1981.

4. OTA, "Staff Draft."

5. "How Many More Lakes?"; U.S. Environmental Protection Agency (EPA), *Acid Rain* (Washington, D.C., July 1980).

6. EPA, *Acid Rain;* "Acid Rain Is Sweden's Most Serious Environmental Problem," *World Environment Report,* July 6, 1981; "Acid Rain a Catastrophe Says a Norwegian Nine-Year Study," *World Environment Report,* April 13, 1981; National Wildlife Federation and Environmental Defense Fund, "Acid Rain."

7. Harold Faber, "Study Reassesses Acid Rain Effect on Adirondacks," *New York Times,* Dec. 19, 1980; EPA, *Acid Rain;* Lois R. Ember, "Acid Pollutants: Hitchhikers Ride the Wind," *Chemical and Engineering News,* Sept. 14, 1981.

8. Ember, "Acid Pollutants."

9. National Academy of Sciences, *Atmosphere-Biosphere Interactions.*

10. G. W. Tomlinson, "Acid Rain and the Forest—The Effect of Aluminum and the German Experience," Québec, Domtar Inc., Feb. 1981; Raymond Brouzes, "A Synopsis of Some Acid Rain–Related Forest Research and the Emerging Conclusions," Québec, Domtar Inc., 1981.

11. United States–Canada Research Consultation Group on the Long-Range Transport of Air Pollutants, "The LRTAP Problem in North America: A Preliminary Overview," Washington, D.C., 1979; "The Acidification of Norway," *Ambio* 4, nos. 2–3 (1981).

12. EPA, *Sulfuric Acid Rain Effects on Crop Yield and Foliar Injury* (Washington, D.C., Jan. 1980).

13. Lloyd Timberlake, "Poland—the Most Polluted Country in the World?" *New Scientist,* Oct. 22, 1981.

14. Jennie E. Bridge and F. Peter Fairchild, "Northeast Damage Report of the Long Range Transport and Deposition of Air Pollutants," prepared for the Northeast States for Coordinated Air Use Management and the New England Interstate Water Pollution Control Commission, Boston, April 1981; National Academy of Sciences, *Atmosphere-Biosphere Interactions.*

15. Bridge and Fairchild, "Northeast Damage Report."

16. Cited in OTA, "Staff Draft."

17. Environment Canada, *Downwind: The Acid Rain Story* (Ottawa, 1981).

18. The reports of the annual meeting of the Coordinating Committee on the Ozone Layer are published by UNEP, and provide essential summaries of emerging trends and theories.

19. U.S. National Academy of Sciences, *Stratospheric Ozone Depletion by Halocarbons: Chemistry and Transport* (Washington, D.C., 1979). A second NAS report, *Protection Against Depletion of Stratospheric Ozone by Chlorofluorocarbons* (Washington,

D.C., 1979), provides an excellent review of the damage that would result from depletion of the ozone layer.

20. J. Hansen et al., "Climate Impact of Increasing Atmospheric Carbon Dioxide," *Science,* Aug. 28, 1981, discusses recent evidence on temperature trends and their consistency with theories about the "greenhouse effect."

21. Council on Environmental Quality (CEQ), *Global Energy Futures and the Carbon Dioxide Problem* (Washington, D.C., Jan. 1981).

22. Ibid.

23. Ibid.

24. Joint WMO/ICSU/UNEP Meeting of Experts, *The Assessment of the Role of CO_2 on Climate Variations and Their Impact* (Geneva, Jan. 1981).

25. Hansen et al., "Climate Impact."

26. CEQ, *Global Energy Futures.*

Chapter 8. Croplands and Wastelands

1. Lester R. Brown, *Building a Sustainable Society* (New York: W. W. Norton, 1981), p. 13.

2. U.N. Food and Agriculture Organization (FAO), Committee on Agriculture, "Soil and Water Conservation," Rome, Nov. 1980.

3. National Agriculture Lands Study, "Executive Summary of Final Report," Washington, D.C., Jan. 1981.

4. Ibid.

5. Statement by Secretary of Agriculture John R. Block, before the Committee on Agriculture, Nutrition, and Forestry, U.S. Senate, Oct. 28, 1981.

6. On Third World land degradation, see Erik P. Eckholm, *Losing Ground: Environmental Stress and World Food Prospects* (New York: W. W. Norton, 1976), and FAO, "The State of Natural Resources and the Human Environment for Food and Agriculture," in *The State of Food and Agriculture, 1977* (Rome, 1977).

7. B. B. Vohra, "A Policy for Land and Water," New Delhi, Department of the Environment, 1981.

8. The main conclusions presented to the U.N. conference are in *Desertification: An Overview* (Nairobi: U.N. Conference on Desertification, Aug. 29–Sept. 9, 1977). More recent calculations about the scale of the problem, the numbers of people affected, and the costs of desertification and control activities are in U.N. General Assembly, "Study on Financing the United Nations Plan of Action to Combat Desertification; Report of the Secretary-General," New York, Sept. 17, 1980.

9. This and other calculations by Dregne that follow are from U.N. General Assembly, "Study on Financing."

10. Club du Sahel/CILSS, *The Sahel Drought Control and Development Programme, 1975–1979; A Review and Analysis* (Paris, Sept. 1980).

11. H. F. Lamprey, "Report on the Desert Encroachment Reconnaisance in Northern Sudan, 21 October to 10 November 1975," Nairobi, UNESCO, undated.

12. Jon Tinker, "Sudan Challenges the Sand-Dragon," *New Scientist,* Feb. 24, 1977.

13. The figures are from interviews with several specialists working in Upper Volta, especially Chris Reij and Robert Winterbottom. See also Jaques-Yves Marchal, "Système Agraire et Evolution de l'Occupation de l'Espail au Yatenga (Haute-Volta)," *Cahiers de l'ORSTOM,* Ser. Sci. Humaines, 14, no. 2 (1977).
14. Michael F. Lofchie, "Political and Economic Origins of African Hunger," *Journal of Modern African Studies* 13, no. 4 (1975).
15. See Michael M. Horowitz, "The Sociology of Pastoralism and African Livestock Projects," Washington, D.C., A.I.D. Program Evaluation Discussion Paper No. 6, May 1979.
16. Dr. Brian Spooner discusses the advantages and limitations of desertification as a conceptual window on development in "The Significance of Desertification," in M. S. Swaminathan and S. K. Sinha, eds., *Global Aspects of Food Production* (London: Academic Press, forthcoming).
17. Dr. H. S. Mann has prepared a useful review of follow-up actions in Asia in "Status of the Implementation of the Plan of Action to Combat Desertification in the ESCAP Region: An Overview," ESCAP, for a workshop in Jodhpur, India, Oct. 1981. He finds the degree of implementation to be generally inadequate.
18. Club du Sahel/CILSS, *The Sahel Drought Control and Development Programme,* p. 74.

Chapter 9. Deforesting and Reforesting the Earth

1. Portions of this chapter are based on material that originally appeared in Erik Eckholm, *Planting for the Future: Forestry for Human Needs* (Washington, D.C.: Worldwatch Institute, Feb. 1979).
2. R. Chakravarti, "Forestry for the Masses," Madhya Pradesh State Forest Department, Bhopal, India, mimeo, 1976.
3. Wood consumption and trade figures are from FAO documents.
4. The Expert Group report on fuelwood and charcoal to the 1981 U.N. Conference on New and Renewable Sources of Energy lays out the dimensions of the firewood challenge. See also FAO, *Agriculture: Toward 2000,* rev. ed. (Rome, 1981).
5. *Entering the Twenty-first Century: The Global 2000 Report to the President* (Washington, D.C.: U.S. Government Printing Office, 1980).
6. Reidar Persson, *World Forest Resources* (Stockholm: Royal College of Forestry, 1974).
7. Adrian Sommer, "Attempt at an Assessment of the World's Tropical Forests," *Unasylva* 28, nos. 112/113 (1976). In "The Present Status and Future Prospects of Tropical Moist Forests" (*Environmental Conservation,* Summer 1980), Norman Myers suggests that conversion rates may be far higher than commonly assumed. The FAO makes much lower estimates of forest losses in its new assessment of tropical forests (see note 8, below).
8. Results of the FAO/UNEP assessment have been published in FAO, *Los Recursos Forestales de la America Tropical* (Rome, 1981); FAO, *Forestry Resources of Africa* (Rome, 1981); and FAO, *Forest Resources of Tropical Asia* (Rome, 1981).
9. Carlos Marx Ribeiro Carneiro, "The Brazilian Forest Cover Monitoring Pro-

gramme," Brazilian Institute for Forestry Development, presented to 14th International Congress of the International Society for Photogrammetry, Hamburg, West Germany, July 1980.

10. Norman Myers, *Conversion of Tropical Moist Forests* (Washington, D.C.: National Academy of Sciences, 1980).

11. On Malaysia, see "Logged Out by 1990," *IUCN Bulletin,* Oct. 1977; "Let's Not Make the Same Mistake," *New Straits Times* (Kuala Lumpur), Sept. 4, 1977; "Tardiness in Timber," *Business Times* (Kuala Lumpur), Feb. 24, 1978; and Sahabat Alam Malaysia, "State of the Malaysian Environment 1980/81," Penang, 1981. On Thailand, see *UNEP—Asia Report 1977* (Bangkok: UNEP Regional Office for Asia and the Pacific, Feb. 1978); "Drastic Thai Action to Save Teak," *The Times* (London), June 8, 1978; "Only 106M Rai of Forest Land Left," *The Nation* (Bangkok), Nov. 6, 1978; "Forestry," *World Environment Report,* Jan. 1, 1979.

12. Population, Resources, Environment and the Philippine Future, *Philippine Scenarios: 2000 A.D.* (Manila: PREPF, 1978); M. Segura and A. V. Revilla, Jr., "A Historical Perspective of the Philippine Forest Resources," PREPF, Manila, mimeo, 1977; A. V. Revilla, Jr., M. L. Bonita, and M. Segura, "An Evaluation of Certain Policies and Programs Affecting Forestry Production Through 2000 A.D.," PREPF, Manila, mimeo, 1977.

13. FAO, *Wood: World Trends and Prospects* (Rome, 1967).

14. Robert F. Skillings and Nils O. Tcheyen, "Economic Development Prospects of the Amazonian Region of Brazil," Johns Hopkins School of Advanced International Studies, Center of Brazilian Studies, Washington, D.C., Nov. 1979. For an excellent summary of the problems of colonization, see Nigel J. H. Smith, "Colonization Lessons from a Tropical Forest," *Science,* Nov. 13, 1981.

15. Lawrence S. Hamilton, *Tropical Rainforest Use and Preservation* (New York: Sierra Club Office of International Affairs, March 1976); "Panama Watershed Management Project Paper," U.S. Agency for International Development, Panamá, Nov. 30, 1978.

16. Robert J. A. Goodland, "Environmental Ranking of Amazonian Development Projects in Brazil," *Environmental Conservation,* Spring 1980; Philip M. Fearnside, "The Effects of Cattle Pasture on Soil Fertility in the Brazilian Amazon: Consequences for Beef Production Sustainability," *Tropical Biology* 21, no. 1 (1980).

17. The Tosi statement is from "Sacred Cow Causing Ecological Disaster in C.R., Local Experts Say," *Tico Times* (San José), Nov. 3, 1978; James J. Parsons, "Forest to Pasture: Development or Destruction?" *Revisita de Biologia Tropical* 24 (1976).

18. M. S. Tomar and S. C. Joshi, "Vanishing Forests Vis-à-vis Energy Crisis in Madhya Pradesh by 2000 A.D.," State Forest Resources Survey Organization, Bhopal, India, Feb. 1977.

19. Turi Hammer, "Wood for Fuel: Energy Crisis Implying Desertification—The Case of Bara, The Sudan," Ph.D. thesis, University of Bergen, Norway, Nov. 1977.

20. Kuswata Kartawinata et al., "The Impact of Man on a Tropical Forest in Indonesia," *Ambio* 10, no. 2–3 (1981).

21. Cited in Norman E. Johnson and Gary F. Dykstra, "Maintaining Forest Produc-

tion in East Kalimantan, Indonesia," presented to the Eighth World Forestry Congress, Jakarta, Oct. 16–28, 1978.

22. UNEP, *Overview Document,* Experts Meeting on Tropical Forests, Nairobi, Feb. 25–March 1, 1980.

23. Dennis Richardson, "Forestry and Environment in the South Pacific," University of Technology, Lae, Papua, New Guinea, mimeo, no date.

24. World Bank, *Pakistan: Forestry Sector Survey* (Washington, D.C., June 1978).

25. Arnold J. Barnett and Chandler Morse, *Scarcity and Growth: The Economies of National Resource Availability* (Baltimore: Johns Hopkins University Press, 1962).

26. Gujarat Forest Department, "Social Forestry Project, Gujarat State, for World Bank Assistance," Baroda, India, Aug. 1978.

27. Robert T. Winterbottom, "Reforestation in the Sahel: Problems and Strategies," presented to Annual Meeting of the African Studies Association, Philadelphia, Oct. 1980.

28. The consequences of firewood scarcity discussed in the following paragraphs are mainly from J. E. M. Arnold, "Wood Energy and Rural Communities," *Natural Resources Forum* 3 (1979).

29. B. B. Vohra, "A Policy for Land and Water," New Delhi, Department of the Environment, 1981; John S. Spears, "Developing Country Forestry Issues in the 1980s: A World Bank Perspective," mimeo, presented at University of Athens, Georgia, Feb. 23, 1981.

30. Samuel H. Kunkle, "Forestry Support for Agriculture through Watershed Management, Windbreaks and Other Conservation Actions," presented to Eighth World Forestry Congress, Jakarta, Oct. 16–28, 1978; Government of Kenya, Ministry of Environment and Natural Resources, "Report of the GOK/UNEP/UNDP Project on Environment and Development" draft, Jan. 1981.

31. The Bihar example is from *World Environment Report,* July 20, 1981, and S. K. Chauhan, "Tree War in Bihar," Earthscan, London, 1981.

Chapter 10. Biological Diversity and Economic Development

1. Portions of this chapter are based on material that originally appeared in Erik Eckholm, "Disappearing Species: The Social Challenge" Worldwatch Paper 22, Washington, D.C., July 1978.

2. Norman Myers, *The Sinking Ark* (New York: Pergamon Press, 1979); Peter H. Raven, Brent Berlin, and Dennis Breedlove, "The Origins of Taxonomy," *Science,* Dec. 17, 1971.

3. Peter H. Raven, "Ethics and Attitudes," in J. B. Simmons et al., eds., *Conservation of Threatened Plants* (New York: Plenum Press, 1976); Grenville L. Lucas and A. H. M. Synge, "The IUCN Threatened Plants Committee and Its Work Throughout the World," *Environmental Conservation,* Autumn 1977.

4. In addition to Myers, *The Sinking Ark,* see projections of species losses by Thomas Lovejoy in *Entering the Twenty-first century: The Global 2000 Report to the President,* vol. 2 (Washington, D.C.: U.S. Government Printing Office, 1980).

5. Paul S. Martin, "The Discovery of America," *Science,* March 9, 1973; C. Vance

Haynes, Jr., "Elephant Hunting in North America," *Scientific American,* June 1966; Jean-Yves Domalain, "Confessions of an Animal Trafficker," *Natural History,* May 1977.

6. Tim Inskipp and Sue Wells, *International Trade in Wildlife* (London: Earthscan, 1979).

7. "Japan as No. 1 in International Wildlife Trade," *Chikyu no Koe* (Voice of the Earth), July 1981.

8. Myers, *The Sinking Ark.*

9. G. T. Prance, "Floristic Inventory of the Tropics: Where Do We Stand?" *Annals of the Missouri Botanical Garden* 64, no. 4 (1977); Peter H. Raven, "The Destruction of the Tropics," *Frontiers,* July 1976.

10. O. H. Frankel, *The Significance, Utilization and Conservation of Crop Genetic Resources* (Rome: Food and Agriculture Organization, 1971); O. H. Frankel, "Genetic Resources," *Annals of the New York Academy of Sciences,* Feb. 25, 1977; Garrison Wilkes, "The World's Crop Germplasm—An Endangered Resource," *Bulletin of the Atomic Scientists,* Feb. 1977; National Academy of Sciences, *Conservation of Germplasm Resources: An Imperative* (Washington, D.C., 1978).

11. Tony Loftas, *Food and the Environment* (Rome: Food and Agriculture Organization, 1976); J. G. Hawkes, "Genetic Conservation: A World Problem," presented to 139th Annual Meeting of the British Association for the Advancement of Science, Aston, England, Sept. 5, 1977.

12. David L. Rhoad, "Milk in My Mouth," *War on Hunger,* March 1974.

13. Hawkes, "Genetic Conservation"; Jack R. Harlan, "Genetic Resources in Wild Relatives of Crops," *Crop Science,* May/June 1976.

14. National Academy of Science, *Genetic Vulnerability of Major Crops* (Washington, D.C., 1972).

15. John Walsh, "Germplasm Resources Are Losing Ground," *Science,* Oct. 23, 1981. On IBPGR activities, see "The IBPGR in the Eighties: A Strategy and Planning Report," Rome, 1981.

16. Paul C. Mangelsdorf, "Introduction," and Richard Evans Shultes, "The Future of Plants as Sources of New Biodynamic Compounds," in Tony Swain, ed., *Plants in the Development of Modern Medicine* (Cambridge, Mass.: Harvard University Press, 1972).

17. Eric Ranawake, " 'Death Flower' Threatened as Its Juice Brings US $115,000 a Pound," Depthnews Science Service, Manila, March 19, 1977; Jerry E. Bishop, "The Curare Mystery: Is Winchester Rifle Linked to Shortage?" *Wall Street Journal,* March 28, 1978; Robert F. Raffauf, "Some Notes on the Distribution of Alkaloids in the Plant Kingdom," *Economic Botany* 24, no. 1 (1970); D. A. Levin, "Alkaloid-Bearing Plants: An Ecogeographic Perspective," *The American Naturalist,* March/April 1976.

18. Philip J. Hilts, "Useful Drugs Found in Sea Creatures," *Washington Post,* Jan. 6, 1981.

19. Winston J. Brill, "Agricultural Microbiology," *Scientific American,* Sept. 1981.

20. Paul Ehrlich and Anne Ehrlich, *Extinction* (New York: Random House, 1981), p. 94.

21. David W. Ehrenfeld, "The Conservation of Non-Resources" *American Scientist,* Nov./Dec. 1976.

22. O. H. Frankel, "Genetic Conservation: Our Evolutionary Responsiblity," *Genetics,* Sept. 1974.

23. Personal interview, Maria Thereze Jorge de Padua, director of the Department of National Parks and Reserves, Brasilia, April 22, 1981.

24. Joseph Hanlon, "Can People Live with Elephants?" *New Scientist,* Dec. 4, 1980.

25. Aldo Leopold, *A Sand County Almanac* (London: Oxford University Press, 1968), p. vii; "Long Live the Wilderness," *IUCN Bulletin,* Dec. 1977.

26. Walter J. Lusigi, "New Approaches to Wildlife Conservation in Kenya," *Ambio* 10, no. 2–3 (1981).

27. Thomas Lovejoy, "We Must Decide Which Species Will Go Forever," *Smithsonian,* July 1976.

28. Information on important countries that have not yet signed the CITES was supplied by Jaques Berney, acting secretary-general of CITES, personal communication, Aug. 25, 1981.

29. Ecological gaps in the Biosphere Reserves system were described by the program's coordinator, B. von Droste, personal interview, March 30, 1981.

Chapter 11. The Conservation of Humanity

1. OECD, *Environment Policies for the 1980s* (Paris, 1980), p. 12.

2. Shirley Hazzard, *Defeat of an Ideal* (Boston: Atlantic Monthly Press, 1973), p. 248.

3. Lance Taylor, "The Costly Arms Trade," *New York Times,* Dec. 22, 1981.

INDEX